Two

Changing Times

se⊗plained

By

Helen J Knox

Knox Publishing

Brentwood, Essex, UK

Sexplained Two — For Changing Times

First published in November, 2014
Updated 2016

This book replaces *Sexplained 2... For Young People*.

© Helen J Knox 1995-2016

British Library Cataloguing in Publishing Data
A catalogue record for this book is available from the British Library

Knox, Helen J
Sexplained Two — For Changing Times
ISBN 10 - 0-9526224-3-2
ISBN 13 - 978-0-9526224-3-7

Typeset by — Helen J Knox
Cover design — Helen J Knox
Printed and bound in Great Britain by Berforts Information Press Ltd
2016 Update printed and bound in Great Britain by 4edge Limited
Published by – Knox Publishing, Brentwood, Essex

Acknowledgements

Although many people have patiently tolerated my questions about contraception and other topics included here, I would especially like to thank the following people.

For guidance on contraception copy

Dr Barbara Hollingworth — Consultant in Sexual and Reproductive Health
Sally Kelsey
    — Contraception Nurse Specialist
Jane Knight
    — Fertility Awareness Nurse Specialist

For guidance on general copy

Justin Gaffney RN
    — Chair of Genito-Urinary Nurses Association (GUNA) UK
Kim Holloway
    — An avid reader of books
Joy Marchese
    — Teacher and Parent Educator at The American School in London
Judith Sherlock
    — Young People's Nurse Specialist
Jeanie Smith
    — Young People's Nurse Specialist
Dr David Wight
    — General Practitioner

For guidance on The Law & Sex

Gary Pankhurst — Police Detective Sgt
Jason Morgan — Police Detective

For medical and cartoon illustrations

Peter Gardiner
Sylvia Rawsthorn
FP Sales
Durex®
Jane Knight / Dr Cecilia Pyper / Fertility UK

For writing the Foreword

Penny Hopkinson
Consultant Editor A Mentor and Longstanding Friend

Thanks

I would like to thank my early medical mentors for their patience as I asked many questions over the years.

First, the late Dr Rimah El Borai, who introduced me to and demystified the specialist field of 'family planning' a long time ago; and Mr Ali Kubba, Consultant Community Gynaecologist, with whom I worked in South London for many years.

They shared their knowledge and their passion for teaching (often explaining complicated topics in a simple way) which helped me to establish a deeper interest in contraception and reproductive healthcare. They helped me to find my own way to teach the subject on to others and build a very interesting and enjoyable nursing career.

Their generosity has enabled me to share some of that knowledge and experience with you, here.

Dedication

This book is dedicated to the memory of my parents, without whose influence my books may not have been finished.

They taught me to keep going and finish what I start, even when I get fed up and want to stop or change direction.

I am grateful for that guidance and am, now, very proud to let you read this updated and extended edition of my second book.

Acknowledgements

Sexplained Two — For Changing Times ® © 1999-2016

There's a big difference between having sex and making love. Just having sex in various ways is all that porn films portray. They don't explain anything about the enjoyable feelings that are involved within a loving, caring sexual relationship – or that it's important to learn about healthy and unhealthy relationships, respect and care for someone else as you mature.

A loving, faithful relationship is built on trust, mutual respect, true friendship and the maturity to work through the tough as well as the good times together. As the bond between two individuals deepens, a natural consequence is often the desire to start a family and create a secure family unit that will lead to emotional fulfilment.

However, this may take many years to achieve and no one person's journey will be the same. The early years of discovering what you want from a permanent relationship can be exciting, confusing and not without problems. Sometimes what one person wants doesn't match the desires of a partner.

Sexplained Two — For Changing Times confronts the many issues that need to be addressed in relation to sex and physical relationships. The book is packed with information applicable to everyone – regardless of age, race, sexual orientation or disability. Issues are addressed and explained head on without embarrassment, 'telling it like it is' from the practical viewpoint.

•   Young people will easily relate to the real questions and real problems from real people from all walks of life – and at every level

•   Parents will find everything they need to teach their children the basics on reaching puberty and then help their children understand the complexities of sexual maturity

•   Those working in sexual health education will find a wealth of information backed up by facts, figures and illustrations in one handy teaching resource

A Little Knowledge ...
Almost everyone has a little knowledge – and a great deal of curiosity – about sex. Helen Knox believes that a little knowledge can be dangerous and, the more young people know about the many other issues that affect physical relationships, the better able they will be to prevent such problems as unplanned pregnancy and sexually acquired infection.

Her book is non-judgmental and packed with facts that will enable young readers to evaluate for themselves the risks and pleasures of sex so that they can make an informed choice related to their own sexual activity and develop their sense of responsibility towards each other as well as themselves – without feeling exploited or exploiting others. Much of the information, facts and figures will shock. Helen makes no apologies.

The Law & Sex
'Changing Times' means knowing where you stand with the Law and sex. The Law & Sex is a major section of **Sexplained Two** which is a thought provoking guide based on the *Sexual Offences Act 2003*. It aims to raise awareness of some of the less obvious but important legal issues in the UK, many of which also apply in other countries. Young people should understand how the Law differentiates between consent and lack of consent. Other important issues tackled include grooming, trafficking, forced and arranged marriage, sexting, online grooming, cyber bullying, stalking, domestic and honour based violence. It also covers The Law related to pornography.

Social Media

The way we communicate with each other has changed dramatically over the last few years. In real life, when we see and speak to people, we pick up on the many 'non-verbal clues' (body language) they give off – e.g. their facial expression, tone of voice, appearance, etc. When it comes to meeting new people, we make up our mind about them within seconds. But, online, unless using a webcam, we can't do this; nor can we pick up on other small clues, which puts us at a disadvantage.

Many young people have a computer in their bedroom. They lock themselves away in a virtual world for hours. Communicating via Social Media takes over their day-to-day life. Many are safe, but some are not, and it is important to understand the Dos and Don'ts and learn how to stay safe online.

FGM – Female Genital Mutilation

UNICEF estimates that FGM/C affects over 130 million girls and women worldwide. Although the practice is starting to decline in some regions, an additional 30 million more girls and young women will be affected within the next 10 years.

This equates to:

- 57,000 per week
- 8,250 per day
- 344 per hour
- 6 per minute
- 1 girl mutilated every 10 seconds

It's important to have FGM/C on the school curriculum because nowadays, more children (and parents) from different cultures mix in school, and some will be vulnerable.

- We have a 'duty of care' towards each other, not just to our friends or family

- Educating the next generation about FGM/C is the best way to influence change

- Once FGM/C is better understood, children can help to protect each other; and increased disapproval of the practice can help to influence change

- Greater understanding of what it involves can also help to support those who have been made to go through it.

People meet, fall in love and live happily ever after in the movies. In the real world, real people experience many changes and face many choices. Making the right choice is so much easier when you have the correct, up to date, and relevant information. Therefore, Helen's qualified advice about the rewards and risks of sex and relationships should become essential reading for everyone.

Penny Hopkinson
Consultant Editor

Foreword

About the Author

Described in 2004 by the UK's **Nursing Times** magazine as 'a courageous innovator', Helen J Knox qualified as a Registered Nurse at **Westminster Hospital**, London SW1 in 1978. She worked as a Senior Staff Nurse at **St Thomas' Hospital** Accident and Emergency Department, London, and later as a District Nursing Sister in West London. In the mid 1980s, she moved into the specialist field of Family Planning and has worked in the area of reproductive health as a Clinical Nurse Specialist in Contraception and Sexual Health ever since.

Initially covering up to seven clinical sessions in West and North-West London and teaching in two or three men's prisons each week, she gained a unique insight into the reproductive and sexual health needs of both genders.

In 1991, a time when there was no-one to base such work on and talking about contraception and sexual health was considerably more risky and 'taboo' than it is today, Helen became the UK's first Outreach Clinical Nurse Specialist in this field, working in the deprived multi-ethnic, inner-city South London Borough of Lambeth.

She introduced 'condom supply points' to South London and by promising organisers a regular supply of condoms for participants or residents, gained access to many unsuspecting audiences.

She could be found in all sorts of unexpected locations, teaching people of all ages about contraception and sexual health. Places included, but were not limited to: homeless hostels, youth clubs, drug agencies, probation centres, pupil referral units, civic centres, sex work projects, job clubs, bus stations, boxing gyms, mental health and learning disabled units, mother and baby projects, women's refuges, schools, colleges, and universities. She even held a session with young people who insisted on sitting in a neighbouring graveyard, rather than their classroom.

All of this contributed to her unique perspective on the challenges of sexual health promotion, and in 1994, led her to become a finalist in the **Nursing Times / 3M National Nursing Awards for Innovation in Nursing and Midwifery** for her outreach work in South London.

In her own time, Helen became **The Virgin Sexpert**, running the first moderated chat room for **Virgin Net.** She then set up her own **Sexplained Cyber Clinics** and her very busy website, **WillyWorries.com**.

Unable to find accessible leaflets to answer questions she was being asked, Helen wrote a booklet to explain some topics, supported by the Special Trustees of St Thomas' Hospital, London SE1. Then, in 1995, she published her highly acclaimed first book, **Sexplained... The Uncensored Guide to Sexual Health,** which changed her life, forever.

About the Author

In 1999, she published it's sequel, **Sexplained 2... For Young People**. In the same year, she formed **Sexplained Ltd.** and went on holiday to Barbados — a trip that took her life in a different direction.

Since 2001, Helen has written a monthly **Sexplained Column** for that country's **Better Health Magazine**. Extracts of which are included in this book to bring the topic to life.

In 2004, Helen became an **Assessor for the RCN (Royal College of Nursing) Sexual Health Skills Course**. Since 2011, she has redesigned **Sexplained Training** to give people a comfortable way of learning about contraception and sexual health subjects in *bite sized* portions, in an enjoyable way; and in 2013 she completed a Post Graduate Diploma in Social Innovation. She plans to offer this training, long-distance, using innovative techniques online, as audio books and as multi-media e-publications.

Also in 2013, she republished her first book, **Sexplained... The Uncensored Guide to Sexual Health** after updating and considerably extending it over a period of several years, as **Sexplained One — Sex & Your Health**; and in 2014 she joined the UKTI (UK Trade and Investment) Passport to Export scheme for assistance taking **Sexplained®** to a global audience.

She has appeared over 200 times on TV and radio in the UK, and overseas, and been invited to speak at national conferences. She has also appeared on stage alongside actors/comedians Robbie Gee and Eddie Nestor, to drive home some health messages in a rather unusual way.

Sexplained Two — For Changing Times updates and extends Helen's second book, **Sexplained 2... For Young People**, for a world in which sexual health is no longer such a taboo topic but for which a greater understanding about contraception and all the related sexual health topics is vital.

This book is as relevant for parents and other adults as it is for young people, today. It is also relevant for healthcare professionals and indeed, for all people influencing others across a wide range of disciplines.

For more information about Helen, her books, **Sexplained Training** and to be kept up to date with developments, please visit **www.Sexplained.com**

Contents

&

Sections

Contents & Sections

Contents & Sections

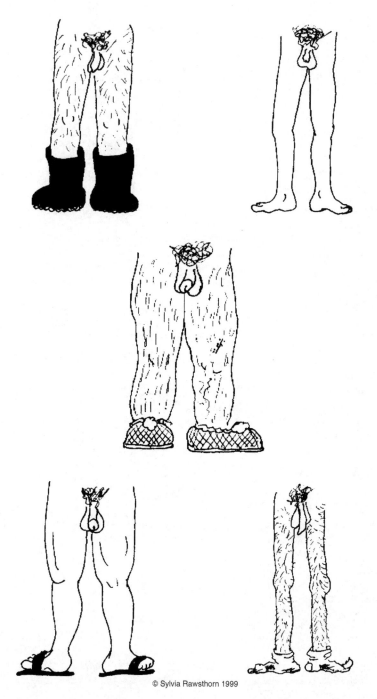

© Sylvia Rawsthorn 1999

Young Men's Changes & Willy Worries

Puberty and Adolescence
Sperm production
Quality of sperm
Some other changes during puberty
Sexuality
How do boys and men get an erection?
Vital note to all men
Does it matter that I have a small penis?
How you measure the length of your penis can add about an inch or two!
How do I measure the length of my penis?
How can I make my penis bigger?
I'm worried that my penis is too small for sex.
How can I make my penis smaller?
Is it normal to have one testicle bigger than the other?
What happens to the unused sperm if I don't have sex?
What are wet dreams and why do I have them?
Why do I have an erection when I wake up in the morning?
Is it normal to have lumps or little bumps on my penis?
If I masturbate and stop the ejaculate coming out by squeezing my penis (or put my thumb over its tip, or behind my testicles and press hard) will it do me harm?
I get a pleasant sensation when I climb frames or ropes in PE from rubbing against my genital area. Is this an orgasm?
My friends say they go on for ages when they have sex, but I ejaculate very quickly. Is this normal?
Why do some men get painful erections, with their penis bending to one side?
How do I put my penis in to my partner so we can have sex and does it hurt?

Will my penis be trapped inside my partner when I have sex and how do I get it out again?
When my penis is inside my partner, will I pass urine?
Why do my testicles ache so much when we're just heavy petting?
Will my penis be too big to go inside my girlfriend if she's never had sex before?
I can get my penis in to my partner but I can't ejaculate. What's wrong and how can I come?
Does it mean I have sperm if I have erections?
At what age will I have sperm?
Should I be able to see sperm in my urine?
Information about sperm!
A good reason for fiddling with your own or your partner's testicles!
How often should I check?
Where should I check them?
How do I check my testicles?
What else should I look out for?
I've noticed something
First, check to see if it is on your other testicle, too.
If it is, it's extremely unlikely to be cancer, as it rarely develops on both sides.
Now what do I do?
What if I've got testicular cancer?
I won't look normal any more
What about sex?
I've heard of torsion of the testicles, what's that?
What's a hydrocele?
What's my prostate?
With infection, you may notice:
Further genital hygiene

Willius Floppius Variegata
The Willy Plant

Puberty and adolescence

✦ Puberty is the time when your body starts to change into that of a young man physically. It happens between the age of about 9 and 18 and lasts for about 4 to 6 years.

✦ Adolescence also occurs around this time, when you mature and change emotionally.

✦ In some cultures young men are treated differently by adults when they reach adolescence and there may be a religious celebration eg. the Jewish Barmitzvah ceremony, when boys reach the age of 13.

Sperm production

✦ During puberty your reproductive organs *(testes)* become active and you produce sperm.

✦ Under the influence of chemical and other messages, your brain sends a signal to the tiny tubular areas deep within your testicles, telling them to start producing sperm and the hormone testosterone.

✦ Each sperm takes about 76 days to mature.

✦ During this time they spend the first 64 days growing into newborn sperm which then move to the epididymis *(an area of your testicles)* where they gather, learn to swim and mature over the next 12 days.

✦ You can now make a girl pregnant if your sperm comes into contact with her egg.

Quality of sperm

✦ From puberty to old age, if you remain healthy, you'll make thousands of sperm every minute.

✦ You'll also have about 3 million sperm in the clear fluid near the tip of your penis each time you get sexually excited.

✦ An average ejaculation *(come / cum)* contains about 200-300 million sperm, which is why, in the field of contraception we have a healthy respect for them. It only takes one to lead to pregnancy from so many! A large number of them will be blanks *(no good)*, but this still leaves millions of healthy sperm.

✦ Sperm may live for up to 7 days inside a female partner if she's at the fertile time of her menstrual cycle and makes fertile mucus for that long.

✦ *See the section 'Young Women's Changes & Women's Worries' on page 33 for information about the menstrual cycle.*

Willy Worries

Testes less than 2.5 cm/1" diameter

Young boy
1 — preadolescent

Testes more than 2.5 cm/1" diameter

Start of puberty
2 — Enlargement of testes; scrotum enlarges, becomes redder and rougher. Sparse growth of long hairs at base of penis

Early teens
3 — penis lengthens; more growth of testes and scrotum. Darker, thicker, curly hair.

Late teens
4— penis broader ; glans develops; scrotum darkens.
Hair is adult in type but not as extensive

Testes 5-6 cm/2-3½" average length

Young adult
5 — adult, hair spreading up towards tummy and to thighs.

Willy Worries

© Peter Gardiner

Some other changes during puberty

✦ Your voice will start to deepen in tone *(break)*.

✦ Hair will start growing on your face, in your pubic area, under your arms, on your chest, arms and legs.

✦ You may develop spots on your face, due to the chemical changes taking place in your body.

✦ The odour *(smell)* of your body may change slightly.

✦ Your penis and testicles will grow in length, width and weight.

✦ You'll grow in height – have a growth spurt.

✦ You may have some wet dreams *(ejaculate in your sleep)* occasionally.

✦ You'll gradually become more inquisitive about sex and the mysteries surrounding it.

✦ You'll start to explore your body and learn to masturbate. This won't make you blind, deaf or drive you mad as people used to say in olden days!

✦ You may become interested in fashion, fast cars, music, members of the opposite sex and in the appearance of your body.

Sexuality

✦ You'll probably wonder about your sexuality *(sexual preference)* as you learn to express yourself in the adult world.

✦ As you mature you may become attracted to members of the opposite sex.

✦ You may, however, become attracted to members of your own sex or perhaps both sexes.

✦ For more information on sexuality see the section called *'Growing Up & New Experiences'.* See page 129.

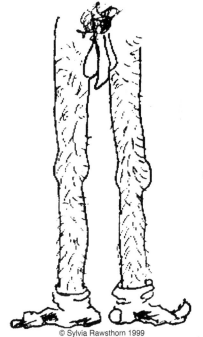

© Sylvia Rawsthorn 1999

Willy Worries

Willy Worries

How do boys and men get an erection?

✦ Several things can trigger an erection.

✦ Usually, it's in response to something sexual or exciting. *(Though sometimes it may happen when you're just sitting at the back of a bus, thinking of your maths homework or even a cheese sandwich!)*

✦ Stimulation may be visual, by touch, smell, using your imagination or from memory.

✦ Sometimes, though, an erection happens because of fear.

✦ When sexually stimulated, the muscle at the base of your penis allows blood to flow in.

✦ It engorges, enlarges, hardens and expands. It then tightens to keep your penis muscles full of blood.

✦ After ejaculation this tight band of muscle relaxes and allows the blood to flow out of your penis again.

✦ You can't pass urine while you have an erection so don't worry that you might pass urine inside your partner during sex — and you may find it difficult to pass urine until your erection goes down — especially early in the morning when you wake up with your early morning erection and full bladder.

How does erection happen?
The penis cut through to show how...

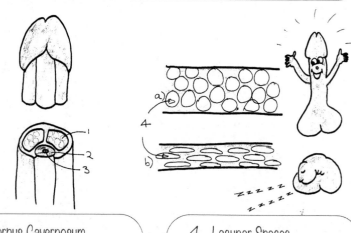

1. Corpus Cavernosum
2. Corpus Songiosum
3. Urethra (urine tube)

4. Lacunar Spaces
a) filled with blood whilst erect
b) collapsed when relaxed

© Sylvia Rawsthorn 1999

... and Willy Worries

Vital note to all men about pregnancy and sexually acquired infections

✦ Penetration and/or ejaculation are NOT always necessary for a young woman to get pregnant.

✦ If your erect unprotected penis comes into contact with a young woman's fertile mucus *(see page 36)* sperm can swim into her vagina, up to her uterus, over to her fallopian tubes and she could become pregnant **without having penetrative sex!**

✦ It's important to realise that there are active sperm *(about 3 million)* in the tiny amount of clear fluid, which usually appears at the tip of your penis on erection.

✦ To ensure absolutely no risk of pregnancy you must keep an unprotected penis away from female genitalia.

✦ If sperm can pass, so can germs, so be extremely careful where you allow your fluids to go, or what you allow them to contact.

✦ Even when protection is used, there's still a risk of passing infection both ways if protection fails.

✦ *Note: You're at your most virile between the age of 14 and 24 and at your sexual peak. At this time your penis has a mind of its own!*

✦ Your penis may not be as choosy as you are! So keep you brain in your head when your erection throbs and remember to protect yourself at all times.

Does it matter that I have a small penis?

✦ Size is no barrier to or indication of pleasure.

✦ A small penis can receive and give just as much pleasure as a bigger one.

✦ Men of all ages, in all countries are obsessed by penis size.

✦ Size is irrelevant when it comes to pregnancy or sexual performance.

✦ Of course, when it's soft it may appear small, looking down on it as you do from above. Try looking at it sideways in the mirror for a more impressive view!

✦ When soft, a small penis can more than double in size by the time it's erect; large penises when soft, don't tend to react so impressively.

✦ At times, it might also look larger or smaller – which is also quite usual.

✦ Many heterosexual *(straight)* men don't see other penises erect for comparison! It's perfectly common to have an erection between 5 and 7 inches *(approx 13 and 18 cm)*.

✦ How you measure the length of your penis can add about an inch or two!

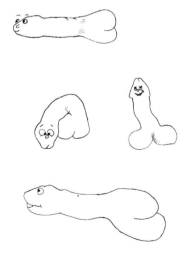

© Sylvia Rawsthorn 1999

Willy Worries

How do I measure the length of my penis?

✦ Measure your penis when you have a good erection. Push it horizontal *(at a right angle to your tummy)* then measure from your hairline to the tip and hey presto, you have its length.

✦ No doubt you could measure from the underside and add an inch or so, with perhaps even more if you measure the back while it's erect instead of horizontal.

✦ There's no reason at all to panic about penis size. It is what it is.

✦ It grows in length, weight and size as you grow up and mature physically.

✦ Some are long, some are short, some are fat and some are thin.

✦ When it's erect, you should feel as proud of it as any other man.

✦ Men often worry about penis size. It's how you use it that really matters, not how much you've got!

How can I make my penis bigger?

✦ Trying to make your penis bigger can cause far more problems than it solves.

✦ Generally you can't enlarge it naturally.

✦ Its size is determined by your genes, which also determine the colour of your eyes, hair etc.

✦ It tends to grow thicker and longer as you mature physically. Your testicles also develop in size and weight.

✦ Some men go to great trouble to try and get surgery or use stretching instruments to lengthen it or have fat injections to make it wider. But many are bitterly disappointed with the expensive lack of results.

✦ Creams, lotions, potions, and surgery are largely a waste of money and just play on your insecurities; they can't guarantee success and often fail to deliver what is eagerly expected.

✦ The psychological damage *(in your mind)* could make the problem far greater and your performance worse than it was before if the result isn't as you hope.

✦ The average vagina is only 3½" — 4" (9 — 10 cms) deep, although it can expand to about twice this, when a penis is inserted slowly and gently, so there's no point in men bragging that they're 12" — 14" long! It simply isn't necessary.

✦ Mr. Average is just fine and preferred, by most partners, long term.

✦ Mr. Huge is OK for novelty value but can cause discomfort.

✦ Believe it or not, it can even lead to couples splitting up.

✦ Remember: try to concentrate on how you use what you've got; not how little or how much you have.

Willy Worries

Willy Worries

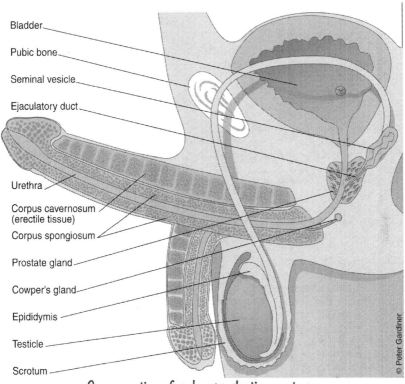

Bladder
Pubic bone
Seminal vesicle
Ejaculatory duct
Urethra
Corpus cavernosum (erectile tissue)
Corpus spongiosum
Prostate gland
Cowper's gland
Epididymis
Testicle
Scrotum

© Peter Gardiner

Cross section of male reproductive anatomy
Image shows flaccid and erect penis positions

I'm worried that my penis is too small for sex and that if someone sees it, they'll laugh and not want me any more

✦ Don't worry – you're not alone. You'd be surprised how many men worry about this unnecessarily.
✦ Young men develop at different rates. For example, seeing someone the same age at school with a bigger penis, when you're having a shower after physical exercise, can do untold harm to some young men's egos.
✦ Few heterosexual *(straight)* men get to see another man's penis except if they're watching a pornography film or in the gents toilet.

✦ Pornographic films sometimes employ trick photography to make a penis look bigger.
✦ A penis that's large when flaccid *(soft)* doesn't usually impress as much as a smaller one does when it erects.
✦ A smaller penis can more than double in size on erection
✦ A larger penis may just increase slightly in length or width. So, you should try not to worry.

Willy Worries

How can I make my penis smaller?

✦ In theory, to make your penis smaller you could have surgery. But it would be a rare man indeed who thinks his penis is too large!

✦ If you're seriously concerned that your penis is too big, you should consult your doctor.

✦ Trying to make your penis larger or smaller can lead to more problems, physical and emotional, than you may already have. Just accept what nature's given you and don't worry about size.

Is it normal to have one testicle bigger than the other?

✦ Yes, it's quite normal to have one testicle bigger than the other.

✦ The left one is often slightly bigger than the right and it usually hangs a little bit lower.

✦ This clever design is probably so that they don't crash into each other and cause pain when you're running!

What happens to the unused sperm if I don't have sex?

✦ After a month or so, the unused sperm degenerate *(break down)* and are absorbed back into your body *(through special areas called sterocilia in the epididymis of your testes)* and are filtered out of your body like any other waste *(eg. in your urine or faeces (poo))*.

What are wet dreams and why do I have them?

✦ Wet dreams are when you ejaculate in your sleep due to something sexually arousing in a dream.

✦ Wet dreams are also called nocturnal emissions.

✦ They're perfectly normal and nothing to worry about.

✦ Your dream may not have been sexy or about someone you fancy. Wet dreams sometimes happen when they're least expected.

✦ Some young men don't have them very often while others have them frequently.

Why do I have an erection when I wake up in the morning?

✦ It's quite usual to have about five erections in your sleep each night, throughout your life.

✦ They're more likely to be a left over erection from the last dream you were having before you woke up.

✦ These are sometimes nicknamed piss hards, morning glories or dawn horns.

✦ They're not, as is often thought, due to having a full bladder when you wake up and need to 'piss'.

© Sylvia Rawsthorn 1999

Willy Worries

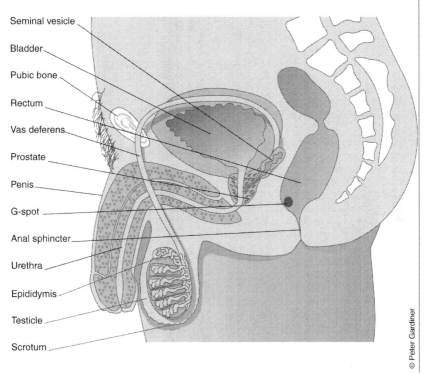

Seminal vesicle
Bladder
Pubic bone
Rectum
Vas deferens
Prostate
Penis
G-spot
Anal sphincter
Urethra
Epididymis
Testicle
Scrotum

© Peter Gardiner

Cross section of male reproductive anatomy

Is it normal to have lumps or little bumps on my penis?

✦ You have lots of tiny glands near the tip *(glans)* of your penis, around the coronal sulcus *(crown/helmet)* which may or may not be easily visible as lumps and bumps when you reach puberty.

✦ If you've had them for years and they haven't changed, they're unlikely to be anything to worry about.

✦ If, however, you notice new lumps or bumps and you've had sex in the last few months, it's worth asking a doctor to check them or visit a Sexual Health Clinic, in case they're genital warts – or another infection called molluscum contageosum.

If I masturbate and stop the ejaculate coming out by squeezing my penis *(or if I put my thumb over its tip, or behind my testicles and press hard)* will it do me harm?

✦ In the short term, this is unlikely to do you harm but it's better to ejaculate into a tissue which you can then throw away.

Willy Worries

I get a pleasant sensation when I climb frames or ropes in PE (physical exercise) from rubbing against my genital area. Is this an orgasm?

✦ It could well be an orgasm – or a similar sensation.

✦ A young man may get a sensation similar to orgasm with or without ejaculation.

✦ Ejaculation and orgasm are two separate things, yet many people think they're the same. You can have an orgasm without ejaculating and you can ejaculate without having an orgasm.

✦ Most young women reach orgasm through clitoral stimulation. So whether you're a young man or a young woman, you're probably getting some form of sexual arousal and pleasure when you rub your genital area against the frame or rope.

My friends say they go on for ages when they have sex, but I ejaculate very quickly. Is this normal?

✦ There's no normal length of time for having sex but this could be called premature ejaculation.

✦ It's extremely common when you're very excited at the prospect of having sex, particularly when you're young or with a new sexual partner.

✦ With practice you can learn to have your orgasm and ejaculation as and when you choose.

✦ You can ejaculate without having an orgasm and you can have an orgasm without ejaculating, though they often happen simultaneously *(together)*.

✦ If you are still worried about it refer to the condom information in the Safer Sex section *(page 204)*.

Why do some men get painful erections, with their penis bending to one side?

✦ Not all penises are straight but a change in direction could be caused by a condition that is more common in middle aged and older men.

✦ It's called Peyronie's disease and is when the muscle on one side of the penis is blocked by little lumps deep inside and it can't fill with blood properly to give a straight erection.

✦ Sometimes sex becomes very difficult and medication or surgery may be recommended.

✦ The reason why it happens to some and not to others is unclear.

© Sylvia Rawsthorn 1999

How do I put my penis in to my partner so we can have sex and does it hurt?

✦ You need to have a firm erection, not a soft penis.

✦ A young woman must be turned on enough for sex, making a welcoming fluid, which then makes penetration *(entry of your penis into her vagina)* easier and more comfortable.

✦ If she's not moist you may need to use extra lubrication otherwise penetration may be uncomfortable.

✦ Gently rub the tip of your penis between the lips *(labia)* of her moist external genital area (vulva) then slowly push your penis inside her vagina.

✦ Sex shouldn't hurt either of you.

✦ *For further information about lubricants, see page 217.*

Willy Worries

Will my penis be trapped inside my partner when I have sex and how do I get it out again?

✦ Your penis cannot become trapped because the vagina doesn't trap or 'bite' it.
✦ So just pull it out gently when you want to withdraw.
✦ Rarely, some women develop a condition called vaginismus. Their vaginal muscles go into spasm and tighten. It doesn't last long and you can still withdraw your penis easily.

When my penis is inside my partner, will I pass urine?

✦ No, you can't pass urine while you have an erection.
✦ A valve at your bladder closes when your penis is erect. This allows semen and sperm to come out through your urethra but it holds your urine back, inside your bladder.

Why do my testicles ache so much when we're just heavy petting?

✦ During sexual arousal your testicles rise towards your body and swell.
✦ At orgasm they relax and return to their usual size quite quickly.
✦ So, if you're just teasing/petting each other for a long time, without ejaculation, they may ache later.
✦ That doesn't mean you have to have sex to prevent this feeling.
✦ It'll wear off on its own or after sex – but you can always masturbate to relieve any discomfort. *(It is natural for most men to masturbate. Many are too shy to admit it to their friends or talk about it in company.)*

Will my penis be too big to go inside my girlfriend if she's never had sex before?

✦ No, it's unlikely that your penis will be too big. As long as you're gentle, and she's nicely relaxed, aroused and wet, it should slide in easily.
✦ She has to be relaxed otherwise the welcoming fluid won't flow to lubricate her vagina.
✦ Her hymen may still be intact if she hasn't used tampons or stretched it during exercise. *(For further information on the hymen, see page 49.)*
✦ You should be very gentle, not in a hurry and be ready to stop if she feels pain or changes her mind – even at the last minute.
✦ If she says stop, and you don't, you will be committing a criminal offence.
✦ There's a band of muscle at the entrance to her vagina, which relaxes when she's ready to allow you to enter.
✦ Her vagina has a dead end so you don't have to worry about going in too far.
✦ Discuss your decision to have sex carefully though, because once it's lost, she can't retrieve her virginity.
✦ You should also make sure you use adequate protection from pregnancy and/or infection.
✦ She may be at risk of infection if you've had sex before.
✦ Many girls are bullied by peer pressure and made to feel they should have sex by a certain age.
✦ There's no upper age limit for having sex, no hurry to start and no right or wrong number of times to do it.

© Sylvia Rawsthorn 1999

Willy Worries

I can get my penis in to my partner but I can't ejaculate. What's wrong and how can I _come_?

✦ Many men worry about not being able to ejaculate inside their partner although they can ejaculate during masturbation.

✦ You need to learn to relax and let go of your worries, and your ejaculate.

✦ The reason you hold back may be as simple as being scared of getting your partner pregnant.

✦ Something might have happened to you when you were younger which you subconsciously block out.

✦ There may be other reasons, which you need to explore and your doctor may be able to help you find the reason or refer you to someone else for help.

Does it mean I have sperm if I have erections?

✦ No. Babies and small boys have erections but don't have sperm.

✦ Sperm start to develop from puberty.

✦ After that, unless a doctor tells you otherwise, you should assume you have millions of sperm at the tip of your penis every time you have an erection.

✦ There could be enough to cause pregnancy if they get near a young woman's fertile mucus (*even externally*) so be very careful where you put your erect penis!

At what age will I have sperm?

✦ You start to have sperm soon after you reach puberty.

✦ This is usually between 10 and 14 years of age.

Should I be able to see sperm in my urine?

✦ No. Sperm are so tiny they're invisible to the naked eye.

✦ The fluid you ejaculate consists of sperm, semen and prostatic fluid – not all sperm.

Information about sperm!

✦ Some people nickname them tadpoles because they look similar under a microscope!

✦ They can swim at about 1/10th of an inch a minute, which is about 6 inches an hour or 0.0001 mph.

✦ They come shooting out at an average speed of about 28 miles an hour, along with semen and other alkaline (*non-acid*) fluid in which they're swept along. Without this they'd be killed as soon as they reach the acid of the vagina.

✦ Some ejaculations may be slower and some faster, some thick and some runny!

✦ Sperm get into the cervix after about 90 seconds after ejaculation.

✦ They can then take only five minutes to reach the fallopian tubes.

✦ They can live inside a woman for half a day or up to 7 days, depending on the woman's fertile mucus, in which they live, and off which they feed.

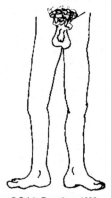

© Sylvia Rawsthorn 1999

Willy Worries

Willy Worries

A good reason for fiddling with your own or your partner's testicles!

✦ All men and boys should be testicle aware - just as ladies are taught to be breast aware.

✦ The aim is to catch early signs of cancer of the testicles or other testicular problems.

✦ Testicular cancer is not a sexually acquired infection but can affect sexual health and fertility, if it's not treated quickly.

✦ Men between the ages of 15 and 35 are most commonly affected.

✦ The incidence of testicular cancer is on the increase. Fortunately it has the highest treatment success rate of all cancers. Don't panic if you notice something unusual.

✦ Other things can cause swellings or lumps, so it's essential that you let a doctor check you quickly – even if you're embarrassed to ensure you get the correct diagnosis and treatment.

The cause of testicular cancer is not proven but the main factors, which may increase your risks, are:

1 – age – highest risk is between 15 to 35 years of age;

2 – if you had undescended testicles when you were born and needed an operation to bring one or both of them down into your scrotum;

3 – infection; and/or

4 – trauma / accident / injury.

How often should I check?

✦ Check them about once a month.

Where should I check them?

✦ Checking them in a bath or shower is a good idea, when your scrotum is relaxed and they hang a bit lower.

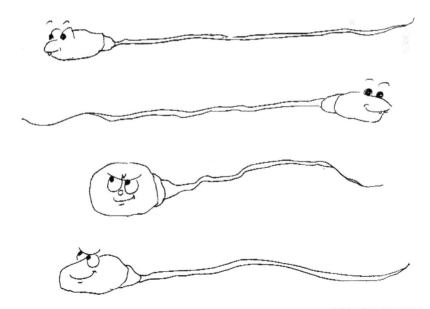

Willy Worries

© Sylvia Rawsthorn 1999

Willy Worries

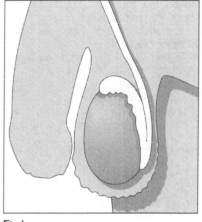

Fig 1

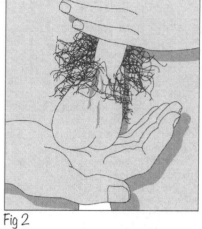

Fig 2

Fig 3

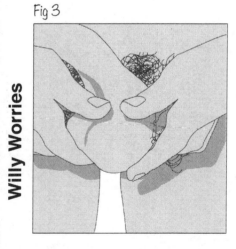

Fig 4

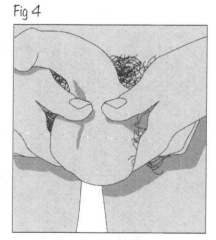

© Peter Gardiner

Willy Worries

Testicular Self-Examination (TSE)

How do I check my testicles?

✦ **Fig 1** - The first time you check them you'll notice various lumps and bumps. Consider these to be your base line from which you can notice any changes.

✦ **Fig 2** - Rest your testicles in the palm of your hand and note their weight and size.

✦ You'll probably notice that one testicle is larger than the other and may also hang lower than the other one, which is quite normal.

✦ **Fig 3** - Then roll each testicle, in turn, between your thumbs and fingers.

✦ **Fig 4** - Feel right round each one and up into your groin behind them.

✦ You'll notice a spermatic cord behind each testicle *(long, thin, round, semi-hard area).*

✦ Look at your testicles in the mirror and notice any visual changes.

What else should I look out for?

✦ Look out for a dull ache in your groin or abdomen.

✦ Heaviness in your scrotum.

✦ Occasionally there may be pain in your testicle itself.

I've noticed something

✦ First, check to see if it is on your other testicle, too.

✦ If it is, it's extremely unlikely to be cancer, as it rarely develops on both sides.

Now what do I do?

✦ Make an appointment to see a doctor – either visit your GP or you can go to a Sexual Health Clinic where the staff specialise in dealing with this part of the body; and appointments are not always necessary.

What if I've got testicular cancer?

✦ When it's detected early, simple removal of the affected testicle is usually all that's necessary.

✦ You may be offered special drug or x-ray treatment afterwards.

✦ There's virtually a 100% cure rate when detected early.

I won't look normal any more

✦ Testicular implants *(false ones)* will probably be discussed with you, so you'll look as you did before.

What about sex?

✦ You'll be able to continue your sex life as before.

✦ The other testicle will continue to produce enough sperm and testosterone so your fertility shouldn't be affected.

© Sylvia Rawsthorn 1999

Willy Worries

Willy Worries — Torsion

I've heard of torsion of the testicles, what's that?

✦ Torsion is when a testicle gets twisted in your scrotum and its blood and oxygen supply are cut off.

✦ It's extremely painful and requires medical attention, quickly.

✦ The affected testicle may have to be removed but you still have the other one to make millions of sperm, so your future fertility shouldn't be affected.

✦ As before, you can have a false one implanted to make you look as you did before.

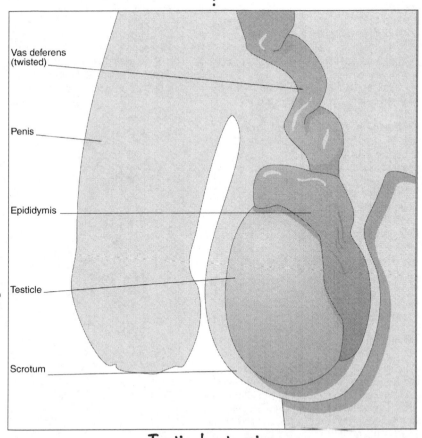

Vas deferens (twisted)

Penis

Epididymis

Testicle

Scrotum

Testicular torsion

© Peter Gardiner

Willy Worries — Hydrocele

What's a hydrocele?

✦ Hydrocele is when fluid gathers in your scrotum and it swells up due to a tiny fluid leak from your abdomen to the area surrounding your testicles.
✦ It's common in babies but also common in adult men.
✦ It may or may not be painful depending upon the cause.
✦ It may be due to injury or infection, though it often develops for no known reason.

Depending on the cause, treatment consists of either:

1. leaving it alone and seeing if it goes away on its own, if it isn't particularly large or painful;
2. antibiotics if there's an infection;
3. draining it with a needle *(aspiration)*; and/or
4. surgical repair if the leak is recurrent, of particular concern or if your scrotum becomes very large and uncomfortable.

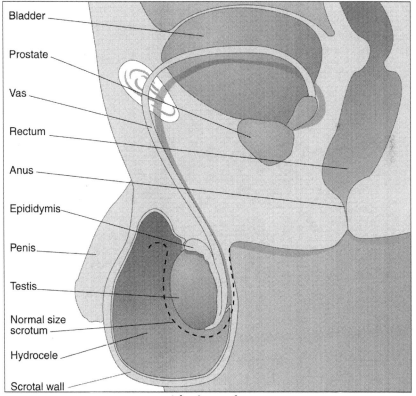

Bladder
Prostate
Vas
Rectum
Anus
Epididymis
Penis
Testis
Normal size scrotum
Hydrocele
Scrotal wall

Willy Worries

Hydrocele

© Peter Gardiner

What's my prostate?

✦ Your prostate is a walnut sized organ or gland, which lies underneath your bladder.
✦ It produces a fluid which mixes with semen and sperm during ejaculation.

There are three conditions you should be aware of, all related to the prostate, and each of which needs medical attention.

1. Inflammation or infection due to sexually acquired infections, which can affect men of all ages.
2. Benign enlargement *(not cancer)* is very common and affects 1 man in 3 over the age of 50. *(This is also called BPH or benign prostatic hyperplasia.)*
3. Cancer of the prostate *(malignant)* causes the second highest number of cancer deaths amongst men after lung cancer.

For all three of the above, you are likely to notice one or more of the following

✦ Altered urination – you may have difficulty or delay when starting to pass urine.
✦ Your urine may not flow normally, but may stop and start.
✦ You may feel your bladder hasn't emptied properly when you've passed urine.
✦ You may have to get up in the night to pass urine, which is not directly related to a drinking binge the night before.
✦ There's a blood test which can detect if you're more likely to develop cancer of the prostate.
✦ **Early detection makes treatment easier and saves lives.**

Willy Worries

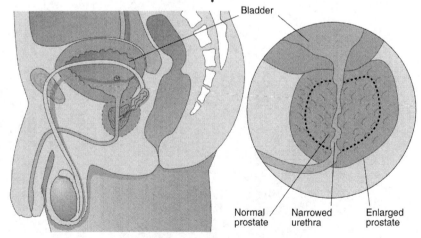

Bladder

Normal prostate   Narrowed urethra   Enlarged prostate

View of enlarged and normal prostate gland

© Peter Gardiner

With infection, you may notice:

- ✦ lower back pain;
- ✦ pain on passing urine;
- ✦ fever and/or chills;
- ✦ discomfort in your genital area.

Treatment depends upon the cause but consist of antibiotics for infection, surgery or chemotherapy if benign or cancerous *(malignant)* plus additional radiotherapy for cancerous enlargement.

Further genital hygiene

✦ Good genital hygiene is important for prevention of infection.

✦ If you haven't been circumcised, you should look after your foreskin.

✦ No man is immune from infection but uncircumcised men are at increased risk of contracting sexually acquired infections.

✦ A creamy lubricant called smegma, forms underneath it, to keep it moving freely over the tip *(glans or head)* of your penis.

✦ Like many other young men, you may know of your smegma by a nickname such as knob cheese!

✦ It's important to wash every day otherwise germs can multiply and your foreskin may become infected, dry and sore, causing it to tighten over the end of your penis *(phimosis)* and become painful.

✦ You should pull your foreskin back along the shaft of your penis, so that the skin lies flat.

✦ Wash away the smegma from around the tip area with soap and water before towelling yourself dry again.

✦ If you're unable to pull your foreskin back to clean underneath it, you may need circumcision.

✦ Women also make a small amount of smegma around their clitoris, so daily washing is recommended for women, too.

✦ Women don't suffer from the same tightening as men, so there's no medical reason for female circumcision, which is more accurately called FGM *(Female Genital Mutilation).*

NOTE: For further information on both male circumcision and FGM, see page 190.

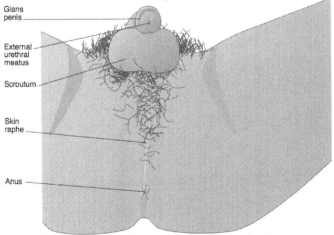

Glans penis

External urethral meatus

Scroutum

Skin raphe

Anus

View of male genitalia from below

Willy Worries

© Sylvia Rawsthorn 1999

Young Women's Changes
&
Women's Worries

What's puberty?

What's the difference between puberty and adolescence?

Fertile mucus

What happens when you have unprotected sex?

Ectopic pregnancy

How periods happen

How much blood is lost during a period?

How long do periods last and how often do they come?

Vaginal discharge

Diary keeping

Other changes during puberty

Sexuality

Menstrual cycle and weight

Cervical maturity

Adolescent development

Smoking

How can smoking cause high blood pressure?

Breast Self-Examination (BSE)

What should I look for when I check my breasts?

Basic BSE technique

What's my clitoris and where is it?

I've heard about the G-spot. What is it and where can I find mine?

Why do I get wet down below when I think of sex?

What is my vagina?

Where is my vagina?

What's my hymen?

If I break it, can it be repaired?

What does the word virgin mean?

If I lose my virginity, how can I find it again?

Will I lose my virginity if I ride a man's bicycle or a horse?

When do girls start their periods?

When will I have my first period, become fertile and be able to have a baby?

Is it common to have irregular periods?

Should I use sanitary pads/towels or tampons when I have my periods?

The Mooncup ®

How is it used?

Toxic shock syndrome (TSS)

Will I bleed when I have sex for the first time?

If I do bleed, how much will it be?

If my Mum gets ill with her periods, will I, too?

Is it OK to have sex during a period?

Weight and dieting

What's contraception?

Why is it important for men/women to know about contraception before we first have sex/make love?

Where can I get contraception?

What should we know about contraception?

What else is on offer?

Do I have to be married or planning a family to go to a clinic offering contraception services or family planning advice?

Do they need to see any identification of who I am?

Will they lecture me?

So, if I inject or use drugs, am I still welcome at the clinics?

Will they tell my doctor (GP) if I go to clinic?

How can I be sure?

Must I return to the same clinic where I started?

Are the doctors male or female at contraception clinics?

How much does it cost?

Can I just go to clinic for condoms?

Where can I find these condom supply points?

Breast development

1 — preadolescent

Start of puberty
2 — breast bud — small mound;
areola enlarges

Early teens
3 — further growth; areola and nipple
not separate from breast curve

Late teens
4— nipple and areola above curve
of breast

Yound adult
5— mature: nipple elevated but areola
flattens into breast curve

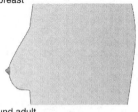

Pubic hair development

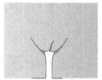

1 — preadolescent

2 — sparse growth of long
hairs on labia

3 — darker, thicker, curly hair
covers junction of pubes

4— adult in type b ut not as extensive

5 — adult in type; spreading up linea alba
and on to medial aspects of the thighs,
especially in males

© Peter Gardiner

Body Changes — Young Women

Young Women's Changes & Women's Worries

What's puberty?

✦ Puberty is the time when your body starts to change from that of a child into a young woman. It happens between the age of about 9 and 16 and lasts for about 3 to 6 years.

✦ You'll start to release your eggs *(ovulate)* and have periods right through until you're about 50, when they stop. This is called menopause.

✦ Your breasts will start to develop.

✦ You may get spots appearing on your face due to hormonal *(chemical)* changes.

✦ Both your pubic and underarm hair will start to grow.

✦ When you start your periods you'll become a young woman, capable of reproduction. Generally, because of this, your parents or other adults will worry about you and become protective.

What's the difference between puberty and adolescence?

✦ Puberty is the time when you mature physically.

✦ Adolescence is the time when you start to mature emotionally.

Egg release *(ovulation)*

✦ From the start of your periods you will usually release one or two eggs (ova) every month.

✦ You were born with your lifetime's supply of eggs in your ovaries.

✦ For this to happen, your brain sends a chemical message in the form of a hormone, FSH *(follicle stimulating hormone)*, to your ovaries.

✦ Your ovaries then start to develop an egg for that month and produce oestrogen.

✦ After the egg is released from your ovary, it is wafted along your fallopian tube towards the lining of your womb (the endometrium) and your ovary then stimulates another hormone called progesterone *(pronounced pro-jes-terone)*.

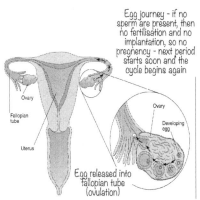

Egg journey – if no sperm are present, then no fertilisation and no implantation, so no pregnancy – next period starts soon and the cycle begins again

View of egg release from ovary

© Peter Gardiner

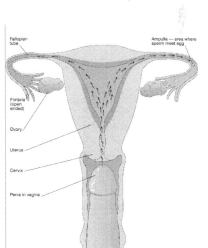

Illustration of unprotected vaginal sex and ejaculated sperm

© Peter Gardiner

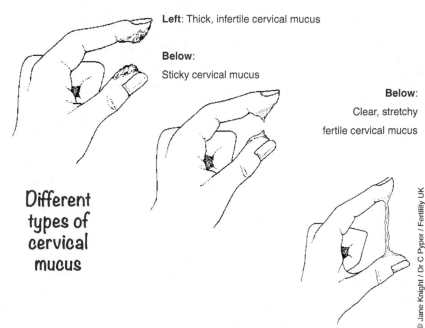

Left: Thick, infertile cervical mucus

Below:
Sticky cervical mucus

Below:
Clear, stretchy
fertile cervical mucus

Different types of cervical mucus

© Jane Knight / Dr C Pyper / Fertility UK

Fertile mucus

✦ The *cervix* (neck of your womb) makes a fertile type of mucus while your egg develops. *(See illustration next page.)*

✦ You can not get pregnant without fertile mucus present.

✦ Some women make 'Spinnbarkeit' fertile mucus for only a day, while others make it for several days.

✦ It's clear and stretchy, rather like egg white and it's essential for sperm to make their way to your egg.

✦ Sperm can live in it and feed off it for the length of time you make fertile mucus. *(This may be up to seven days.)*

✦ After egg release, it changes to infertile or thick mucus which sperm can't get through and lasts until you have your next period.

What happens when you have unprotected sex?

✦ At any time, but especially at the fertile time of the month, sperm can travel through the fertile mucus in the neck of your womb *(cervix)*, up through your uterus *(womb)* and into your fallopian tubes where they may meet an egg. They may then join together *(fertilise)*, start to divide and multiply as a zygote. This spends five days travelling back towards the lining of your womb *(endometrium)* before it finds somewhere suitable to implant *(settle)*. The zygote then becomes a blastocyte and starts growing into the placenta and an embryo. This, in turn, becomes a foetus.

✦ When implantation occurs, a signal is sent from your ovary, telling the lining of your womb to stay in place so you don't have your next period.

✦ It then takes nine months for the foetus to fully develop into a baby.

✦ You may also be at risk of catching a sexually acquired infection (SAI) when you have unprotected sex.

Ectopic pregnancy

✦ An ectopic pregnancy is when a fertilised egg *(ovum)* and pregnancy develops outside the uterus eg. in the fallopian tube, ovary or abdomen.

✦ The most common area for ectopic pregnancy is in the fallopian tube, when the fertilised egg *(ovum)* gets stuck and settles, growing there, instead of travelling to the lining of your womb to settle.

✦ Ectopic pregnancy can be life-threatening and you would need emergency treatment or surgery to prevent serious illness or even death.

✦ You may have pelvic pain and abnormal vaginal bleeding with ectopic pregnancy.

✦ If worried, you should be checked by your doctor; or visit your local Sexual Health Clinic or Emergency Department, without delay.

Illustration of ectopic pregnancy

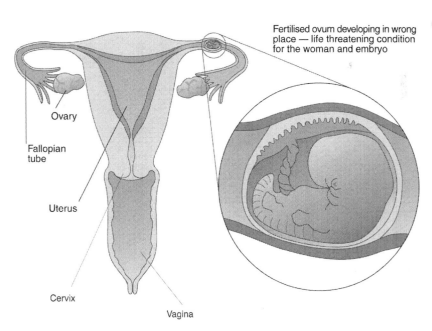

Fertilised ovum developing in wrong place — life threatening condition for the woman and embryo

Ovary

Fallopian tube

Uterus

Cervix

Vagina

© Peter Gardiner

How periods happen

✦ Periods happen because of a series of events throughout your menstrual cycle.

✦ While the egg is being produced in your ovary, the lining of your womb *(endometrium)* builds a ripe cushion for an ovum *(fertilized egg)* to implant.

✦ If one doesn't implant, it gets a signal from your ovary and the cushion or lining sheds away.

✦ This shedding is what happens when you have your menstrual *(i.e. monthly)* period.

How much blood is lost during a period?

✦ On average 1-2 tablespoons of blood are lost each month.

✦ Many people think pints of blood are lost, but this is not true. A little bit of blood can go a long way!

✦ Some women have heavier periods and may benefit from using hormonal contraception to reduce their blood loss.

✦ If you are worried about your periods, speak to your doctor or nurse.

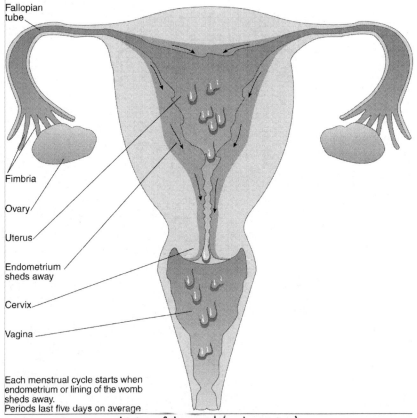

Fallopian tube

Fimbria

Ovary

Uterus

Endometrium sheds away

Cervix

Vagina

Each menstrual cycle starts when endometrium or lining of the womb sheds away.
Periods last five days on average

© Peter Gardiner

Lining of the womb (endometrium) shedding during a period

How long do periods last and how often do they come?

✦ Each period will usually last between three and 10 days.
✦ Periods may be irregular for many months while your body adjusts but they usually settle into a pattern of coming between every 21 and 35 days.
✦ You'll develop your own menstrual pattern and release your egg somewhere between 10 and 16 days before the first day of your *next* period – not always, as is often stated, on the 14th day into your cycle.
✦ Life would be simple if this were the case – there would be fewer unplanned pregnancies. Unfortunately life isn't quite that easy!
✦ Some people call periods menses, monthlies or the curse.

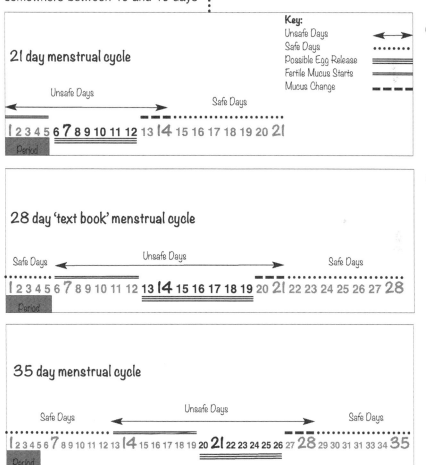

Illustration of different length menstrual cycles, with safe/unsafe days

NOTE: Also see the section on Fertility Awareness Methods.

© Helen Knox 2014

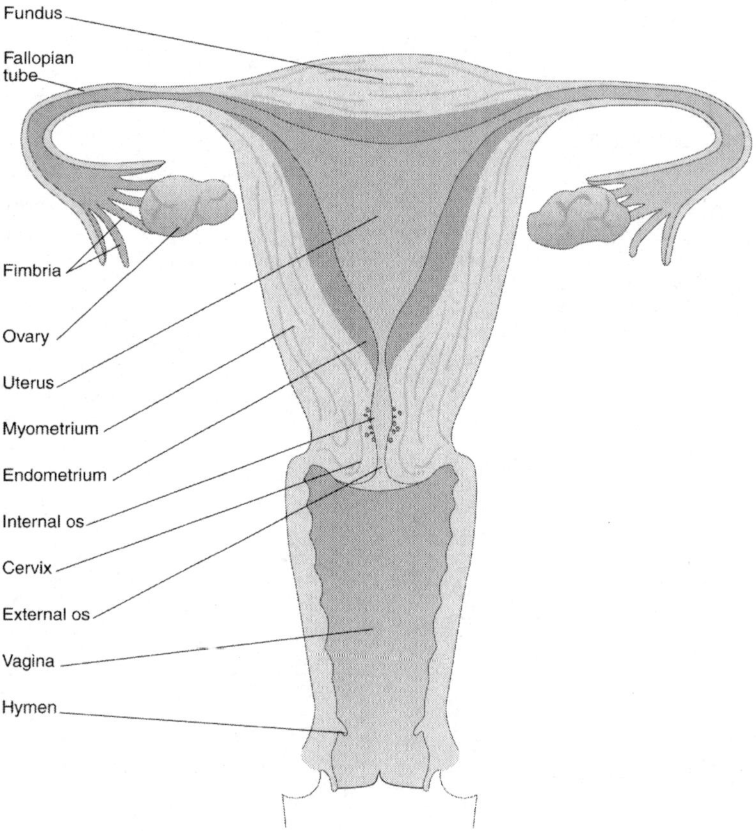

Fundus

Fallopian tube

Fimbria

Ovary

Uterus

Myometrium

Endometrium

Internal os

Cervix

External os

Vagina

Hymen

© Peter Gardiner

Female Reproductive Tract

Vaginal discharge

✦ Vaginal discharge occurs, and changes, throughout the menstrual cycle.
✦ Each menstrual cycle starts with a period, which lasts for about five days. You will need to use external sanitary pads, internal tampons or a Mooncup® to protect your clothing.
✦ After that, your vagina will probably appear to be quite dry for a few days, before fertile mucus is produced at the neck of your womb *(cervix)*.
✦ Mucus is cloudy at first then goes clear and stretchy, appearing just like egg white.
✦ After egg release, the mucus gets thicker and your vagina becomes drier, though you'll still have a general moistness to keep you comfortable.
✦ It's perfectly normal to have a clear or slightly white and occasionally watery vaginal discharge, which stains your knickers and doesn't really smell.
✦ But, if the discharge seems unusual, heavier or smells, it's wise to get tested at a Sexual Health Clinic incase you've been passed a sexually acquired infection.

Diary keeping

✦ Keeping a note of your periods is very useful.
✦ This can help you to predict when your next period will arrive.
✦ Many times throughout your life you'll be asked for the date of the **first** day of your last/most recent period. So it's wise to keep a note in your diary each month to check the length of your menstrual cycle *(cycle)*. This helps to assess your fertile times and whether your body is working as it should.
✦ To measure your cycle length in days, you count the number of days from the *first* day of your period, until the *day before* the first day of your *next* period.
✦ Sometimes your period might be longer or shorter than other times, as might the length of your menstrual cycle.
✦ The number of days in a calendar month can vary, which is why it's a good idea to count the days by looking at calendar dates rather than guess when you think your next period should come.

Other changes during puberty

✦ You'll continue to grow in height and weight.
✦ Your figure will start to change with your breasts growing, your hips getting wider, your waist becoming more defined; and you might develop a wiggle as you walk!
✦ Your general body odour may change slightly and you'll gradually become more inquisitive about sex and its mysteries.
✦ You'll probably start to explore your body and start to masturbate.
✦ Masturbation won't make you blind, deaf or drive you mad as people used to say in olden days!
✦ You may become interested in make-up, fashion, music, members of the opposite sex and the appearance of your body.

© Sylvia Rawsthorn 1999

Sexuality

✦ You may wonder about your sexuality at some stage and the people you find attractive.

✦ You might not be attracted to members of the opposite sex but to members of your own or even, to both sexes.

✦ *For further information on sexuality, see p147.*

Menstrual cycle and weight

✦ If you're under or overweight for your age and height your menstrual cycle could be affected.

✦ Your periods may become irregular or perhaps stop until you return to your correct weight.

Cervical maturity

✦ Even if you appear physically mature by your mid teens, your reproductive organs, in particular the neck of your womb *(cervix)* takes until you're about 23 years of age to mature.

✦ Therefore, if you have sex, particularly under this age you'd be wise to use condoms to protect it from infection.

✦ *See p65 for information about the HPV vaccine, developed to protect the cervix.*

Adolescent development

✦ You may think that all adults are stupid and don't have a clue how you feel.

✦ This is just part of your development.

✦ You might think you can't talk to any of them, but don't forget, they've all gone through similar confusing years, too. They really aren't stupid aliens from outer space!

✦ They know more about the ways of the adult world. They'd like to help you avoid many of the mistakes they made when they were your age; and you never know, you might even grow to like them if you give them a chance!

✦ They'll be happy to help if they know the answers to your questions.

✦ If you're too shy to talk to your parents or another adult you know well, try asking other people; for example your teacher, school nurse, youth worker, doctor, practice nurse, trusted aunt, uncle, older brother, sister, cousin or family friend.

✦ You may prefer to find information by talking to friends, reading books, watching films, or drop into your local Sexual Health Clinic where the staff are clued up about sex.

✦ You'll find that there's a lot more to having sex than just the physical act of intercourse and that there's another side to it.

✦ You'll learn about the risk of contracting sexually acquired infections and of unplanned pregnancy in addition to the fun, joy and pleasure of sex.

✦ By looking after yourself and asking the right questions, sex will also be enjoyable and give you pleasure.

✦ Remember, though, that with sex you have responsibilities: to your partner as well as yourself.

✦ It is wrong for an adult to interfere with you sexually. You must tell someone, whatever they say, even if you're scared, so you get help for it to stop.

✦ *For information about abuse, see page 171.*

Smoking

✦ There are one or two very good reasons not to smoke!

✦ Smoking is, as you'll probably know, bad for your health.

✦ Each time you smoke a cigarette hundreds of chemical reactions take place throughout your body.

✦ Apart from smelling like an old ashtray with bad breath, there's a strong link between smoking and cancer of the lungs, heart disease, bronchitis, shortness of breath, emphysema, leg ulcers; bladder, stomach, mouth and throat cancer; strokes, high blood pressure and lots more.

✦ In women, smoking is linked to cancer of the cervix.

✦ In men, it's linked to reduced sperm count *(reduced fertility)* and later in life, with impotence *(the persistent inability to get and keep an erection, sufficient for intercourse)*.

✦ Would you really choose to gamble with your ability to have good sex for many years, even if you don't have any problems now?

✦ Therefore not smoking could improve and protect your sex life!

✦ Smoking ages your skin, so by the time you're about 30, you might look about 50 years old!

✦ Smoking can also lead to incontinence of urine and of faeces.

✦ If you smoke and want help to give up, ask your doctor for advice and referral; otherwise, just quit!

✦ It may be hard to stop smoking, but living with long term discomfort because of it, is much harder and more painful than the craving for nicotine.

✦ Smoking other drugs is illegal and can have damaging effects on your body and your sex life.

✦ The choice is yours, you only have one life, so why damage it with a dirty, expensive habit, which may cause years of suffering if you continue?

✦ It seems daft!

How can smoking cause high blood pressure?

✦ There are several causes of high blood pressure *(hypertension)*. Commonly it's due to the gradual build up of atheroma *(fatty substances)* on the lining of your arteries and veins. This causes blood to flow less freely along them and your heart has to pump more forcefully to send the same amount of blood around your body.

✦ Think about it another way. When a house is built, the plumber instals clean pipes and water flows freely to your bath, washing machine, sink etc.

✦ Gradually tough scale deposits inside the pipes, as in your kettle, causing them to fur up and block.

✦ As you get older, depending on what you eat and your general lifestyle, blood or fat cells stick to the lining of your arteries and veins causing rough areas of atheroma to develop, which can form a clot, and block them.

✦ Due to the extra pressure at which your heart pumps, the clot may be pushed off its resting place and travel around your body.

✦ If it lodges in your brain, it causes a stroke *(CVA or cerebro vascular accident);* in the muscle of your heart it causes a heart attack *(myocardial infarction)*; in your lungs it causes a pulmonary embolism; and in your calf or other muscles, it causes a DVT *(deep vein thrombosis)*.

✦ Smoking is a major factor, which increases the stickiness of your blood and greatly increases your risk of developing problems.

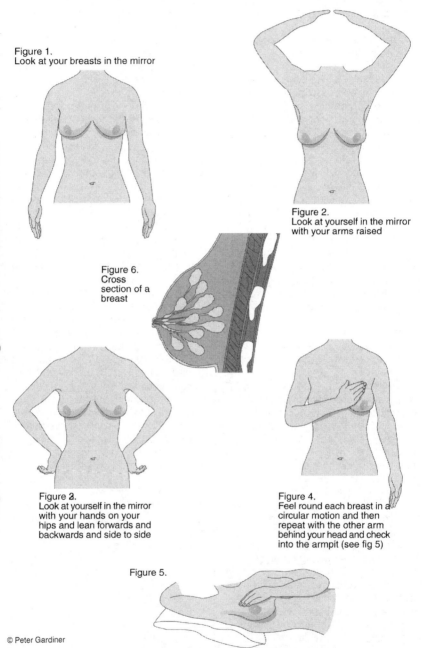

Figure 1.
Look at your breasts in the mirror

Figure 2.
Look at yourself in the mirror
with your arms raised

Figure 6.
Cross
section of a
breast

Figure 3.
Look at yourself in the mirror
with your hands on your
hips and lean forwards and
backwards and side to side

Figure 4.
Feel round each breast in a
circular motion and then
repeat with the other arm
behind your head and check
into the armpit (see fig 5)

Figure 5.

© Peter Gardiner

Breast Self Examination (BSE)

Young Women's Changes & Women's Worries

Breast Self-Examination (BSE)

✦ It's sensible for all men and women to be breast aware.
✦ WOMEN **and** MEN should check their breasts regularly using the same technique.
✦ Partners can check each other's breasts.
✦ You may be shown other techniques but they all aim to check your vulnerable areas.
✦ You should know the look, shape and texture of your breasts.
✦ Breast cancer affects one woman in 12 in the UK.
✦ It's rare for men, but not unknown.
✦ Nine out of 10 lumps found, are not malignant – ie. they are benign / non-cancerous – so, if you find a lump, act quickly and let a doctor check it out.
✦ Either visit your doctor or go to a Contraception / Sexual Health Clinic.
✦ In the UK, women aged 50 to 65 are automatically invited for free mammography *(special breast X-ray)* every three years.

What should I look for when I check my breasts?

Watch for:
✦ any changes to the usual look or feel of your breasts;
✦ any change to your nipple*(s)* and any discharge or secretion from them;
✦ any change in the direction your nipple*(s)* point;
✦ any puckering or swelling of your breast skin;
✦ any bulges in your breast contour;
✦ 'orange peel' skin, dimpling or tethering – i.e. as if something is stuck to the inside of it;
✦ any swelling of your upper arm or armpit.

Basic BSE technique

Looking at yourself in a mirror:

✦ stand upright, then lean forwards, then tilt sideways with your arms by your sides;
✦ put your hands on your head – to stretch the breast tissue – and repeat looking, moving and checking as before;
✦ place your hands on your hips and repeat viewing, moving and checking again, as before.

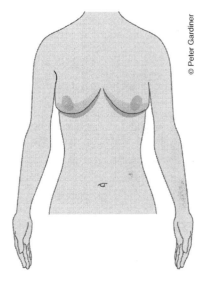

© Peter Gardiner

Fig I - Look at your breasts in the mirror

Then
✦ Be comfortable and relaxed whilst checking.
✦ You can do this in a bath or lying on the bed – wherever you're most comfortable.
✦ With one arm stretched behind your head, feel your opposite breast in a firm but gentle manner, with the flat of your other hand.

Young Women's Changes & Women's Worries

Fig 2 - Look at yourself in the mirror with your arms raised

✦ Start by squeezing your nipple and look for fluid coming out.
✦ Feel in a Catherine wheel motion around your nipple area with your hand, round and round the breast area and up into your armpit.
✦ All this time, be aware of the lumps you are feeling.
✦ You will find lumps the first time you check, as your breasts are made up of many glands, surrounded by fat.

Fig 4 - Feel round each breast in a circular motion, then repeat with other arm behind head, checking in to armpit (Fig 5)

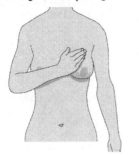

Fig 3 - Look at yourself in the mirror with your hands on your hips, leaning forwards and backwards, side to side

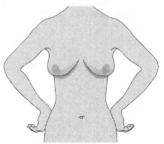

✦ These lumps and bumps form a base line from which you can notice any changes.
✦ When you make breast awareness part of your routine health care, the stress of regular checking is reduced.
✦ If in doubt, ask your doctor or Contraception / Sexual Health Clinic to check them for you.

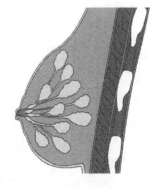

Fig 6 - Cross section of a breast

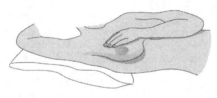

Fig 5 - see Fig 4

© Peter Gardiner

It's OK to look at your bits!

© Sylvia Rawsthorn 1999

What's my clitoris and where is it?

✦ Your clitoris is a small area of erectile tissue situated at the front of your genital area *(vulva)* which is covered by a little hood of skin.

✦ Looking down on yourself, it sits just infront of your urine passage *(urethra),* before the vaginal entrance.

✦ It also extends to encompass the whole of your vulva, hidden from view.

✦ It has a large supply of blood vessels and nerve endings, which make it very sensitive to touch.

✦ It swells in size and becomes erect when you're sexually aroused; just as a penis gets larger and hard when a man is sexually aroused.

✦ The area that is on view would have developed into a penis if you'd been a boy instead of a girl.

✦ Like your clitoris, the tip of a penis is sensitive. But the nerve endings of your clitoris are concentrated into a smaller area – hence its 'super-sensitivity' when touched.

✦ To learn about your anatomy, have a look at yourself in a mirror and explore your genital area *(vulva).*

NOTE: For information about Female Genital Mutilation (FGM), see page191.

I've heard about the G-spot. What is it and where can I find mine?

✦ While the term G-spot was popularised by a pop song, it doesn't appear in general anatomy text books.

✦ The area is mythical and not so much a physical but psychological area for sexual arousal.

✦ In women it's said to be about 1-1½ inches (2-3 cms) inside the vagina, underneath the bladder; and for men, in the rectum, below the bladder, where the nerve endings change.

✦ The muscle in this area is said to be slightly thicker and rubbing it gently is said to be pleasurable.

✦ Not everyone finds it so, so don't worry. You can still have perfectly good sexual arousal and orgasm without experiencing the amazing, but possibly mythical, G-spot.

✦ No two orgasms are the same anyway and no two people are the same, so don't start worrying about whether you have a G-spot or not.

✦ Worrying about your anatomy will spoil your enjoyment.

✦ Simply enjoy sex safely when you have it.

Young Women's Changes & Women's Worries

Why do I get wet down below when I think of sex?

✦ Just as young men get erections to show they're sexually aroused *(turned on)*, when you're sexually aroused you make a welcoming fluid so that a penis can slip into your vagina easily and painlessly.

✦ Sometimes foreplay *(heavy petting)* is necessary to make this moisture appear.

✦ If you feel hurried or pressured into sex, it's unlikely to flow!

✦ Just because you're wet, it doesn't mean you HAVE to have sex or necessarily WANT to have sex, just that you're becoming aroused!

What is my vagina?

✦ It's a self-cleansing passage, between your external genital area *(vulva)* and your cervix and womb.

Where is my vagina?

✦ Your vagina is situated in your genital area *(vulva)* between your anus and your urine passage *(urethra)*.

✦ It has a dead end and is only linked to your womb *(uterus)* – not to your bladder or your bowels. No urine or faeces *(poo)* can leave your body through it.

✦ It's also called the birth canal.

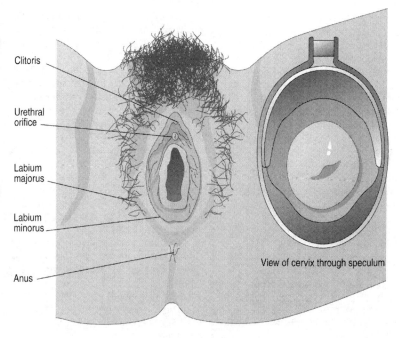

Clitoris

Urethral orifice

Labium majorus

Labium minorus

Anus

View of cervix through speculum

© Peter Gardiner

Illustration of female genitalia

What's my hymen?

✦ Your hymen is a very thin layer of skin, which almost covers the entrance to your vagina. As you grow up it may stretch without you realising.
✦ Sometimes it doesn't stretch but is broken or torn when you first insert a tampon or finger. It may stretch during certain athletic movements.
✦ It's broken when you have sex for the first time *(lose your virginity)*.
✦ This may or may not make you bleed a little bit.

If I break it, can it be repaired?

✦ It's possible for a hymen to be repaired surgically, but it's not common practice to do so.

What does the word *virgin* mean?

Virgin means:
✦ being the first or happening for the first time;
✦ a person who has never had sexual intercourse.

If I lose my virginity, how can I find it again?

✦ You can't get your virginity back after you've lost it.
✦ That's why you should be sure you really want to lose it before giving it away when you have sex for the first time.

Will I lose my virginity if I ride a man's bicycle or a horse?

✦ No. You won't lose your virginity by riding a bicycle.
✦ Although there are male and female saddles, the male saddle doesn't have anything which could penetrate you.
✦ The lady's saddle is wider and is designed to be more comfortable for women.

✦ There's a possibility that with some athletic movements your hymen may stretch, eg. horse riding, gymnastics and perhaps with certain Yoga positions.
✦ However, just because your hymen may have stretched, it doesn't mean you aren't still a virgin – particularly if you haven't had sex.

When do girls start their periods?

✦ Girls usually start their periods between the ages of 9 and 16.

When will I have my first period, become fertile and be able to have a baby?

✦ It's impossible to tell when you will start your periods.
✦ You could, however, become fertile and get pregnant from just before your first period.
✦ Don't think that because you haven't had a period you can't get pregnant. You might!
✦ This is because your egg is released before your period, not after. Because you can't tell when your first egg will be released, you can't tell, for sure, when your period will start.
✦ Many young women get caught out by this and become pregnant before they ever have a period.

I'm worried because all my friends have started their periods and I haven't. What should I do?

✦ Wait until you're about 16 or 17, then see your GP who may do some simple tests to make sure your hormones are working properly.
✦ Alternatively the Sexual Health Clinic staff can advise you.
✦ Many sexual health doctors are gynaecologists *(specialists in women's health and medicine)* so they're good to talk to about things like this. They will listen to your fears and give good advice.

Is it common to have irregular periods?

✦   Many young women have irregular periods in the first few years.
✦   Many continue to have irregular periods for many years, although they many settle into a regular pattern.
✦   There is also a common condition called polycystic ovary syndrome *(PCOS)* which causes irregular bleeding cycles and a few other side effects, such as excess hairiness.
✦   Taking a combined method of contraception, such as the Combined Oral Contraceptive Pill *(COC)* can help control irregular bleeding, as long as the woman is otherwise medically fit.

✦   If you're worried about your periods you should seek medical advice from your doctor or Sexual Health Clinic.

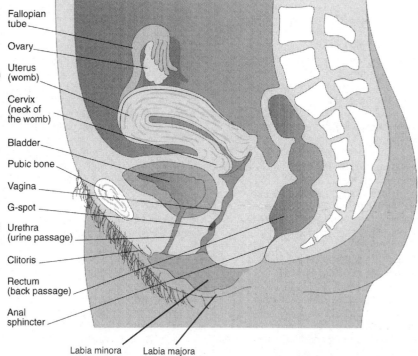

Fallopian tube
Ovary
Uterus (womb)
Cervix (neck of the womb)
Bladder
Pubic bone
Vagina
G-spot
Urethra (urine passage)
Clitoris
Rectum (back passage)
Anal sphincter
Labia minora   Labia majora

© Peter Gardiner

Illustration of female reproductive organs

Should I use sanitary pads/towels or tampons when I have my periods?

✦ The decision about which type of protection to use is up to you.

✦ Each has their use. Sometimes you may choose a tampon *(internal sanitary protection)* and other times you may choose a pad.

✦ Your choice may depend upon what you're wearing, where you're going and how heavy your flow is that day.

✦ If you use tampons, it's important not to leave them in for more than the recommended 8 hours.

✦ Don't use tampons if you have a vaginal infection or an abnormal discharge.

✦ Don't use a tampon of greater absorbency than you need. Many women change their tampons 3-4 hourly.

✦ Some women use more absorbent tampons than they need, thinking that they can then leave them in longer, but it's not recommended.

✦ Stale tampons become smelly and there's then the possibility of bacterial *(germ)* growth in the vagina. *(See p52)*

✦ Tampons should be removed before you pass urine to ensure that you empty your bladder properly.

✦ This will help you to prevent cystitis *(inflammation of the lining of your bladder).*

✦ Pads should be changed as often as necessary to be comfortable.

Mistakes happen: At the end of each period, it is important to check that you have removed your last tampon.

✦ **Many** women forget.

✦ Some have sex, some don't, but either way they then develop a foul smelling vaginal discharge.

✦ They attend their doctor or clinic for a check up, only to find that they've left their last tampon in place!

✦ They are usualy mortified about it.

✦ Try to avoid this mistake.

The Mooncup®

✦ The Mooncup®, launched in 2002, is NOT a method of contraception but one type of device to use instead of tampons or pads. *(There are other brands.)*

✦ It's a smart sanitary protection choice that's worn internally and collects rather than absorbs menstrual fluid;

✦ Holding three times as much as a tampon, it's helpful for heavy days; and being made of soft medical grade silicone, is reusable.

How is it used?

✦ The Mooncup® is folded and inserted into the vagina.

✦ It opens up once it's inside.

✦ It should be removed and emptied every 4 to 8 hours, depending on the flow and then rinsed out, or wiped, before being reinserted.

✦ Unlike a tampon, it's non-absorbent, so it won't cause dryness on light days.

✦ It comes in two sizes, depending on the woman's age and if she has had a baby; and, since it can last for years, only one Mooncup®, is needed, it's an ecomical solution to a monthly problem!

✦ The Mooncup® is discreet, whatever you're wearing; and it can be used when you are travelling, swimming, exercising and also, overnight.

✦ For more information about this item, see www.Mooncup.co.uk

The Mooncup®

Young Women's Changes & Women's Worries

Toxic shock syndrome (TSS)

✦ Although this condition is very rare it is something you should be aware of.

✦ TSS is an infection caused by the bacteria *staphylococcus aureus*.

✦ If tampons are left inside your vagina for a long time *(or forgotten)*, in the presence of the bacteria, they can alter the normal conditions in your vagina and trigger problems.

✦ TSS can cause headache, sore throat, aching muscles and joints, high temperature, a rash, dizziness, diarrhoea and even coma from blood poisoning *(septicaemia)*. This is a life-threatening condition and has to be treated quickly with antibiotics, probably in hospital.

✦ The use of sanitary towels rather than tampons on light flow days may be helpful and does not carry the same risk.

✦ It is advisable to use tampons with an applicator or wash your hands before and after inserting your tampon.

✦ Many women have changed from using tampons to sanitary pads / towels or e.g. a Mooncup® to avoid the risk of developing TSS.

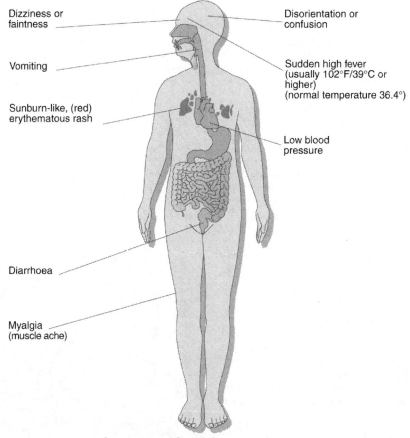

Dizziness or faintness

Vomiting

Sunburn-like, (red) erythematous rash

Diarrhoea

Myalgia (muscle ache)

Disorientation or confusion

Sudden high fever (usually 102°F/39°C or higher) (normal temperature 36.4°)

Low blood pressure

Symptoms of Staphylococcus Aureus

© Peter Gardiner

Will I bleed when I have sex for the first time?

✦ Some people believe that bleeding the first time you have sex proves you're a virgin. That's not true because not all women bleed when they first have sex, and you may be one of them.

If I do bleed, how much will it be?

✦ You should only bleed a little if you bleed at all – when you first have sex.
✦ The bleeding shouldn't continue.

If my Mum gets ill with her periods, will I, too?

✦ No, not necessarily.
✦ Girls often copy role models and think they're expected to feel ill too, but this isn't usually the case. There could be many other reasons for feeling ill.

Is it OK to have sex during a period?

✦ Yes, it's OK.
✦ There are no rules about it and it's down to personal preference.
✦ There's nothing dirty or shameful about having your period.
✦ Some women feel more sexy during their period while others don't want anyone to see or know anything about it.
✦ Generally, the risk of pregnancy is less at this time, although the risk of infection is higher.
✦ It's equally OK not to want sex during your period.
✦ Your vagina and the neck of your womb (cervix) may feel more tender so you may choose to have sex in a position where you're more in control of the depth of penetration.
✦ Some women like to use the contraceptive cap (diaphragm) as additional protection to hold back their flow of blood.
✦ Others prefer to place a towel underneath themselves to protect their bedding or their furniture.

✦ Sex is never compulsory. Don't do anything you feel uncomfortable about just to please someone else.
✦ The main rule about sex is that whatever you get up to should be by mutual consent (agreement) and not harm anyone else.
✦ In some countries and cultures, people still believe that women are unclean during their period and their men won't go near them at this time.
✦ Sometimes it's used as an excuse to have sex elsewhere.
✦ This has obvious dangers for sexually acquired infections if the man returns to their regular partner after having casual sex elsewhere.
✦ Attitudes change as men learn more about women's, and their own, health risks from having multiple sexual partners.
✦ Furthermore, since most men wouldn't like their mother or sister to be treated with such disrespect, it would be wise not to cheat on your partner for such a reason.

© Sylvia Rawsthorn 1999

Weight and dieting

✦ You may become conscious of your weight and your diet. This may be influenced by the fashion industry – from pictures you see of super-models in magazines – and want to copy.

✦ Some young people, both male and female, develop anorexia *(almost stop eating)* or become bulimic *(make themselves sick after they eat a meal)* to keep their weight low.

✦ Many young women have the mistaken belief that men prefer skinny women or that they'll be more popular if they look like some fashion models.

✦ What you may not realise is that most men actually prefer a woman who has some padding on her and aren't particularly attracted to the 'walking skeletons of high fashion'.

✦ It's important to realise that a certain amount of fat is essential for healthy growth and development.

✦ Dieting or weight loss regimens whilst you're young could harm your development if you deprive it of essential food and nutrients when your body's meant to be growing.

✦ These are particularly important for healthy bones and regularity of periods.

✦ You should only diet if a doctor says you're overweight and that it's of medical concern because some larger people may be healthy; and some people who appear to be of average appearance may be unhealthy on the inside.

✦ Any dieting should then be under their supervision, to make sure that you don't do more harm to yourself by dieting than by being overweight in the first place.

✦ To maintain health, having a regular medical check-up is a sensible thing for everyone.

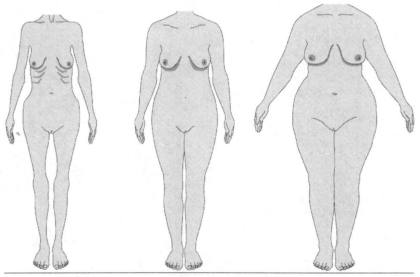

Female Body Shapes:

Anorexic — Average — Overweight

© Peter Gardiner

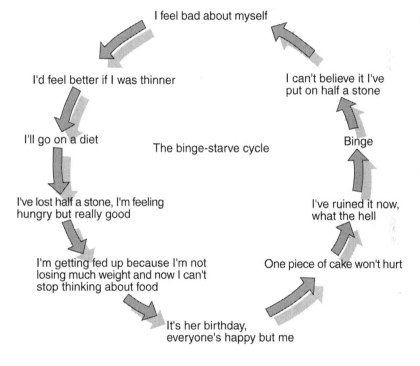

The binge-starve cycle

- I feel bad about myself
- I'd feel better if I was thinner
- I'll go on a diet
- I've lost half a stone, I'm feeling hungry but really good
- I'm getting fed up because I'm not losing much weight and now I can't stop thinking about food
- It's her birthday, everyone's happy but me
- One piece of cake won't hurt
- I've ruined it now, what the hell
- Binge
- I can't believe it I've put on half a stone

The Binge-Starve Cycle

Sexplained Two — For Changing Times ® © 1999-2016

What's contraception?

✦ Contraception is a method used by a man or a woman to prevent a pregnancy; also called birth control.

Why is it important for men/women to know about contraception before first having sex / making love?

✦ It is important to know about contraception if you want to avoid unplanned pregnancy; or you don't want to catch a sexually acquired infection.

✦ Sex is not always as simple as it appears in the movies. So-called roll models don't always provide us with good examples of how to behave.

✦ They don't tell you about pregnancy or catching an infection.

✦ If you consider yourself mature enough to start having a sexual relationship, you should be fully aware that there's much more to healthy sex than just doing it for pleasure. You should take responsibility for your sexual health.

✦ Apart from pregnancy and sexually acquired infection, there could be serious side effects, physical and emotional, from having sex.

✦ As a young man you should be aware that if you make a girl pregnant – and she continues with the pregnancy – YOU will have to pay money to her for your child every week until s/he leaves full-time education. This could be until they are 25 years of age, so all of this is very important for young men. It's a huge commitment and not one to be taken lightly.

✦ If a young couple doesn't use contraception correctly and consistently, it's extremely common for girls to get pregnant the first time they have sex.

✦ Although a natural occurrence, pregnancy can be dangerous for a woman's health.

✦ Condoms, alone, don't always offer enough protection, particularly when neither of you is practised at putting them on a penis or keeping them on during sex.

✦ Why not share the responsibility and use the Double Dutch approach — ie. routinely use condoms AND another method of birth control. So called because it is widely practised in Holland, where there is one of the lowest rates of unplanned pregnancy and sexually acquired infection in the world.

✦ By using the Double Dutch *(dual protection)* approach you can then relax and enjoy each other without the added anxiety of an unplanned pregnancy or risk of infection.

✦ Always seek advice if you didn't use your method of contraception correctly and you're worried that you might be pregnant.

Where can I get contraception?

In the UK, previously, contraception was only available from GPs *(family doctors)* or Contraception Clinics but at present it is available, free, from:

✦ any Sexual Health Clinic that offers it;

✦ most family doctors *(GPs)*;

✦ many areas have special clinics for young people under the age of 25;

✦ and some private clinics provide it, for a fee.

© Sylvia Rawsthorn 1999

What should we know about contraception?

✦ In addition to the condom, which should be used routinely for safer sex, there are many other methods of contraception.

✦ Only celibacy is 100% safe.

Methods of Contraception (birth control)

Hormonal Methods:
(1) combined pills *(The Pill or COC Pill)*;
(2) combined vaginal ring;
(3) combined patch;
(4) progestogen only pills *(POP)*;
(5) injections;
(6) sub-dermal implants;
(7) intrauterine system *(IUS)*;
(8) emergency hormonal contraception.

Non-hormonal methods:
(9) intrauterine contraceptive device *(IUD)* or coil;
(10) female barrier methods:
  — contaceptive diaphragm: flat, coil or arcing spring, which lie across the vagina;
  — cervical caps, which fit neatly over the cervix; and
  — female condoms, which line the vagina;
(11) advice on fertility awareness / natural family planning *(e.g. safe time)*;
(12) referral for vasectomy *(male sterilisation)*;
(13) referral for female sterilisation;
(14) male condoms *(see Safer Sex)*;
(15) new technologies; and
(16) other methods may be used in different countries.

✦ Throughout your life you might try several methods, not just one or two.

✦ Each has advantages and disadvantages.

✦ No single method is likely to suit you for life.

✦ To feel happy about using contraception effectively, you should always have a choice.

✦ Different methods of contraception are advised at different times or with certain medical conditions.

✦ Men should understand how each method works. Taking responsibility for understanding how contraceptive methods work is important for men and women alike as each must / may rely on the other to prevent unwanted pregnancy.

© FP Sales Ltd

What else is on offer?

In the UK, and many other countries, clinics also offer:

+ free pregnancy testing;
+ pre-pregnancy advice;
+ advice and counselling about rape, impotence, premature ejaculation, and other common sexual worries;
+ referral for unwanted pregnancy counselling;
+ post-abortion support and counselling;
+ breast awareness for women of all ages and / or teach you how to be breast aware;
+ routine cervical *(papanicolaou / pap)* smear screening tests for women of 20-64 years of age *(25 in England)*;
+ hysterectomy advice and support;
+ menopause advice/support and referral for HRT *(hormone replacement therapy)*;
+ relationship counselling;
+ some may offer tests for rubella *(German measles)*, or disorders of the blood called sickle cell disease and thalassaemia;
+ blood pressure and weight checks for both men and women;
+ advice on testicular health and testicular self-examination techniques;
+ contraception *(Family Planning)* clinics, or sessions within a Sexual Health Clinic, are NOT for women only.
+ some areas offer specific sessions for men's health issues.
+ Sexual Health Clinics are commonly staffed by both male and female healthcare professionals and you can ask to see someone of your preference.
+ Many young men find it difficult to visit a clinic and talk their problems through. But after attending they wish they'd taken the opportunity before.

Do I have to be married or planning a family to go to a clinic offering contraception services or family planning advice?

+ No, you don't – clinics care for young and old, male and female, married or single without age limit.
+ In recent years, in most areas in the UK and some other countries, family planning clinics have been renamed Sexual Health Clinics. This is because they have integrated services to offer screening and treatment for sexual infections and conditions, as well as contraceptive care.
+ Staff don't sit in judgement. They are there to help you. So there's no need to feel shy, scared or worried about what they may think.

Do they need to see any identification of who I am?

+ No, they don't. They accept what you say.

How old do I have to be to be seen?

+ They will see you at any age – even if you're under 16.

If I'm under the legal age of consent, won't they judge me?

+ No, they won't.
+ They're not there to judge you.
+ Just because you seek advice, it does not mean you are or plan to be sexually active, merely that you want guidance.
+ Sex is an adult activity, with adult consequences. There is no rush to be sexually active before you are sure you want to be, and you are ready to accept responsibility for your actions if anything goes wrong.
+ They respect you for taking responsibility and the maturity which prompted you to seek advice.

Will they contact the Police, social workers, parents, guardians, or hostel workers etc?

✦ No, no-one is contacted without your permission or you being aware.
✦ They can only work with what you tell them and they do so in your best interests.
✦ Their only concern is for YOU.

Will they lecture me?

✦ No, they won't.
✦ What you do and how you do it is your business.
✦ Any questions you may have about contraception, safer sex, sexual health – even drugs, drug taking or injecting – can be discussed freely with the nurse or doctor.

So, if I inject or use drugs, am I still welcome at the clinics?

✦ Yes, you are.

Will they tell my doctor *(GP)* if I go to clinic?

✦ No, they won't. The service is strictly confidential and your doctor *(GP)* is only contacted with your permission – even though some clinics may encourage you to let them write to your GP.
✦ Remember: the choice is yours and yours alone.

How can I be sure?

✦ You can give only a contact address / number. But do make sure you can be contacted somehow, just in case.

Must I return to the same clinic where I started?

✦ No. You don't have to return to the same clinic.
✦ If you ask, they can write a transfer note for you to take to another clinic or healthcare provider about any treatment you are given or method of contraception you are using.
✦ However, it's sensible to stay with one healthcare provider, so that you have continuity of medical care.
✦ Once again, the choice is yours.

Won't they laugh at my problems?

✦ No, they won't. They're only interested in helping you.

Are the doctors male or female at contraception clinics?

✦ The doctors are commonly female in the clinics because they're aware that the majority of women prefer female doctors.
✦ If you prefer a male doctor, you can enquire at reception when you first visit.
✦ The doctors are all specialists in contraception care, with considerable medical experience in this field.

How much does it cost?

✦ At the time of writing, all NHS sexual health services and supplies are FREE of charge in the UK.

Can I just go to clinic for condoms?

✦ Yes and they're free in the UK.

✦ They will usually ask for minimal information in the clinics but some areas offer free condoms at condom supply points where no questions are asked.

✦ Other areas run a 'C-card' scheme, where condoms are issued free of charge to people under the age of 25 at various locations within their borough, on production of a card.

✦ This runs like a membership or club card scheme.

Where can I find these condom supply points?

✦ Each area is different but if you phone your local hospital and ask for the Sexual Health Clinic, they should be able to tell you what your area offers.

✦ Some GPs offer condoms free at reception — check with yours.

✦ BUT, remember, condoms are also available at all Contraception and Sexual Health Clinics in the UK, FREE of charge.

Why is it called a clinic when I'm not ill?

✦ Good question! Clinic means *"centre at which advice and assistance in matters of health, hygiene, maternity etc. are given"*.

If I have or have had many partners, am I still welcome?

✦ Yes, of course.

✦ They won't judge your lifestyle or lecture you in any way.

What may a clinic need from me?

✦ You'll always be asked to give the date of the FIRST day of your last period.

✦ If that's today then say so, otherwise try and work out the date before you're seen.

✦ If you want a pregnancy test, they need something to test! So, take a sample of that day's urine *(wee)* for testing.

✦ The first wee is the most concentrated but other samples can usually give a reliable result three weeks after unprotected sex; a pill or a condom accident; or one week after a missed period.

✦ You don't need a special container. A clean jar or bottle will do and only a few drops are needed for a pregnancy test.

✦ BUT: pregnancy tests look for a specific hormone, human chorionic gonadotrophin *(HCG)*, at specific amounts in the body.

✦ This means that a pregnancy test is not commony reliable until three weeks after the incident of unprotected sex.

✦ If you had unprotected sex within the last few days and don't want to get pregnant, see the section on Emergency Contraception because you may need that, rather than a pregnancy test.

Can I take a friend or an interpreter with me?

✦ Yes you can. Having company can also help to make you less nervous.

✦ Some clinics have interpreters but it sometimes helps the clinic staff, too, if English isn't your first language.

✦ However, your friend may not be allowed to act as an interpreter during your consultation or accompany you to that part of your visit because of rules relating to confidentiality.

Will they show me how to use whatever they give me?

✦ Yes, they teach you how to use your contraceptive method(s) properly and make sure you understand what to do if things go wrong.
✦ If you are ever in any doubt, PLEASE ASK FOR HELP.
✦ Even if your clinic runs by appointment rather than letting you just walk in to be seen without appointment, you don't need an appointment to ask for help.
✦ Alternatively you could phone for advice, when the clinic is open.

I don't want to have a period when I go away on holiday. What can I do?

To avoid a period when you go away on holiday there are two options.
1) If you are using a combined method of hormonal contraception (The COC Pill, The Ring or The Patch), you can avoid taking the break between cycles and continue in to the next cycle; complete that cycle, as advised, and then take your usual break.
2) Your doctor may prescribe a special course of the progestogen called norethisterone, to take daily, for the duration of your holiday; but this may not be suitable for everyone.

Are there any help lines I can ring for advice about my method?

✦ You can ring any Contraception / Sexual Health Clinic and ask to speak to a doctor or nurse.
✦ Details of clinics can be found in the phone book, at the library or online.
✦ You can ring and ask to speak to your own doctor or practice nurse, or, you can see or speak to any doctor who offers contraceptive services – even if they are not the doctor you are registered with.
✦ You can also ask your pharmacist *(chemist)*.

© Sylvia Rawsthorn 1999

Young Women's Changes & Women's Worries

What does having an internal examination involve?

✦ It involves a gentle examination of your genital area by a doctor or nurse.
✦ You may be embarrassed, but they will only want to make sure that everything is healthy.
✦ They sometimes use a special instrument called a speculum.
✦ This enables them to look inside your vagina and check that your cervix (neck of your womb) is healthy.
✦ Staff appreciate that some young women find this embarrassing.
✦ But, it's the only way to check if you really are OK.
✦ There is often a healthcare support worker or nurse or with you to reassure you and hold your hand. If there's not and you'd like one to be there as a chaperone, just ask.
✦ It's always better to pluck up courage and be sure you're alright, than neglect your health simply because you're embarrassed.

Will it hurt?

✦ No, it won't hurt.
✦ It may be slightly uncomfortable but the more relaxed you are the more comfortable it will be.
✦ Afterwards many people say, "Is that it? I didn't feel a thing. I don't know why I was so scared."

Do I HAVE to have one?

✦ An internal examination is NOT compulsory at your first visit or before you receive contraception.
✦ It may only be necessary if you, yourself, have any health concerns.

What's a smear (Pap) or cervical cytology test?

✦ This is when the neck of your womb (cervix) is wiped with a special type of spatula or brush.
✦ The spatula is then wiped across a piece of glass, which is then fixed with a special solution and sent to the laboratory — or — the brush is shaken within a pot of special liquid to release the collected sample (this is called liquid based cytology / LBC).
✦ The laboratory checks the sample to see if any of the cells covering your cervix have changed from the normal pattern.
✦ Sometimes abnormal cells are noticed, which can gradually lead to pre-cancer, if not treated. If that's then left untreated it can lead to cancer of the cervix, travel to your womb and on to the rest of your body.
✦ Treatment of early abnormality is now easy, quick and highly successful.
✦ Regular smear tests are designed to detect any abnormal cell changes at your cervix before they turn into pre-cancerous ones.
✦ The test is named after the person who invented it, called Papanicolaou.
✦ Cervical cytology means 'the study of cervical cells'.

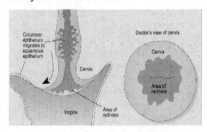

© Peter Gardiner

Cervix:

Image shows the area from which a cervical smear test is taken, and a harmless area of redness which some women have; but others don't.

Is cervical cancer a sexually transmitted infection?

✦ Yes cervical cancer is a sexually acquired infection .... and No.

✦ There are two types of cervical cancer.:

✦ They are squamous cell carcinoma and adenocarcinoma.

✦ Regular smear tests are made to detect early abnormalities of the cervix, which sometimes lead to squamous cell carcinoma.

✦ This type is considered to be sexually related, and strongly linked to HPV *(human papilloma virus)*.

✦ The other type, adenocarcinoma, is much less common and is more difficult to detect. It usually develops further inside the cervical canal towards the inside of the womb and the cause is less clear.

✦ A smear test does NOT, however, check you for sexually acquired infections, although sometimes one may be detected.

When should I have my first smear test?

✦ Different countries have different regimens.

✦ You should have your first test at or near the age of 25 if you have ever been sexually active, unless there are specific reasons to have one earlier.

✦ At present, in the UK, it is routinely offered, free, to all women between 25 and 65 years of age.

✦ It's important that you're honest with your doctor or nurse about when you first had sex, about your sexual history and your lifestyle in case other tests or earlier testing are appropriate.

Why can't I have a smear test earlier?

✦ The body commonly rids itself of early cervical abnormalities.

✦ By testing later, persistent abnormalities can then be detected and treated appropriately.

Conventional Smear Test Technique

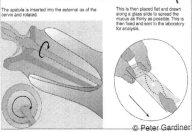

The spatula is inserted into the external os of the cervix and rotated.

This is then placed flat and drawn along a glass slide to spread the mucus as thinly as possible. This is then fixed and sent to the laboratory for analysis.

© Peter Gardiner

Conventional Papanicolaou (Pap) cervical smear test, with which the sample is smeared straight to the glass slide and 'fixed' for the lab to analyse.

Can cervical cancer be prevented?

✦ Yes, it can. If abnormalities are found in the early stages, treatment can be given to remove the abnormal cells and prevent this form of cancer developing.

✦ Although having regular cervical smear tests may be embarrassing and you may not like having them, they really are the only way abnormalities can be detected.

✦ You owe it to yourself to have this simple test.

✦ There is a vaccine against some strains of HPV, which is strongly advised for young women, today.

✦ *See page 65 for information about HPV vaccination.*

NOTE: HPV and analysing samples

✦ Some areas now look for the presence of HPV *(human papilloma virus)* in cytology *(cell)* samples first, and only proceed to further investigation if it that been detected.

✦ In the future, young women who have been vaccinated against HPV are anticipated to need fewer smear tests than young women who have not been vaccinated.

Young Women's Changes & Women's Worries

My friend's worried because she had an abnormal smear test result and nobody's explained what the different test results mean.

✦ A simple and general translation of smear test results, starting with the most minor follows.

✦ The term **CIN** stands for **cervical intraepithelial neoplasia** or changes in the cells of the surface of the neck of the womb *(cervix)*.

✦ Cervical cancer develops relatively slowly which is why there is such a high success rate when abnormalities are treated in the first stages of development.

Inadequate — unsatisfactory smear

✦ This may be due to blood or discharge making it difficult to view the other cells easily or the cell sample may have dried too quickly.

✦ These smears should be repeated within 3 months, preferably about two weeks after your period starts.

Negative — normal — no abnormal cells seen on this sample

✦ At present, repeat after 3 to 5 years if your previous smears have been normal.

✦ Occasionally thrush, gardnerella, trichomoniasis or other bugs are detected. However, smear tests do not check for SAIs, so you mustn't assume you are clear.

Borderline *(previously, Inflammatory)*

✦ Smear should be repeated after 6 months, depending on your medical history.

✦ The majority of these smears return to normal on their own.

✦ If the problem persists, colposcopy would be advised.

✦ If you smoke, giving up may help.

✦ HPV *(human papilloma virus)* or genital wart virus, *(the most common SAI)* may be associated with these smear results.

Mild Dyskaryosis — CIN 1 — low grade changes noticed

✦ Repeat smear after 6 months – by then some revert to normal.

✦ CIN1 is often associated with HPV/genital wart virus.

✦ If problem persists, colposcopy is advised.

Moderate Dyskaryosis — CIN 2

✦ You would be referred for colposcopy.

Severe Dyskaryosis — CIN 3 — high grade abnormalities noticed

✦ You would be referred for colposcopy.

Is there a vaccine against HPV?

Yes. Two vaccines have been available against four different types of HPV since 2006. *(see next page)*

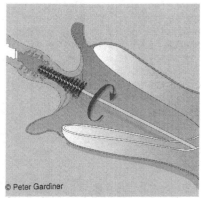

© Peter Gardiner

Cervical smear test, using a cervical brush and LBC (liquid based cytology) technology.

Different techniques are used in different parts of the world.

What's colposcopy?

✦ Colposcopy is when a specially trained doctor or nurse looks at the neck of your womb with a special microscope *(colposcope)* to check for any abnormalities. They paint your cervix with a weak solution of acetic acid *(similar to vinegar)* which may sting a little. Abnormal cells show up white and are then viewed more closely.

✦ They may also apply some iodine to your cervix and perhaps take a small sample (biopsy) of the abnormal area, to send to the laboratory for further checking. Treatment usually depends on what is seen at colposcopy and/or as a result of the laboratory test.

Does it hurt?

✦ It's similar to having a smear test but you lie on a special bed and may have the opportunity to see what's happening inside by a special video / TV link.

✦ The biopsy may pinch a little bit but it doesn't last long.

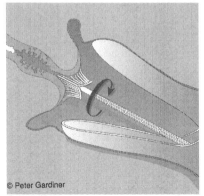

© Peter Gardiner

Cervical smear test, using a cervical broom and LBC (liquid based cytology) technology.

Who is the HPV vaccine suitable for?

The HPV vaccine is licenced for use by young men and women aged nine to 26 years of age, who have never been sexually active.

If their doctor agrees to prescribe it, older people who have only had a few sexual partners may still benefit from having it, but they may have been exposed to one or more types of the virus already and not gain as much, if any protection.

There are two vaccines available.

One is only, but greatly, effective against HPV types 16 and 18.

The other is greatly effective against HPV types 6, 11, 16 and 18 which are the types associated with 90 per cent of genital warts (6 and 11) and 70 per cent of cervical cancer (16 and 18), respectively.

Since one vaccine protects against the most common types that cause genital warts, several public health experts also recommend it for young men and boys — especially young gay men who may have multiple sexual partners and who may be more exposed to the virus in the future.

For more information about smear tests and cervical cytology, see: http://www.jostrust.org.uk

Brush technique and sample deposit in LBC pot containing preservative.

© Peter Gardiner

Section 3

Visiting a Sexual Health Clinic

When I am visiting a clinic, what should I be aware of?

What else is available?

Is everything confidential?

If they keep notes about me, what information do they need?

Who will I see?

How can I help the staff?

Can I have an HIV test at a Sexual Health Clinic?

What's a contact slip and why do some people get one?

Can I do a test for HIV at home?

Is contraception available at all sexual health clinics?

Can I just visit a clinic for condoms if I don't want to be seen?

Do they need to see identification of who I am?

How can I be sure?

Can I take a friend with me as an interpreter?

Apart from contraception or testing for sexual infections, what else is available at this type of clinic?

General information

Wound care

When I am visiting a clinic, what should I be aware of?

✦ *Sexual Health Clinic* is the new name for a GUM *(genito-urinary medicine)* or an STI Clinic. It is also the new name for family planning / contraception clinics.

✦ Many now offer an integrated service, combining contraception and sexual health services under one roof.

✦ Previously, these were known as special clinics, VD *(venereal disease)* or nicknamed 'clap' clinics.

✦ Traditionally these clinics are open Monday to Friday, from 9 am to 5 pm. but many areas now offer evening and weekend services.

✦ Ring your local hospital to check their opening times and whether they run an appointment system, a walk-in clinic – or both services.

✦ If you have symptoms or need to have emergency contraception, you will be seen on the day you decide to attend. Other times, it may be possible to make an appointment, to save waiting so long when you arrive.

✦ You don't need to be referred to this clinic by your doctor. You can walk in and ask to be seen.

✦ Sometimes you may have to wait if they are very busy but they can sometimes diagnose test results while you wait.

✦ This takes time but you'll be given the correct treatment for your specific infection, FREE OF CHARGE (UK).

✦ Some have a special fast lane or prioritised and speedy walk-in service for male and female sex workers *(also known as working women / men, or prostitutes)*.

What else is available?

✦ All counselling and medication is provided FREE OF CHARGE.

✦ If you're on 'income support' benefit, your fares may be reimbursed *(UK)*.

✦ Hepatitis B vaccination is available. Usually, it's 3 injections over 7 months but may be given to different regimens.

✦ Sexual Health Clinics provide emergency contraceptive pills up to 120 hours after unprotected sex.

✦ Emergency IUDs (coil) are not always offered in Sexual Health Clinics. However, they usually are in services that offer both screening and contraception.

✦ If you have a pelvic infection at the time, an IUD / coil is not advisable.

✦ Some integrated Sexual Health Clinics do *(Pap)* cervical smear tests but check before attending.

✦ If any abnormalities are found, further tests and treatment can also be done quickly and accurately.

Is everything confidential?

✦ By Law, their service must be confidential.

✦ They won't tell you what your partner has or is using, nor will they tell your partner what you have or are using – unless you request their help and intervention.

✦ They won't inform your doctor of anything unless you give permission.

If they keep notes about me, what information do they need?

✦ They will ask you for:
  – a name;
  – date of birth;
  – contact address.

✦ The details should be your own – but this is not essential. You can make up a name.

✦ The name and date of birth you give are used purely for internal administration and filing.

✦ If you give a false name / address you'll need to remember it for future visits to the clinic – without the correct details they won't find your notes quickly and / or easily.

Visiting a Sexual Health Clinic

Visiting a Clinic

Who will I see?

✦ Doctors and nurses, help you with method of contraception or symptoms of infection; healthcare assistants, who help with screening if you don't have problems; health advisors, who can spend more time with you and clerical staff, who assist the team.
✦ A psychosexual counsellor *(to talk sexual problems through)* often works in the Sexual Health Clinic, too.

How can I help the staff?

To ensure better results:

✦ MEN can help by not passing urine for 3 to 4 hours before any swabs or specimens are taken.
✦ WOMEN can help by working out the date of the first day of your last period before you are seen.
✦ It's OK to attend when you have a period but the staff are unlikely to do a smear test or colposcopy – and may ask you to return. However other tests can be carried out.
✦ If you want a pregnancy test, either take a specimen of that morning's urine with you in a clean jar or ask the receptionist for a specimen pot when you arrive in clinic and do your sample in before you are seen.

Can I have an HIV test at a Sexual Health Clinic?

✦ Yes. Totally confidential HIV counselling, and testing, are available.
✦ Nowadays, same day HIV test results are available at many clinics.
✦ Treatment is available for those who are HIV antibody positive, with referral to other hospital departments, including dental, community and social care.

What's a contact slip and why do some people get one?

✦ A contact slip is a specially coded piece of paper, which tells another doctor which specific infection*(s)* should be checked.
✦ If you're given a contact slip they will ask you to give it to your sexual partner*(s)*.
✦ They can then take it into any Sexual Health Clinic in the country for examination and receive the appropriate treatment.
✦ Following the treatment you are given is the best way you can help the doctors and avoid re-infection.

Can I do a test for HIV at home?

✦ Yes, in some countries, you can.
✦ The use of home based HIV tests was legalised in the UK in 2014.
✦ Some sexual health services offer home sampling, with which specimens are sent in the post to the local laboratory and results sent to the patient by the local service, which also offers ongoing support and care as needed.
✦ The safety and reliability of tests purchased over the Internet is often of concern, as is the availability of support if a tests reacts, suggesting but not confirming a positive result.
✦ Reactive home tests MUST be followed by a laboratory analysed blood test before HIV infection can be safely diagnosed.

Is contraception available at all sexual health clinics?

Yes, and no.
✦ Emergency hormonal contraception is available at all of these clinics but other methods and ongoing contraception may only be available at specific times or by appointment.
✦ To avoid frustration, check what they offer at your local service before you visit.

Can I just visit a clinic for condoms if I don't want to be seen?

✦ Yes, you can.

Do they need to see identification of who I am?

✦ No. In the UK, they don't ask for identification or proof of address.
✦ They accept what you say.

How can I be sure?

✦ If you are that worried, you can give a different name and address but make sure it is something you will remember for future visits.
✦ It is sensible to provide a safe way to contact you, though, incase the clinic needs to speak to you again.

Can I take a friend with me as an interpreter?

✦ Yes, and no.
✦ You can take a friend with you for support but they should not be asked to act as your interpreter.
✦ This may seem silly, but the staff are likely to want to see you on your own when they ask you about your medical and sexual history and, for reasons of confidentiality, it is not always appropriate for a friend or a partner to act as such a translator.
✦ The clinic will either use their own interpreter; make an appointment for you to be seen with an approved interpreter; or they may use a telephone based interpreting service to translate each question and obtain your reply.

Apart from contraception or testing for sexual infections, what else is available through this type of clinic?

Other things available through these clinics include:
✦ free pregnancy testing;
✦ pre-pregnancy counselling;
✦ advice and counselling about rape, domestic violence, sexual abuse, impotence, premature ejaculation, and other common sexual worries;
✦ referral for unwanted pregnancy;
✦ post-abortion counselling;
✦ breast checks for women of all ages and/or they will teach you how to be breast *aware*;
✦ in some areas, routine cervical *(Pap)* smear screening tests for women aged 20-64;
✦ hysterectomy advice and support;
✦ menopause advice/support and by appointment, in some clinics, HRT *(hormone replacement therapy)*;
✦ referral for relationship counselling;
✦ blood pressure and weight checks;
✦ advice for men on testicular health and testicular self examination techniques;

Visiting a Clinic

Visiting a Clinic

◆ these clinics are NOT just for women;
◆ some areas have dedicated Well Man Clinics.
◆ There are male doctors at some clinics but women can ask to be seen by a woman, and men can ask to be seen by a man.
◆ If you need further help, ask and you will be guided how to access it.

General information

◆ Don't be shy. Answer all questions openly and honestly. You won't shock anyone working in a Sexual Health Clinic.
◆ Most infections are treatable. If you delay treatment because of embarrassment, the problem could get worse. So, go early and get a problem sorted out.
◆ If you think you have an infection, NEVER take a friend's medication or some that you see lying around. It could make the problem worse.
◆ Visit the clinic for correct diagnosis and in date medication for what you HAVE got.
◆ If you notice any abnormal lumps, bumps, blisters or discharge, particularly in your genital area, get it checked. And if you can't go straight away, take a clear digital picture of what you can see, so you can show the staff.
◆ A good picture may help with diagnosis, especially if you can't be seen for a few days and it heals in the meantime.
◆ Everyone should have a check up, from time to time.
◆ Germs can spread genitally *(down below)* or orally *(by mouth)* so – safer oral and penetrative sex is vital.
◆ Remember: having a sexually acquired infection increases your risk of contracting HIV or HEPATITIS.
◆ Many SAIs which cause open wounds, are highly infectious. Therefore, when treating an open wound or sore from a SAI you must avoid cross infection, either to a different area of your own body or to the body of someone else.
◆ The consistent, correct use of all methods of contraception is important to prevent pregnancy.
◆ If you feel you have made a mistake or have questions, don't hesitate to ask for help.
◆ Depending on what the people ahead of you need, the wait to be seen can sometimes be quite long. Therefore, take a good book with you or something else to do while you wait for your turn. You, in turn, will get the amount of time that you need.

Wound care

◆ Wear disposable latex gloves when treating a wet or oozing wound/sore.
◆ Dispose of any soiled dressings in a plastic bag. Wrap or seal the bag, before throwing it out with the rubbish.
◆ Alternatively, ask a qualified nurse to teach you how to change a dressing, using an aseptic or no-touch technique.
◆ Do all you can to prevent cross infection. Don't put others at risk.
◆ To prevent cross infection / contamination, always wash your hands with soap and hot water after passing urine, opening your bowels, touching your own or anyone else's genitalia, or changing a baby's nappy – especially if you'll be preparing food.
◆ You don't always receive immunity against future infection by having an infection once.
◆ It's possible to get some sexually acquired infections more than once, so protect yourself at all times.

Contraception
(Birth Control)
(Family Planning)

Emergency Hormonal Contraception

Combined Hormonal Contraception (CHC)

Progestogen only methods

Intra-Uterine Contraception

Barrier Methods

Sterilisation

Natural Methods

Contraceptive Hormones

Contraception — Family Planning — Birth Control

Oestrogen
(Estrogen USA)

Natural OESTROGENS are:
— produced in the ovaries,
— by the maturing follicle,
— in increasing amounts.

They are produced in the form of:

Oestradiol
— an inactive form;

Oestrone
— a relatively inert form — found mostly after the menopause;

Oestriol
— not very active, but large amounts are found in pregnancy.

Contraceptive Method Oestrogens

Estradiol valerate
(derivative of natural oestrogen)

Ethinylestradiol (EE)
(a synthetic oestrogen)

Other
— cyproterone acetate (CPA),
— drospirenone (DRSP), and
— Ulipristal acetate (UPA).

Progesterone

Natural PROGESTERONE is produced:
— in the ovaries,
— by the corpus luteum,
— in large amounts — after ovulation.
Synthetically, it is called **progestogen**.

Contraceptive Method Progestogens by Generation

First generation: (oldest)
— ethynodiol diacetate,
— lynestrenol (LYN);
— norethisterone (NET),
— norethynodrel, and
— norethindrone (NE);

Second generation:
— levonorgestrel (LNG), and
— norgestrel (NG);

Third generation:
— desogestrel (DSG),
— etonogestrel,
— gestodene (GSD), and
— norgestimate (NGM);

Fourth generation: (newest)
— dienogest (semi synthetic),
— norelgestromin,
— nestorone,
— nomegestrol acetate, and
— trimegestone.

Injectable methods use:
— DMPA
   Depot Medroxyprogesterone Acetate,
— Hydroxiprogesterone Caproate, and
— Norethisterone oenanthate.

Third and fourth generation progestogens are thought to carry a slightly higher risk of venous thromboembolism (VTE / blood clots) in susceptible women. Pregnancy carries more risk.

Emergency Hormonal Contraception

Levonorgestrel — Levonelle®
Ulipristal acetate — ella® / ellaOne®
E-IUD — Emergency IUD / Coil

Combined Hormonal Contraception (CHC)

Combined Pill (COC) — The Pill
Combined Transdermal Patch — The Patch
Combined Vaginal Ring — The Ring

Progestogen only methods

Progestogen only Pills (POP) — The POP / Mini-Pill
Subdermal Implants — The Implant
Injections — The Injection

Intra-Uterine Contraception

Intra-uterine Device — IUD / Coil / Copper Coil
Intra-uterine System — IUS / Mirena® / Jaydess®
(contains progestogen)

Barrier Methods

Cap — Cervical Cap
Diaphragm — Dutch Cap / Diaphragm
Female Condoms — e.g. Femidom® / Reality®
— e.g. Women's Condom
Male Condoms — Latex Condoms
— Non-Latex Condoms

Sterilisation

Female Sterilisation — Tubal Ligation / Essure®
Male Sterilisation — Vasectomy

Natural Methods

Natural Family Planning — Fertility Awareness Methods
New Technology — Electronic Devices

Contraception — Family Planning — Birth Control

Contraception — Family Planning — Birth Control

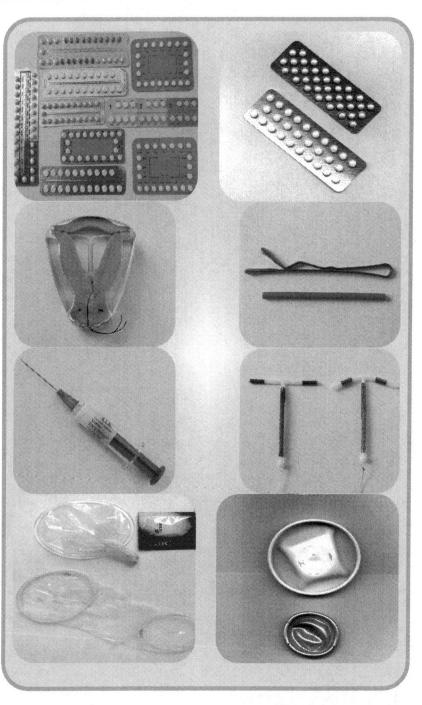

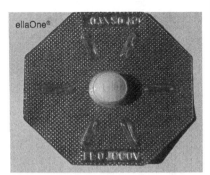

ellaOne®

What's Emergency Contraception?

✦ There are two types of emergency contraception available in the UK, which aim to prevent unplanned pregnancy, after sex has taken place.

There are pills and devices.
1) Previously called '*the morning after pill'* its new name is Emergency Hormonal Contraception *(EHC)*.
2) An IUD *(intra-uterine device / coil)* can also be used as an emergency method of contraception.

Why has the 'morning after pill' been renamed EHC?

✦ That's because it works later than just the morning after unprotected sex.

OK! So what's EHC?

At the time of writing, there are two types of EHC available *(UK)*.
✦ There are over 70 brand names of EHC available world-wide, and of these, there are three main types.
✦ **First**: a high, single dose of the progestogen hormone, levonorgestrel, taken within 72 hours *(three days)* of unprotected sex: e.g. if you've had an accident with your chosen method of contraception, to try and prevent an unplanned pregnancy. This medication has a long list of alternative names, and what your prescriber calls it will depend on where you are in the world. In the UK it is called Levonelle®

✦ **Second**: a single dose of a different hormone, Ulipristal acetate *(UPA)*, as ella® *(USA)* / ellaOne® *(UK and Europe)*, licenced for use up to 120 hours *(five days)* after unprotected sex. *(Internationally, this is also known as UPRIS® / Duprisal® and Dvella® .)*
✦ **Third** and no longer used in the UK, is a combined oral contraceptive method, available for emergency situations, comprising of four tablets. Worldwide, this method has a long list of alternative names.
✦ For information about the **emergency IUD** / coil, please see the pages about the IUD as a main method.

What would EC do to me?

✦ Each emergency hormonal method delays ovulation if it has not already occurred in a particular cycle.

What should I do after I take EHC?

✦ No methods of EHC provide ongoing contraception, only the IUD, which is non-hormonal.
✦ If you continue to have sex in the same cycle, you should return to using your usual birth control immediately.
✦ You if you are using hormonal contraception as your regular method, you should also use condoms or avoid sex for seven days following EC with levonorgestrel, or 14 days following ulapristol acetate if you are using hormonal contraception. *(This extends to 9 or 16 days respectively if using the pill called Qlaira consisting of natural hormones rather than synthetic.)*
✦ However, if you take pills, the manufacturers recommend that you have no sex or use a condom until your next menstrual period to avoid further risk.

Contraception — Family Planning — Birth Control

Contraception — Family Planning — Birth Control

What if I miss the 72 hours or don't want to take hormones?

✦ If you miss the 72 hours *(three days)* ellaOne® is licenced for use up to 120 hours *(5 days)* or don't want to take hormones, an emergency IUD / coil can generally be fitted up to five days after unprotected sex *(sometimes later)*.

Where can I get EHC?

✦ The pills are available at a pharmacy, but can be obtained free from all Contraception and Sexual Health Clinics, most family doctors, and some hospital casualty departments.
✦ At the doctors you may have to explain to the receptionist why you need an emergency appointment, otherwise you may not be seen until it's too late to prescribe the pills.
✦ Some private clinics offer EHC, but you will have to pay for it.

When should I get my period after taking EHC?

✦ Whichever hormonal method you use, you should bleed within three weeks of taking emergency contraceptive pills.
✦ If you have a lighter bleed than usual or no bleed, see your doctor or Sexual Health Clinic to check that you're OK.

Will EHC make me sick?

✦ It is OK to take it on an empty stomach or if you have eaten.
✦ You're VERY unlikely to be sick but if you vomit within three hours of taking EHC you should seek medical attention, the same or next day, to obtain more pills or have an emergency IUD *(intra-uterine device)* / coil fitted.
✦ Sometimes an anti-emetic tablet is given with the pills *(anti-sickness)*.

How reliable is EHC?

✦ It's most effective when taken nearer the time of unprotected sex.
✦ In some countries, women who weigh over 75kg may be guided towards an UPA pill instead of levonorgestrel, especially if they are close to the middle of their cycle; or, they may advised to have an emergency IUD instead.
✦ As with other methods of birth control, you should appreciate that it can fail and should never be used as an alternative to more reliable method.

Is it suitable for everyone?

✦ If you're pregnant you shouldn't take it.
✦ If you had unprotected sex more than 72 hours ago or are mid-cycle *(half way between two menstrual periods)* you may be offered ulapristol acetate or an emergency IUD / coil.
✦ In countries where the third hormonal method is available, and you have a migraine at the time you need to take it, you may be prescribed the progesterone only method instead of a combined hormonal product – or offered an IUD.

How many times can I use it?

✦ There is no limit to the number of times you can have it, although, ulaprisol acetate can only be given once in a particular menstrual cycle
✦ Levonelle can be given more than once in a cycle.
✦ If you need to use it often, you should consider using a more reliable method of regular contraception.

Will it make my periods heavier or lighter?

✦ Your next period is unlikely to be any different but if it's lighter than usual or you develop tummy pains, tell your nurse or doctor. There's a very small risk it may not work for you *(less than one in 100)* in which case, you may become pregnant or develop an ectopic *(tubal)* pregnancy.

What should I be aware of if my girlfriend's using it?

✦ If you used a condom and it broke or came off, practise the correct way to wear them and try to avoid this happening again.

✦ If you had unprotected sex and didn't bother to use a condom, you should be better prepared next time you have sex and perhaps more responsible.

✦ Don't rely on emergency contraception instead of a regular method of birth control since it can fail.

✦ Go "Double Dutch" and use a reliable method of contraception routinely to protect against pregnancy, AND a condom to protect against infection. This gives much better protection.

✦ If either of you develops an unusual discharge, sores or pains after needing Emergency Contraception, seek a full check-up at a Sexual Health Clinic just in case you've acquired an infection.

✦ This is especially important if you were having casual sex or if either of you was unfaithful, while in a regular relationship.

If EC fails, will it harm the baby?

✦ As far as is known, levonorgestrel does not harm the baby.

✦ However, as it is newer, Ulipristol acetate is not as well studied yet.

✦ But, no-one can guarantee a normal, healthy baby.

Will EC make me put on weight?

✦ No.

Will EC protect me from infection AND pregnancy?

✦ No, just pregnancy.

Will it cause me to have an abortion?

✦ This has been argued extensively around the world and no, it does not cause an abortion.

Do recreational drugs affect the reliability of Emergency Contraception?

✦ No, they don't.

NOTE: For information about an emergency IUD, please see the section about the IUD / coil.

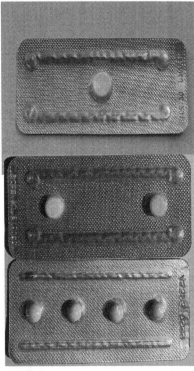

Top: Levonelle®
Middle: Levonelle-2® (LNG 1500)(POP)
Bottom: PC4® (an older, combined emergency method)

Contraception — Family Planning — Birth Control

Contraception — Family Planning — Birth Control

What is the COC Pill?

✦ It's a drug combination of two of the female hormones you already make, oestrogen and progesterone, in the form of progestogen.

How does the COC Pill work?

✦ It's an oral contraceptive pill, which fools a woman's body into thinking that she's already pregnant, because pregnant women don't ovulate or release more eggs until they've had the baby.

✦ It makes the mucus at the cervix thicker so sperm can't get into the womb *(uterus)*; it also changes the conditions in the lining of the womb *(endometrium)*; and fallopian tubes.

✦ This ensures that a steady level of the hormones filter into the body, to keep the ovaries *(where eggs are made)* asleep – thereby ensuring that pregnancy cannot happen.

How do I take it?

✦ Your active COC Pill should be taken at the same time every day for, usually 21 days, then you take a break for seven days, starting your COC Pill again on the 8th day.

✦ *(Note: Some brands have 22 or 24* active pills in a packet with different rules)*

✦ Some COC Pill packets also contain seven placebo *(dummy or substitute)* pills, which provide a useful reminder to help you take your pill on the days where you take a break between your active pills.

✦ They are known as ED *(every day)* combined oral contraceptive pills.

✦ ED COC Pills are taken EVERY day of the year. *(They differ from the POP / mini-pill, which only contains one drug but is also taken every day).*

✦ *(* 24 day pills require only a four day break between packets).*

What if I miss a COC Pill?

✦ Many people think that it takes several months to start releasing eggs again after coming off the COC Pill. This isn't true. Ovulation occurs by Day 9.

✦ **Manufacturer's guidance and that of local organisations differs.**

✦ **This gives manufacturers' licenced guidance, which is VERY safe, reliable and easy to remember.**

✦ If you miss a COC Pill but take it within 12 hours from the time it should be taken, you will still be protected.

✦ If, however, it's over 12 hours from the time you should have taken your COC Pill, you will no longer be protected.

✦ Don't stop the pills.

✦ Continue to take your pills as usual, but use extra protection ie. a condom, cap, diaphragm or not have sex *(abstain)* for the next seven days.

✦ If those seven days go into what would have been the 7-day break between packets – don't take the break but start a new packet and take it to the end of the course *(one day at a time).*

✦ At the end of that packet, have the 7-day break as usual.

✦ This will not harm you.

✦ During the seven-day break your ovaries start to wake up. If they're not sent back to sleep in time then, there's a risk of an egg being released.

✦ See the nearby charts for manufacturer's guidance and that developed by the World Health Organisation, adapted by the UK Faculty of Sexual & Reproductive Health *(FSRH).*

✦ If you understand them both well, you can then decide which set of guidance you prefer to follow, carefully.

Simple Missed COC Pill Guide

	Manufacturer's Guide	WHO / FSRH Guide		This guide is for 21-day COC Pills ONLY
Pill Pack **Week** **One** **Days** **1-7**	**1 missed COC Pill** **Late by less than 12 hrs** - carry on, no problem **Late by more than 12 hrs or more than one pill** - continue pills normally - extra protection 7 days - EC may be required ** **D, V, M** - continue taking Pill - use extra protection during illness or medication and the next 7 days *	**1 missed COC Pill** **Late by less than 24 hrs** - carry on - no problem **D,V, M** - as manufacturer's guide. **BUT** If you had unprotected sex in 7-day break and started your pill packet late, EC may be required * & **	**2 or more missed COC Pills** **Late by 48 hrs or more:** - take last missed pill and carry on as normal - OK to take two pills in one day - use extra protection for 7-days - EC may be required ** **D,V, M** - as manufacturer's guide (see left) *	**Key:** - Diarrhoea (**D**), - Vomiting (**V**), - Interacting Medication (**M**) * Starting pill packets late or missing pills in the first or last week lengthens the pill-free interval. **** If you have unprotected sex; or a condom breaks during any time that extra protection is advised; or if you miss more than one pill more than once in a packet, seek advice about Emergency Contraception (EC)
Pill Pack **Week** **Two** **Days** **8-14**	**1 missed COC Pill** **Late by less than 12 hrs** - carry on, no problem **Late by more than 12 hrs or more than one pill** - continue pills normally - extra protection 7 days **D, V, M** - continue taking Pill - use extra protection during illness or medication and the next 7 days	**1 missed COC Pill** **Late by less than 24 hrs** - carry on - no problem	**2 or more missed COC Pills** **Late by 48 hrs or more** - take last missed pill and carry on as normal - but extra protection 7 days **D,V, M** - as manufacturer's guide (see left)	
Pill Pack **Week** **Three** **Days** **15-21**	**1 missed COC Pill** **Late by less than 12 hrs** - carry on, no problem **Late by more than 12 hrs or more than one pill** - continue pills normally - extra protection 7 days **D, V, M** - continue taking COC Pill - use extra protection during illness or medication and the next 7 days **AND** - **AVOID THE BREAK**	**1 missed COC Pill** **Late by less than 24 hrs** - carry on - no problem	**2 or more missed COC Pills** **Late by 48 hrs or more** - take last missed pill and carry on as normal - extra protection 7-days **D, V, M** - as manufacturer's guide (see left) **AND** - **AVOID THE BREAK**	**NOTE:** If you are taking '22-day pills', '24-day-pills' or pills with 'natural' hormones, please follow the manufacturer's guidelines instead of this outline.
Pill Pack **Week** **Four** **Days** **22-28**	**HORMONE FREE WEEK** To maintain contraception, only take the 7-day break if there are no missed pills, diarrhoea or vomiting during the previous week. If so, don't take the break but start your next pack on Day-22. Take each pill, in turn, and take your break at the end of that packet. Doing this, you are unlikely to bleed but you are also unlikely to get pregnant this way!			If ever in doubt about interacting medication or herbal remedies, use extra protection or avoid sex until the risk is confirmed.

If in doubt, don't have sex without a condom and follow the manufacturer's guidance from the leaflet inside your Pill packet

WHO = World Health Organisation
FSRH = Faculty of Sexual & Reproductive Health - UK

Contraception — Family Planning — Birth Control

Contraception — Family Planning — Birth Control

Do diarrhoea, vomiting or medication affect the COC Pill?

✦ If you have bad diarrhoea or vomiting, are taking some prescription medicines *(particularly drugs used to treat TB, epilepsy and HIV)* or the herbal antidepressant, St John's Wort, you should assume that protection has been lost. *(If you are on long term treatment, you may need to use an alternative method of contraception.)*

✦ Extra protection *(or no sex)* is essential during any illness or when taking interacting medication or herbal remedies, and for seven days afterwards.

✦ If any of that time goes into what would have been your 7-day break between pill packets, after completing the present one you should start taking the pills, in turn, from the next pill packet – and then have your usual break *(as before)*.

✦ If you're in any doubt as to which medicines cause problems, assume they will until you check with the person who prescribed them, ring any Contraception / Sexual Health Clinic; or ask a pharmacist.

✦ If you miss one COC Pill, continue as usual with the rest of your packet but if you have less than seven days left in that packet, do NOT take the break but continue in to the next packet.

✦ Take all of those in turn, and then have your 7-day break, as usual.

✦ If you miss two or more pills, and have unprotected sex or an accident with a condom, seek immediate medical advice because you may require Emergency Contraception.

How reliable is The COC Pill?

✦ The COC Pill is extremely reliable if you remember to take it as directed – ie. it can be up to 99.8% effective when taken properly. In other words, only two women in 1,000 are unlucky enough to get pregnant each year, even if they take the COC Pill properly.

Do I have to be having sex to use the COC Pill?

✦ No, you don't have to be having sex to use or continue using the COC Pill. Few people seem to realise that there are many benefits from taking the COC Pill apart from preventing pregnancy.

Who CAN take the COC Pill?

✦ Generally, the COC Pill is suitable for fit, healthy young women – particularly non-smokers *(or those who only smoke a little)* aren't very overweight and don't have any serious medical conditions.

✦ Its use also depends on the medical history of your close blood relatives *(mother, father, brother(s) and sister(s))*.

Why is the health of my parents and siblings important when I want to use the COC Pill?

✦ The aim is to keep you healthy and safe, as well as protected against unplanned pregnancy when you use hormonal contraception.

✦ It is generally very safe but occasionally the risks of using a particular method are greater than the benefits of using it.

✦ Some medical conditions that close relatives have can suggest that you may be at increased risk of a particular condition, too.

✦ And for the sake of your health, it is extremely important that you are open about your family medical history when you are asked about it by healthcare practitioners.

✦ In these circumstances, a different method of contraception would be suggested.

✦ Your health is too important to hide information just because you think you want to use a particular method, for which you may not be suited.

Who can NOT use the COC Pill?

It's not recommended for women who:
(a) are pregnant;
(b) have epilepsy – because of drug interactions that may alter the efficiency of the COC Pill. *(But check with your prescriber as it may be OK.)*
(c) have hypertension *(high blood pressure);*
(d) are already pregnant;
(e) get migraine, with aura;
(f) have or have had circulatory problems e.g. blood clots in your system *(DVT / deep vein thrombosis, or PE / pulmonary embolism – clot in the lung);*
(g) are breast feeding;
(h) smokers who:
    1) are under 35 and smoke over 40 a day;
    2) are over 35 years of age;
    3) are over 35 and stopped smoking less than a year ago;
    4) smoke shisha / hookah, regularly; *(one hour is equal to smoking 200 cigarettes* Ref: BBC.co.uk/WHO)
    5) and people who chew tobacco;
(i) have active liver disease *(hepatitis);*
(j) have breast cancer;
(k) have diabetes – with complications;
(l) have unexplained vaginal bleeding;
(m) have sickle cell disease *(a blood disorder)*, but not sickle cell trait;
(n) have tuberculosis *(TB)* – because of interacting drugs;
(o) have high cholesterol;
(p) have severe varicose veins;
(q) are bedridden *(immobile)* or use a wheelchair;
(r) have current gall bladder disease or some other rare medical conditions;
(s) are obese, with BMI more than 35 *(ratio of height to weight calculation)* or are a smoker with BMI over 30;
(t) are using St John's Wort *(herbal antidepressant)*; or are taking certain medication *(enzyme inducers);*
(u) women who do not want to use hormonal methods of contraception;
(v) and women with multiple risk factors.

What are the advantages of using it, apart from avoiding pregnanacy?

If you take it properly, some of the advantages may include:
(a) fewer acne-type spots (with some pills);
(b) less non-cancerous breast disease;
(c) regular withdrawal bleeds *(periods);*
(d) less painful periods;
(e) (generally) lighter periods;
(f) less anaemia;
(g) no ovulation pain;
(h) less unwanted hair growth;
(i) some protection against cancer of the ovaries and endometrium *(lining of the womb)*, and also the bowel, which lasts long after the method is stopped;
(j) less endometriosis *(a condition where tissue, similar to the lining of your womb, bleeds outside your womb into your pelvic cavity and causes pain);*
(k) fewer ovarian cysts *(small sacs of clear fluid on the ovary);*
(l) less troublesome fibroids *(non-cancerous/benign tumours or growths in your uterus);*
(m) less rheumatoid arthritis;
(n) no anxiety over unwanted pregnancy; and
(o) it doesn't interfere with sex.

What are the disadvantages of using the COC Pill?

Disadvantages may include:
(a) an initial and temporary sense of minor headache, nausea, mood swings and / or breast tenderness, which settles as the COC Pill's hormones and your own balance;
(b) increased blood pressure;
(c) spotting and/or breakthrough bleeding i.e. bleeding on pill taking days whilst the COC Pill and your body settle together.
d) in some women, a *very* small increased risk of breast cancer, which reduces after stopping.

Contraception — Family Planning — Birth Control

Contraception — Family Planning — Birth Control

Does the use of CHC increase the risk of cervical cancer?

◆ Yes, and no. Women who use methods of CHC *(combined hormonal contraception)* do not tend to use condoms regularly in stable relationships.
◆ Extended use of CHC may increase the risk of cervical cancer cells developing so regular cervical screening is advised to detect this promptly.
◆ However, this may be related to other factors, such as acquisition of HPV (human papilloma virus) and/or smoking.

Are there any risks associated with using the COC Pill?

◆ Most women are safe to use the COC Pill and don't have any problems.
◆ The COC Pill is safe for women whose personal and family medical history give no cause for concern during careful assessment.
◆ However, women with some medical condtions *(or whose family medical history suggests increased risk)* may develop thrombosis *(blood clots)* and other medical problems if they use it.

When should I contact someone if I am worried about something new?

You should consult your healthcare professional if you experience any of the following for the first time:
◆ sudden, severe chest or abdominal pain;
◆ lower leg pain, particularly if you raise your toes towards your knee, if there is any redness or associated swelling;
◆ migraine *(severe type of headache)*, especially 'with aura' *(see information about migraine)*;
◆ breathlessness or coughing up blood;
◆ strong tingling, weakness or numbness in your arms or legs;
◆ fainiting; or, if you collapse.
These may not be associated with your COC Pill but it may not be safe for you to continue using it with such conditions.

For how many years can I take it?

✦ If you remain fit and well – and don't smoke – you can use it until you're 50, without a break.
✦ If you're a smoker, you'll be taken off it, automatically, by the time you're 35.

Do I need to stop taking the COC Pill after a few months, to give my body a break?

✦ No. Your body gets a break from it every four weeks, anyway, and you are merely suppressing *(resting)* ovulation whilst you take it.
✦ By the end of the 7-day break between your packets, the drugs are virtually out of your system and you will be at risk of pregnancy if you don't start your next COC Pill packet on time.
✦ That's why you must use extra protection, or avoid having sex, if you start your next packet late.

Will the COC Pill control my periods?

✦ Yes, it will. Your bleeding will be regular and you may be able to predict them, right down to the hour they start.

Will it make my periods heavier or lighter?

✦ Generally, the COC Pill makes periods extremely regular, much lighter and less painful with fewer, if any, pre-menstrual symptoms.

What should I be aware of if my girlfriend's using it?

✦ You have an interest and a responsibility to understand about the COC Pill and how it works to prevent your girlfriend becoming pregnant.
✦ Her outward appearance will not change, so you'll have to trust her to take it properly because if your girlfriend were to become pregnant, with or without a terminationyou'd have to deal with some difficult emotions.

Without a termination you'd be responsible for paying child maintenance for up to 25 years.

✦ When you understand it, you will realise that there will may be times when you will need to use condoms for protection against pregnancy, as well as for routine protection against infection.

✦ The only way to protect yourself in case she hasn't taken it properly is to use a condom routinely for safer sex.

Do recreational drugs affect the COC Pill's reliability?

✦ No. Not as far as is known.

✦ Drugs can, however, be bad for your long-term physical and mental health and can increase your risk of contracting sexually acquired infections.

✦ If you dehydrate you are more likely to develop thrombosis (blood clots).

Will the COC Pill make me put on weight?

✦ There is no evidence that it causes weight gain. Some women put on a little bit of weight *(3-4 lbs / 1-2 kg)* in the first couple of months due to water retention, but this wears off.

✦ A little extra weight is safer than pregnancy so, if you do put on weight, don't stop taking your pills but watch what you eat and drink.

✦ Try to give it three months before deciding it doesn't suit you. Although contraceptively protected when taken properly, it takes a little time for your body to fully adjust.

✦ Some women become aware of a slightly nauseous sensation in their throat – but this should wear off soon and you're most unlikely to vomit.

✦ Don't stop taking your pills. Try taking it at night instead, so you can sleep through or; take it after breakfast, which may be an easier time to remember to take them routinely.

✦ It's often blamed for things it's not guilty of!

When I take it for the first time, how long does it take to start working?

✦ You're contraceptively protected from the moment you take your 1st pill on the 1st day of your period.

✦ Manufacturers guide that if you start it later than day two of your period, you need to use extra protection or abstain *(avoid sex)* for 7 days.

✦ The same applies if you are re-starting to use the COC Pill after having stopped using it for some time.

✦ In both cases, you're protected from pregnancy if you continue to take it properly, thereafter.

✦ Other guidance states that you are protected if you start it from the 1st to 5th day of the initial period, and that you are then protected if you carry on as prescribed.

✦ Be advised by your prescriber.

Why are smokers taken off the COC Pill but non-smokers are allowed to continue?

✦ Smokers are taken off the COC Pill to protect their health.

✦ Smoking makes blood more sticky and so can oestrogen in combined methods of contraception.

✦ With age, the risk of having a heart attack or stroke from a sticky blood clot *(thromboembolism)* lodging in heart muscle or the brain increases.

✦ If you stop smoking for at least a year before you are 35, you may be allowed to stay on it.

✦ This is why you will be advised to stop smoking, if you are using combined hormonal contraception.

✦ If you're a non-smoker, and want to continue using it, you may be able to do so right up until your menopause *(when periods stop, commonly between 48 and 52 years of age)* and then, if you would like, transfer to HRT *(hormone replacement therapy)*.

Contraception — Family Planning — Birth Control

Contraception — Family Planning — Birth Control

I was reading something about blood clots being serious if a woman is using hormonal contraception.
I have blood clots during my period. Is this dangerous?

✦ No. Although period blood clots, can appear to be quite large, this type of clot is not the same as thromboembolism.
✦ Clots from venous thromboembolism *(VTE)* travel around the body via the circulatory system.
✦ Period blood clots are leaving the body, not circulating inside it.
✦ It's the internal type of blood clots that cause major risk to life and may kill.

What's venousthromboembolism *(VTE)* and why is it so serious?

✦ Thrombos means clot.
✦ The clot forms an obstruction, which is called an embolus.
✦ When an embolism *(clot)* gets stuck in a vein, it is called venous thromboembolism ***(VTE, also called venous thrombosis)***.
✦ VTE commonly develops as a deep vein thrombosis *(DVT)* or a clot in a vein, deep inside the body, rather than in a vein you can see near the surface of your skin.
✦ Sometimes, instead of the clot being formed from blood, it is formed from a fatty deposit or plaque that has stuck to the lining of an artery or vein and become dislodged in a similar way.
✦ This is called atherosclerosis and such plaque develops in medium or large arteries and may also be called 'hardening of the arteries'.
✦ Unfortunately, across the general population, VTE is common and can be deadly.

What are the main risks for the development of VTE?

✦ Thromboembolism is a rare but serious complication, that can occur when using combined hormonal contraceptive methods.
✦ This is why each woman's medical history is assessed carefully.
✦ Risks are higher during the first year of use or when re-starting combined hormonal contraception after a break of four or more weeks.
✦ Examples of conditions caused by thromboembolism are:
— D.V.T *(deep vein thrombosis)*;
— M.I. *(myocardial infarction or death of heart muscle / heart attack)*;
— C.V.A *(cerebro-vascular accident / stroke)*;
— P.E *(pulmonary embolism or clot in the lung(s))*; and
— gastrointestinal embolism, which presents with severe abdominal pain, nausea, vomiting and shock.

Comparison DVT risk examples:
— general population 4 per 10,000
— women using combined methods of contraception - 6-10 per 10,000;
— pregnant women - 20 per 10,000.

And the chance of actually dying from a blood clot whilst using combined hormonal contraception is roughly one in a million. In other words, rare!

Is this why so many questions are asked about my health when I just want to use contraception?

✦ Yes. The questions are designed to protect your health.
✦ If you are worried about your risks, ask your doctor or nurse to guide you.

What might I notice if I develop VTE?

You may notice one or more of the following signs or symptoms, which may or may not be due to VTE, BUT if you are using combined hormonal contraception, you should not ignore:

✦ sudden, severe, shortness of breath unrelated to recent exercise;
✦ a persistent dry cough;
✦ chest pain;
✦ severe headache;
✦ pain in the lower leg, *particularly* if it is in one leg only, which increases when you raise your toes towards your knees, the area is red, swollen, warmer to touch than the other leg and/or tender;
✦ abnormal nerve sensations such as pins-and-needles, tingling, burning, prickling or similar feelings *(known as parasthesia)*;
✦ weakness, particularly one sided;
✦ weak pulse;
✦ coughing up blood; and even perhaps
✦ personality change.

Indeed, anything worrying should be reported to an emergency service, so a correct assessment can be made and appropriate treatment organised.

© Sylvia Rawsthorn 1999

Who is most at risk of developing VTE?

People at higher risk of developing VTE include, but are not limited to, those who:
✦ have already had a DVT;
✦ smoke, use shisha, snuff or chew tobacco;
✦ get migraine with aura;
✦ are obese *(overweight)*;
✦ have high blood pressure;
✦ fly long distances without walking about or drinking much water during the flight;
✦ are pregnant;
✦ have major surgery, especially abdominal surgery;
✦ are on bed-rest, for extended periods of time *(immobile)*;
✦ have had a stroke and are not able to keep mobile;
✦ taking some types of medication;
✦ have various medical conditions that affect their blood and/ or circulation;
✦ have some types of cancer;
✦ have had a heart attack;
✦ have a heart and lung condition called 'congestive cardiac failure';
✦ are increasing in age *(esp. over 40)*;
✦ have high cholesterol;
✦ have a close family member who have had VTE; and also
✦ people who have had VTE are at higher risk of developing another.

This list is not exhaustive, and a combination of factors increase individual risk. But, this list shows how common VTE can be and why it is vital to ask relevant questions about someone's medical history before a woman is given combined hormonal contraception; and why it is important to answer honestly.

Contraception — Family Planning — Birth Control

Contraception — Family Planning — Birth Control

What is the difference between a headache and a migraine. I thought they were the same thing?

No. They are not the same. There are different types of headache but they are usually limited in duration and severity. They are:
+ common headache;
+ tension headaches;
+ migraine.

Migraines, however, tend to last longer than a simple headache and there are two types:
+ simple or common migraine (without aura); and
+ migraine with aura.

How can I tell if I get a common migraine or migraine with aura?

Adults who get migraine with aura tend to notice a recognisable set of symptoms during the hour before the headache starts (although it is possible to have the aura without an associated headache) e.g:
+ an unpleasant smell;
+ confused thoughts;
+ zig-zag lines / blind spots on one side;
+ the perception of a strange light / or a beam of light (as if looking at the light at the end of a dark tunnel). This is commonly followed by a migraine of moderate severity, which occurs on one side of the head, is made worse during movement, and may have other symptoms, such as:
+ sensitivity to noise / sound; ringing in the ears; nausea; and / or vomiting and / or spinning sensation (vertigo);
+ noticing strange odours (smells) or tastes;
+ sometimes muscle weakness, tingling, numbness, 'pins and needles';
+ it may last from a few hours to a few days; and rarely, there is fainting and/or paralysis during the migraine.

Will the COC Pill protect me from pregnancy AND infection?

+ No, it won't. You will still need to use condoms for protection against sexually acquired infection.
+ The barrier of mucus, which forms at your cervix, may slow down the progress of an infection into your womb and tubes, but it won't prevent you from catching it.

Are the effects of the COC Pill reversible?

+ Yes, they are. It's virtually out of your system by the end of your 7-day break.
+ But remember: you can get pregnant after that if you have unprotected sex. So use condoms from the day after your last pill, if you decide to stop using it, if you don't want to get pregnant.

Is it safe to have sex during my 7-day break between packets?

+ Yes it is. As long as you took your previous pack correctly, start your next packet of pills on time; you don't have diarrhoea or vomiting; you aren't taking medication which can interfere with the COC Pill; you're contraceptively protected.
+ If in doubt; ask your doctor, nurse, or pharmacist for advice.

If I'm going on holiday and don't want to bleed while I'm away, is there anything I can do?

+ Yes there is. To avoid your withdrawal bleed (period) — instead of taking your 7-day break between packets of pills/active pills, simply start your next packet of pills when you finish your present pack — take all of those in turn — and then take your usual break.
+ It's OK to do this occasionally, but not wise to do it every month without medical advice.

When should I call my doctor?

✦ Despite the many precautions used to ensure that only women who are medically fit to take it are given the COC Pill, sometimes complications do occur.

✦ If you notice sudden severe shortness of breath with chest pain, or a painful hot tender swelling in your calf *(lower leg)*, contact your doctor immediately or Emergency Dept. in case a DVT has formed, for which you will need urgent medical treatment.

✦ Thrombosis is very rare in young, fit, healthy women but is an important reason why you should be open and honest with whoever asks you about your and your family's medical history.

✦ When you visit to collect more pills, tell the doctor about any worries or concerns you may have however minor or silly you think they are.

✦ They may be very important.

How old do I have to be to start taking the COC Pill?

✦ You can start taking The COC Pill once you have regular, established periods. As already seen, it has many helpful, non-contraceptive uses than just protection against pregnancy.

Will they show me what to do if I go to a clinic, my doctor, practice nurse or pharmacist?

✦ Whoever prescribes you the COC Pill should teach you how to use it correctly before you leave them.

✦ They should also give you an instruction leaflet to keep as a reference – ie. in case you need to check what you were told at any time.

✦ If, for some reason you're not shown how to take your Pill, ask them to make time to teach you before you leave, so you are sure of what to do.

✦ This is especially important for women who have dyslexia or are not able to read very well.

What should I do if I bleed on my COC Pill taking days?

✦ If you bleed on COC Pill-taking days, check that you are taking it at the same time each day.

✦ Continue taking your COC Pill and check with your healthcare provider.

✦ If you have not had a sexual health screen since changing sexual partner or in the last 12 months, it would be wise to do so incase the bleeding is caused by a sexual infection.

What should I do if I don't bleed during my 7-day break?

✦ As long as you have taken all of your pills correctly, start your next packet of pills on time.

✦ However, if you're worried or you think you made a mistake during the previous packet, check with your healthcare provider.

✦ They may suggest doing a pregnancy test, to make sure you are not pregnant, so don't be too alarmed when they suggest this.

When should I stop using the COC Pill if I want to get pregnant?

✦ It used to be thought that it took some time for fertility to return after stopping the COC Pill, but it is now known that ovulation occurs by day 8 or 9 after the last COC Pill.

My boyfriend doesn't like the idea of me taking hormones as our method of contraception.

✦ Your health is monitored closely and you are taking medication that is similar to what your body makes.

✦ Hormonal contraception is very safe and there are many non-contraceptive benefits.

✦ Pregnancy is not risk free!

Contraception — Family Planning — Birth Control

Contraception — Family Planning — Birth Control

When can I use the COC Pill after I have a baby, have a miscarriage or an abortion?

After having your baby:
✦ If you ARE breastfeeding, you will be guided away from the COC Pill and other combined hormonal methods of contraception *(The Patch and The Ring)* until you stop, and guided towards another method, such as the progestogen only pill *(POP)*, implant, IUS *(intra-uterine system / Mirena®)* methods or an IUD (copper coil).
✦ If you are NOT breastfeeding, the COC Pill *(Patch or Ring)* can be used after the baby is 21 days old.

After having a miscarriage or an abortion:
✦ The COC Pill can be used straight after an abortion or a miscarriage.

I've tried the COC Pill before and didn't like it but I'm older now. If I try it again, will I get the same effects or will I feel better this time?

✦ It is impossible to predict how you will react to the COC Pill but if you're still medically fit to take it, it would be sensible to try it again.
✦ You could either try the same one again or ask to try a different one.
✦ Remember, though, that you should allow three months for the COC Pill hormones to settle again, before saying you don't like the new pill.

NOTE
Never take unnecessary risks
✦ Check with your prescriber or your pharmacist if if you are in doubt about anything.
✦ Use extra protection unless you're reliably informed that it's not necessary.
✦ Take the pill you've forgotten, even if this means taking two pills on one day.
✦ There are many different types of pill, so if you think one doesn't suit you, ask to try others until you find the one that is right for you.
✦ But remember to allow at least three months with a new hormonal method before deciding that it doesn't suit you.

SMOKELESS TOBACCO
Surprise Information

✦ Chewing tobacco is shredded like short cut grass, generally mildly acidic and intended to be chewed throughout the day as desired.
✦ Snuff is chopped into particles like large coffee grounds, moistened and used by holding between gum and cheek.
✦ Swedish snus (typically moist), is a variant on snuff but processed differently so that some must be kept refrigerated.
✦ Gutkha and other oral smokeless tobacco products are used in India and South-East Asia.
(ret WHO)

WATERPIPES
Surprise Information

Hookahs, Bhangs, Narghiles, Shisha, Hubble-Bubble

Smoking these for 1 hour is equivalent to smoking 200 cigarettes.

(ref BBC.co.uk quoting World Health Organisation 2011)

Combined hormonal contracpetion may not be the first method of choice for women using these products regularly.

Healthcare professionals prescribing them should consider the use of these products when taking a woman's medical history — and not just ask about their use of cigarettes!

Risk factors, which indicate that combined hormonal methods of contraception should NOT be used by a particular woman:

If the woman has or has had any of the following:

— pulmonary embolism;
— heart attack;
— stroke (cerebro-vascular accident);
— TIA (transient ischaemic attack or mini-stroke).

If she knows she has:

— a higher risk of developing blood clots;
— a history of migraine with aura;
— diabetes with circulation problems;
— blood pressure above 140/90 - the risks of using CHC outweigh the benefits;
— blood pressure above 160/95 - CHC is absolutely contraindicated;
— very high cholesterol in her blood;
— current gall bladder or liver disease;
— periods of immobility e.g. having major surgery, after which she will be on 'bed rest' for a while. In this case, she should stop the method for four weeks before surgery and until two weeks after she is fully mobile again.

If a woman has two or more of the following, she may be advised NOT to use combined hormonal contraception but a progestogenic or a non-hormonal method:

— she is aged 35 or more;
— her BMI *(body mass index / weight to height ratio)* is over 30;
— she smokes; uses 'shisha' or chews tobacco;
— her blood pressure is above 140/90;
— a close blood relative *(mother, father, brother(s), sister(s))* had a VTE under the age of 45 - e.g. a stroke, heart attack, DVT or other similar conditon; or if they have / have had high cholesterol;
— she has diabetes;
— she travels *(sits)* for four or more hours a day *(or has a particularly sedentary occupation)*;
— she has given birth in the last six weeks;
— she has any cardiovascular *(heart)* conditions;
— she has other medical conditons that could increase her risk of VTE, such as cancer, ulcerative colitis, Crohn's disease, sickle cell disease, systemic lupus enythematosus or other disorders of the circulatory system.

As with insurance companies, it is much better to declare a condition than to hide it.

If anything has changed since the woman was last seen for medication, it should be noted; likewise, if anything is going to change e.g. an operation is planned for the future etc.

To the woman:
If in doubt, mention it !

To the practitioner:
If in doubt, err on the side of caution while you check it out.

© FP Sales Ltd 1995

Sexplained Two — For Changing Times ® © 1999-2016

Contraception — Family Planning — Birth Control

Contraception — Family Planning — Birth Control

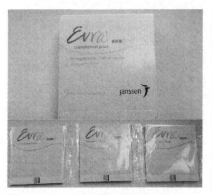

What is the Combined Transdermal Patch and how does it work?

✦ The Patch is a disposable combined hormonal delivery system that is stuck to the skin by a woman once a week, to prevent pregnancy.

✦ In the UK, it is known by the names OrthoEvra® and Evra® and is a 'combined transdermal *(across skin)* contraceptive patch' or **CTP**.

Here, it is referred to as The Patch.

✦ It is a device that, once stuck to the skin, slowly releases the hormones, oestrogen, as ethinyl estradiol *(ethi-nile-eestro-di-ol)* and the progestogen as norelgestromin *(nor-el-jes-tro-min)* into the bloodstream.

Once in the blood stream, the hormones work in the same way as the COC Pill to prevent pregnancy:

✦ the hormones temporarily prevent ovulation *(egg release)*;

✦ alter the conditions within the uterus *(womb)* and fallopian tubes;

✦ form a 'plug' of mucus at the cervix *(neck of the womb)*;

✦ and stop sperm from being able to access an egg to fertilise.

Who can use The Patch?

✦ The Patch is a combined method of contraception, therefore women who are medically safe to use the COC Pill and The Vaginal Ring can use it, too.

✦ The risk of developing blood clots may be slightly greater with the type of progestogen in The Patch *(norelgestromen)* than with the progestogens used in some low-dose combined oral contraceptive pills.

How effective is The Patch?

✦ The Patch is over 99% effective when used correctly.

✦ In other words, extremely reliable, with less than one woman in 100 who use it becoming pregnant each year.

How do I use The Patch?

✦ The total cycle is 28 days, as with The Pill.

✦ The Patch cycle consists of 21 days of active hormonal treatment, carried through three sticky patches, worn consecutively, for seven days each — followed by one week without a Patch, during which a withdrawal bleed can be expected.

✦ It should be applied on day one of the first cycle to obtain full protection immediately but can be applied up to day five of a regular 28 day cycle.

✦ If your cycle is shorter than 24 days, and if it is applied between days two and 5, protection is not sufficient until the 8th day.

✦ In this case you should either avoid sex in that time or carefully use a condom, to prevent pregnancy.

Where is The Patch worn?

✦ The Patch can be worn on most areas of the body, but should not be applied to:
— the breasts; or
— broken or irritated skin.

What if I forget to put a new Patch on?

✦ The same 'rules' apply as with forgotten or missed COC Pills.
✦ If you are late with your next Patch, for more than 48 hours, protection is lost.
✦ Replace the patch and, to avoid pregnancy, use extra protection or avoid having sex for the next seven days.

What are the advantages of The Patch?

The Patch provides:
✦ a discreet way to use hormonal contraception;
✦ a weekly option, rather than a daily method so you only have to remember to do something once a week to maintain your contraceptive protection;
✦ you don't have to worry if you vomit or have diarrhoea as it doesn't have to be swollowed;
✦ as with most other methods, it use doesn't interfere with sex; and
✦ withdrawal bleeds are regular, usually lighter and less painful than natural periods.

What are the disadvantages of The Patch?

The Patch:
✦ can be seen;
✦ does not offer any protection against sexual infections; and
✦ as with other hormonal methods, there may be spotting *(bleeding at unexpected times)* and other side effects during the first few months.

The Patch is pink in colour, so can I colour it or draw a design on it?

✦ No. Do not alter The Patch.
✦ There could be an interaction between the dyes in your ink and the hormones in The Patch.

What if The Patch falls off?

✦ The same guidance applies as with forgotten COC Pills.

Will The Patch fall off when I have a shower or a bath?

✦ The Patch is very sticky and does not generally fall off, either in the bath, shower or with general wear.
✦ If it does, follow the guidance for forgotten Patch and missed COC Pills.

Is using The Patch like using a 'stick on' form of The Pill?

✦ Yes. In many ways The Patch is a 'stick on pill', but for many women, it is easier to use and to remember.

When can I use The Patch after I have a baby, a miscarriage or have an abortion?

✦ See this question in relation to the COC Pill because the answer is the same *(page 88)*.

NOTE: your prescriber should ensure that you understand how to use it correctly before issuing you with The Patch..
✦ However,if you decide to use it, excellent instructions and answers to many more questions are provided by the manufacturer.
✦ Keep their leaflet for reference.

Contraception — Family Planning — Birth Control

What is the Vaginal Hormonal Ring ?

✦ The vaginal hormonal ring *(VHR)* is an increasingly popular choice of disposable combined hormonal delivery system which is inserted in to the vagina by a woman once a month.

✦ It contains a low dose of both female hormones, oestrogen *(ee-stro-gen)* and progestogen *(pro-ges-toe-gen)*, in the same way as in the combined oral contraceptive pill *(the COC Pill)* and The Patch *(Evra®/OrthoEvra®)*.

✦ The hormones are delivered through a slow release mechanism, which activates when the ring is in contact with the woman's vaginal mucose membrane *(vaginal lining)*.

✦ The oestrogen, ethinyl estradiol *(ethi-nile-eestro-diol)* in The VHR is the same as that used in many other combined hormonal methods of contraception.

✦ The progestogen, etonogestrel *(eto-no-ges-trel)*, is the same as that used in the progestogen implant, Nexplanon®/ Implanon®.

✦ Here, the combination is called **The Vaginal Hormonal Ring or VHR**.

How effective is The VHR?

✦ The Vaginal Hormonal Ring is over 99% effective when it is used correctly.

✦ In other words, extremely reliable, with less than one woman in 100 who use it becoming pregnant each year.

Who can use The VHR?

✦ The VHR is a combined method of contraception, therefore women who are medically safe to use The COC Pill or The Patch can choose to use it.

✦ According to the manufacturer the risk of getting blood clots may be slightly greater with the type of progestogen in NuvaRing® *(etonogestrel)* than with the progestogens used in some low-dose combined oral contraceptive pills.

How do I use The VHR?

This relates to the first and best known monthly vaginal ring, called **NuvaRing®:**

✦ **Starting on day one** of your menstrual cycle *(first day of your period)*, squeeze the ring and insert in to your vagina and you will be protected against pregnancy immediately.

✦ **Starting on days two to five**, insert as above but you must use extra protection or avoid sex for the first seven days.

✦ Unlike the contraceptive diaphragm or cap, The VHR is a standard size and 'one size fits all' women, so you do not have to worry about fitting it correctly inside the vagina. It cannot get lost or go too far because the vagina is an enclosed space, with the cervix at the internal end.

✦ Leave it in place for 21 days, then remove and dispose of it in household waste, inside the pouch it came in.

✦ After two to three days without The Ring in your vagina, you should expect a withdrawal bleed *(induced period)*.

✦ After a 7-day break, known as a 'ring free interval' *(whether you are still bleeding, or not)* insert your **next** *(a NEW)* Vaginal Hormonal Ring on the eighth day *(now day one again)* and continue with this 21-7-21-7 routine to maintain your contraceptive protection.

How can I check that it is still there?

✦ You can check that The VHR is there by inserting a finger in to your vagina and feel it.

Will we notice it during sex?

✦ During sex you, or your partner, may notice that it's there but it's rarely a problem.

✦ Some men enjoy the sensation produced as their penis passes over it.

✦ If the sensation is a problem, The VHR can be removed for up to three hours, and then replaced.

Does it hurt to put it in or remove it?

✦ No. It should not hurt to insert or remove The VHR.

✦ To remove it, just insert your finger and hook the device, then pull it out.

✦ If it does hurt, mention this to your doctor or nurse.

Am I protected from pregnancy during the seven day interval?

✦ Yes. You're protected from pregnancy during the 7-day interval, as long as you put the next VHR in on time.

✦ If you don't plan to do this, you must use another method of contraception as soon as you remove your VHR.

Can The VHR fall out of my vagina?

✦ No. The VHR is held in place by your vaginal muscles.

✦ If in doubt, check, as before.

What if I forget to take it out?

✦ If you forget to take it out and have unprotected sex, you may require emergency contraception if you do not change it before the 28th day *(in the same way as missed or late COC Pills)*.

What if I forget to put a new VHR in on time?

✦ If you are late inserting your next Ring, follow the rules as if you were restarting your COC Pill late.

✦ Insert as soon as possible and use extra protection *(a condom)* or avoid sex for seven days.

✦ If you had sex during the break between rings, seek medical advice as you may require emergency contraception to prevent pregnancy.

NOTE: There are very clear instructions with each box of NuvaRing®, so make sure you read this when you start to use the method and keep the leaflet handy, for reference.

✦ The leaflet explains what to do if you encounter situations that could put you at risk of pregnancy.

✦ It also explains what to do if you are using certain medication, experience bleeding at unexpected times or don't bleed when you expect to.

✦ There is no need to stop using the method to give your body a break from the hormones. They disappear from your body by the end of your ring free interval.

If you are ever concerned about using this method, please speak to your prescriber.

Each month, many women use it, very happily, around the world.

NEWS

A 12-month vaginal ring is expected to become available soon, which will give many women increased contraceptive freedom.

Contraception | Family Planning | Birth Control

The Progestogen Only Pill (POP)
Progestogen Only Hormonal Contraception

Contraception — Family Planning — Birth Control

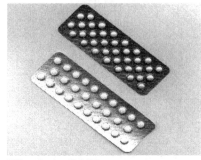

What it the POP?

✦ The POP, or mini-pill as it's also known, is an oral contraceptive pill which contains just one hormone – progestogen.
✦ There are two types of POP:
– traditional and desogestrel *(DSG)*

How does the POP work?

✦ The POP forms a barrier of thick, infertile mucus at your cervix *(neck of your womb)*, so that sperm can't swim through to meet an egg.
✦ It also effects the lining of your womb – helping to prevent pregnancy.

When or how do I use the POP?

✦ The pills must be taken EVERY DAY of the year at exactly the same time – without a break.

Will the POP control my periods?

✦ No, it won't control them at all.
✦ No-one can tell how it will affect your periods.

Will the POP make my periods heavier or lighter?

✦ Generally, you'll have lighter periods, which may stop whilst you use it.
✦ But some women get irregular light bleeding *(spotting)* in the first few months while other women continue to bleed as they did before taking it.

If I forget a POP, what should I do?

1) If you're using a 'traditional' POP, and remember within three hours of your usual time just take it and continue as usual.
2) If you're using a 'desogestrel' POP, and remember within 12 hours, continue as usual.
✦ If you've forgotten for more than three / 12 hours** respectively, continue taking the POP as usual when you remember, but to be safe you must use extra protection or have no sex (abstain) for 48 hours / although the manufacturer advises seven days*, for the destogestrel *(DSG)* POP.
✦ If you had sex before realising you'd forgotten your pill, seek emergency contraception *(EC)*.
✦ If in doubt, ask your pharmacist.

Are all POP used the same way?

✦ No. There is one, which contains the progestogen 'desogestrel', and has a 12 hour window if forgotten, instead of just 3 hours.
✦ If you use this one, please read the manufacturer's information leaflet that comes with the medication and follow their guidance about the 12 hour / 7-day rule.
✦ **Here, where important information relates to desogestrel *(DSG)* POPs, it is indicated by the symbol *, since the manufacturer recommends 7-days.**
✦ **This information largely relates to 'traditional' POPs.**

Key:
* Manufacturer states seven days
** Manufacturer states 12 hours

How reliable is the POP?

✦ When taken properly it's nearly as reliable as the COC Pill, especially in women over 35.

Do diarrhoea or vomiting affect it?

✦ Yes they do – your protection will be reduced if you have bad diarrhoea or vomiting, especially within three hours of taking your POP.

✦ EXTRA PROTECTION is important during illness and with some medication.

✦ To be absolutely sure, and for the infertile mucus plug to be maintained at the cervix, continue taking your pill; but you should use extra protection for 48 hours *(*7-days DSG)* after recovery.

Do antibiotics or other prescription drugs affect the POP?

✦ Yes. Drugs for TB and some other medication can affect it; as can

✦ St John's Wort *(herbal antidepressant)*; but

✦ antibiotics don't affect it.

✦ But, if you're worried about drug interactions it's safer to use extra protection before checking with your doctor, pharmacist, or clinic.

Will my weight make a difference?

✦ Be guided by your prescriber.

✦ Manufacturer's licenced guidance states that one pill per day should be taken, every day.

✦ It used to be said that women who weigh over 70 kgs should take two traditional POPs a day to maintain protection, so you may hear this advice.

✦ Likewise, if you are over 100 kg and taking a desogestrel *(DSG)* POP, you may be advised to take two of these, per day.

For how many years can I use the POP?

✦ This excellent method can usually be used up to the age of 55.

Who is suitable to use the POP?

It's suitable for most women but also if you:
1. are a smoker over 35 years of age;
2. are breast feeding;
3. have high blood pressure;
4. get migraines;
5. are diabetic;
6. have sickle cell disease *(type of blood disease)*; and/or
7. if you don't want to take or don't like the combined pill for some reason.

Who is NOT suitable to use it?

Most young women are safe to use it but it's not suitable for everyone.

✦ You should discuss with your Doctor if you or someone in your family has had or have:
1. breast cancer;
2. ectopic pregnancy;
3. unusual vaginal bleeding;
4. active liver disease *(hepatitis)*; or
5. circulatory or cardiac *(heart)* problems..

Should I stop using the POP and give my body a break?

✦ No, you shouldn't. It's a very safe form of contraception.

✦ If you are someone who stops having periods whilst using it, your doctor *may* ask to test your blood after three years, and may give you additional hormone treatment for a short while.

Can I use the POP safely, if I smoke?

✦ Yes, you can.

✦ If you're taking the COC Pill and smoke, when you reach 35 years of age you'll be automatically transferred to the POP, or another progestogenic method if you still want to use hormonal contraception.

Contraception — Family Planning — Birth Control

The Progestogen Only Pill (POP)
Progestogen Only Hormonal Contraception

Contraception — Family Planning — Birth Control

Do I have to have sex to use it?

✦ No, you don't.

What should I be aware of if my girlfriend's using the POP?

✦ You have an interest and a responsibility to understand the POP and how it works to prevent your girlfriend becoming pregnant.

✦ Her outward appearance won't change when she's taking the POP, so you'll have to trust her to take it properly.

✦ If your girlfriend were to become pregnant, with or without a termination you'd have to deal with the difficult emotions. Without a termination you'd be responsible for paying maintenance for up to 25 years.

✦ There will also be times when you will need to use condoms for protection against pregnancy and routine protection against infection.

✦ The only way to protect yourself in case she hasn't taken it properly is to use a condom routinely for safer sex.

✦ Since most women would find it hard to trust a man saying he was taking the POP, you should read about how it works, as you also rely on it for protection against pregnancy.

Do recreational drugs affect the POPs reliability?

✦ No. Not as far as is known.

✦ Drugs can, however, be bad for your long-term physical and mental health and can increase your risk of contracting sexually acquired infections.

✦ If you dehydrate you may be more likely to develop thrombosis (blood clots).

Will it make me put on weight?

✦ There is no evidence that the POP makes you put on weight.

✦ Simply watch what you eat!

Will it protect me from pregnancy AND infection?

✦ No, it won't. You will still need to use condoms for protection against sexually acquired infection.

✦ The barrier of mucus, which forms at your cervix, may slow down the progress of an infection into your womb and tubes, but it won't prevent you from catching it.

Are the effects of the POP reversible?

✦ Yes, they are. It's out of your system after 27 hours.

✦ But remember: you can get pregnant after that if you have unprotected sex. So, if you don't want this, use condoms from the day after your last pill.

When does the POP start to work when I begin to take it?

✦ You're contraceptively protected from the moment you take your 1st pill on the first day of your period.

✦ If you start it later than the second day of your period, you need to use extra protection or don't have sex for two days (**7-days DSG pills).

✦ You're safe from pregnancy if you continue to take it properly, thereafter.

Also:

✦ never take unnecessary risks;

✦ check with your clinic, GP or pharmacist if in doubt about anything;

✦ use extra protection unless you're reliably informed that it's not necessary;

✦ always take the pill you've forgotten, even if this means taking two pills on one day and use extra protection (a condom) or don't have sex (abstain) for 2 days (**7-days DSG pills);

✦ there are many different types of pill. If you think one doesn't suit you, you can always try others until you find the one which is best for you.

Missed POP

POP pack	Manufacturer's Guide **Desogestrel (DSG) Pills**	Manufacturer's Guide **Traditional POPs**	
Week 1 **Days 1-7**	POPs are taken every day of the year There is NO break between packets X 1 or more missed Desogestrel (DSG) containing POP	POPs are taken every day of the year There is NO break between packets X 1 or more missed POPs	* If you are ever in doubt about interacting medication or herbal remedies, use extra protection or avoid sex until the risk is confirmed
POP pack **Week 2** **Days 8-14**	**Late by less than 12 hrs** - carry on - no problem **Late by 12 hrs or more, or more than one DSG POPs missed** - continue pills normally - extra protection 7 days*	**Late by less than 3 hrs** - carry on - no problem **Late by more than 3 hrs or more than one pill missed** - continue pills normally - extra protection 48 hours	Some POP packs contain 35 pills Traditional rules apply
POP pack **Week 3** **Days 15-21**	**Diarrhoea (D), vomiting (V), interacting medication (M)** - continue taking your POP - use extra protection during illness or medication and for the next 7 days* *	**Diarrhoea (D), vomiting (V), interacting medication (M)** - continue taking your POP - use extra protection during illness or medication and for the next 48 hours (2 days)	**NOTE:** No hormonal methods of contraception provide protection against sexual infections.
POP pack **Week 4** **Days 22-28**	(World Health Organisation (WHO) and UK Faculty of Sexual & Reproductive Health (FSRH) state 48 hrs) ** In the UK this pill is called Cerazette®		Dual protection (condom and other method) are routinely advised.

Contraception — Family Planning — Birth Control

Contraceptive Injection
Progestogen Only Hormonal Contraception

Contraception — Family Planning — Birth Control

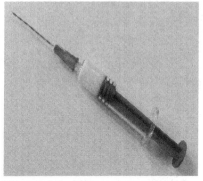

What is injectable contraception?

✦ It's an extremely effective form of pregnancy prevention.
✦ Some types of injection contain oestrogen and progestogen; some just progestogen.
✦ This only explains the progestogenic injections given by intramuscular injection eight weekly *(Noristerat®)* or every twelve weeks *(maximum 14 weeks)* for DepoProvera® / Sayana Press®.
✦ Depo-Provera® is the most common contraceptive injection used in the the world and contains only one drug – the progestogen called DMPA / Depot Medroxyprogesterone Acetate.
✦ This is also available as Sayana Press®. *(See page 100)*

How does it work?

✦ Its action is similar to that of the POP/Progestogen-only-Pill.
✦ It also suppresses *(suspends)* ovulation for the duration of use, alters the conditons within the uterus and fallopian tubes and forms a mucus plug at the cervix. This is the same as in the second half of a woman's menstrual cycle, after ovulation has occurred.

Who's suitable to use it?

✦ It's suitable for most women.

How reliable is this form of contraception?

✦ It's extremely reliable. It can't fall out, be forgotten *(on a daily basis)* and, it can't split or come off.

Who's not suitable to use it?

✦ It's not suitable for pregnant women or women with some potentially serious medical conditions.
✦ You should discuss with your doctor if you or someone in your family have or has had:
1. breast cancer;
2. unexplained vaginal bleeding;
3. active liver disease *(hepatitis)*;
4. circulatory or cardiac *(heart)* problems or abnormal blood test results when checking for cholesterol or lipids *(fats)* in your circulation; or
5. other serious medical conditons.

Are there any other benefits from using the injection?

Yes there are several benefits from using injectable contraception. It:
1. gives some protection against cancer of the lining of your womb;
2. reduces your risk of ectopic *(tubal)* pregnancy;
3. reduces your risk of developing ovarian cysts;
4. reduces your risk of developing ovarian cancer;
5. reduces the possibility of having PID *(pelvic inflammatory disease)*; and
6. women with sickle cell disease experience fewer problems than with other methods of contraception.

When or how do I use it?

✦ Depo-Provera is usually given in the first five days of a menstrual cycle and then repeated after 12 weeks *(maximum 14 weeks)*, for as long as you need contraceptive protection.

Contraceptive Injection
Progestogen Only Hormonal Contraception

When does it start to work?

✦ The injection starts to work as soon as you have it, provided that it's given in the first two days of your period.
✦ If you start it later you need to use extra protection or avoid sex *(abstain)* for 7-days to be sure of preventing pregnancy.

Will it control my periods?

✦ No, it won't control your periods.
✦ Over half the women who use it stop having periods or have a very light bleed every few months.
✦ Other women get irregular bleeding.

Will it make my periods heavier or lighter?

✦ Periods are generally much shorter and much lighter when using injectable contraception.

Should I stop using it and give my body a break?

✦ Safe, long term use of this method is widely practised world-wide.
✦ There is debate about 'bone mineral density' and long term use of injectable. progesterone leading to boney changes but staying on it, rather than stopping and starting has many advantages, especially if it's important not to get pregnant.
✦ In some countries, if you stop having periods whilst using it, you may be offered a blood test after three years and may be given additional hormone treatment for a short while to balance your system and protect your bones from breaking more easily than if you weren't using it.
✦ Also, in some areas, women over 40 years of age may be guided towards an alternative method.
✦ Each woman is assessed separately, for safe use of this method.

For how many years can I use injectable contraception?

✦ You can, most probably, use it for many years without worry.
✦ See the previous question.

Is it affected by diarrhoea, vomiting or antibiotics?

✦ No, it's not.

What should I be aware of if my girlfriend's using it?

✦ You have an interest and a responsibility to understand the injection and how it works to prevent your girlfriend becoming pregnant.
✦ Her outward appearance will not change when she's taking the injection, so you'll have to trust her to take it properly.
✦ If your girlfriend were to become pregnant, with or without a termination you'd have to deal with the difficult emotions. Without a termination you'd be responsible for paying maintenance for up to 25 years.
✦ There will also be times when you will need to use condoms for protection against pregnancy and routine protection against infection.
✦ The only way to protect yourself in case she hasn't taken it properly is to use a condom routinely for safer sex.
✦ Since most women would find it hard to trust a man saying he was taking the injection, you should read about how it works, since you also rely on it for protection against pregnancy.

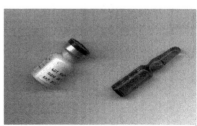

Contraception — Family Planning — Birth Control

Do recreational drugs affect its reliablilty?

✦ No. Not as far as is known.

✦ Drugs can, however, be bad for your long-term physical and mental health and can increase your risk of contracting sexually acquired infections.

✦ If you dehydrate you are at risk of developing thrombosis *(blood clots)*.

Will it make me put on weight?

✦ It may. However, some women put on weight but some lose weight or stay the same.

✦ No-one can tell how you will react before you use it but it may increase your appetite, so be careful of what types or amount of food you eat and what you drink.

✦ If you do put on weight, you initially need to weigh up the risks of this to your health against the risk of getting pregnant and discuss options with your healthcare provider.

Will it protect me against pregnancy AND infection?

✦ No, it won't. You will still need to use condoms for protection against sexually acquired infection.

✦ The barrier of mucus, which forms at your cervix, may slow the progress of an infection into your womb and tubes, but it won't prevent you from catching it.

Is it reversible?

✦ Yes, and it's the first method of choice for many young women.

✦ It's out of your system by the end of the 14th week after injection, which is why extra protection is vital if you forget to turn up on time for each injection.

✦ Some women only take a few months to become pregnant after they stop the injection; others take longer. This is because in nature some women are more fertile than others.

✦ Some women experience a delay in return to fertility.

NEWS

Sayana Press®
A new version of this method has been developed.

✦ Called Sayana Press® it is given subcutaneously *(just under the skin)* via a special device *(compared with into the muscle, as required by DepoProvera® and Noristerat®)* every 13 weeks.

✦ The big advantage is that a woman can learn to give it to herself and avoid the need for regular visits to healthcare settings to get it.

Combined Hormonal Injections

✦ Combined monthly hormonal injections are available in some parts of the world but at the time of writing, they are not used in the UK.

What is the subdermal contraceptive implant?

✦ Subdermal means 'under the skin'.
✦ Subdermal contraceptive implants consist of small rods, about the length of a hair grip, which contain the hormone, progestogen.
✦ They're inserted under the skin *(sub-dermally)* of the upper arm and slowly release the hormone into the woman's body for various lengths of time, depending upon the implant used.
✦ Internationally, there are several different types available.
✦ At the time of writing, the implant of choice in the UK is Nexplanon®.

How does the implant work?

Its action is similar to that of the contraceptive injection.

The implant
✦ suppresses *(suspends)* ovulation for the duration of use;
✦ forms a barrier of thick, infertile mucus at your cervix *(neck of the womb)*, so that sperm can't swim through to meet an egg;
✦ and affects the lining of your womb – preventing pregnancy.

What is the progestogen called, that's used in the implant?

✦ Two types of progestogen are used to make contraceptive implants.
✦ The first is levonorgestrel *(lee-vo-nor-jes-trel) (LNG)*.
✦ The second is etonorgestrel *(e-toe-no-jes-trel)*.
✦ They are both used in other methods of hormonal contraception.

For how long do implants work?

Implants work for different durations.

1) Nexplanon®/ Implanon® works for up to three years, consists of one rod and contain the progestogen called **etonogestrel**. *(Duration advice may change.)*

2a) Jadelle®, Jadelle Sine Inserter® Sinoplant®, Sinoplant II/Sino-implant II® or Zarin® works for up to five years and consist of two rods *(formerly called Norplant II®)* which contain the progestogen called **levonorgestrel**.

2b) Norplant®, the original implant, consists of six rods and now works for up to seven years. In China, it is called Sinoplant I® and also contain the progestogen called **levonorgestrel**.

This relates to the etonorgestrel based implants, Nexplanon® and Implanon®

What's the difference between Nexplanon® and Implanon®?

✦ They contain the same progestogen and act in exactly the same way.
✦ Implanon® preceeded Nexplanon®.
✦ Nexplanon®, which has a different introducer, is designed to make insertion easier and safer.
✦ And, Nexplanon® is visible on x-ray, which Implanon® is not.

Contraception — Family Planning — Birth Control

Subdermal Implant (SDI)
Progestogen Only Hormonal Contraception

Contraception — Family Planning — Birth Control

How is the implant put in (inserted)?

✦ Local anaesthetic is used to numb the area, then the implant is injected under the skin of the upper arm using a special type of syringe, or introducer.

✦ The woman, and the practitioner, feel the area to check that it has been implanted properly before the small wound is covered with a plaster, which is worn for 3-5 days.

✦ To minimise bruising, discomfort and swelling, the manufacturer recommends that a compression bandage should be provided, and worn for 24 hours. Some places offer this, while others no longer do.

✦ The area should not be knocked or allowed to get wet for 3-5 days.

✦ Although not always necessary, a follow-up visit may be advised a few weeks later, to check that the user is happy with their implant.

Does it hurt when it's put in?

✦ No. Injection of the local anaesthetic may sting a little, but after that, insertion of the implant does not hurt.

What might I notice after insertion?

After insertion you *may* notice one or more of the following:
✦ pain or discomfort *(as local anaesthetic wears off)*;
✦ bruising or swelling *(temporarily)*;
✦ redness *(temporarily)*;
✦ infection *(at site of insertion)*;
✦ scarring *(small)*;
(Colleague observation: skin pigmentation change over implant site, is more often noticed on darker skin; Asian in particular).

If concerned about anything, speak to your inserting practitioner.

How is the implant removed?

✦ As with insertion, local anaesthetic is used to numb the area before a small incision *(cut)* is made beside the lower end of the implant, and it is gently pulled out using a special instrument.

✦ A dressing is then applied, in the same way as after insertion.

Can I have another inserted at the time of removal, through the same incision?

✦ Yes. This is a common request and contraceptive protection continues immediately when a replacement is inserted straight after removal.

Does it hurt when it's taken out?

✦ No. Implant removal does not hurt because local anaestetic is used to numb the area.

Who is suitable to use the implant?

✦ As with other progestogen only methods, the implant is suitable for most women, even if they have different medical conditions.

How reliable is the implant?

✦ The implant is one of the safest and most reliable methods of contraception available.

✦ However, as with other methods, there is a small failure rate, with a small risk of ectopic *(tubal)* pregnancy.

Who MAY not be to use it?

The implant is NOT suitable for women who are pregnant or who undiagnosed vaginal bleeding, active liver disease, known or suspected breast cancer and some other potentially serious medical conditions.

You should discuss with your practitioner if you've had or have:
1. breast cancer;
2. unusual vaginal bleeding;
3. active liver disease *(hepatitis)*;
4. circulatory or cardiac *(heart)* problems;
5. a history of thrombosis;
6. epilepsy;
7. TB *(tuberculosis)*;
8. high blood pressure *(if over 100 kg your implant may be changed sooner than three years)*;
9. are overweight;
10. a history of chloasma *(a skin pigmentation that occurs in sunlight, commonly on the face)*;
11. an allergy to any of its constituents.

If you are in doubt about the importance of something in your own, your parents' or brother's/sister's medical history, disclose it *(tell them)*.

What are the advantages of using an implant?

Advantages of implants are that:
✦ it is highly effective, very reliable, low dose, long acting, reversible contraception that are low in total cost;
✦ it can last for three or more years;
✦ they are very safe to use;
✦ they can be used by women who are breastfeeding;
✦ they are helpful for women who experience heavy, painful periods;
✦ implants do not interfere with sexual spontaneity;
✦ their use can't be forgotten on a daily basis.

What are its disadvantages?

The list of possible side effects looks frightening but it does NOT mean that they will be experienced.

There may be one or more of the following:
✦ unpredictable, irregular bleeding;
✦ an itch around the insertion site;
✦ nausea, vomiting and / or dizziness;
✦ acne *(may improve or worsen)*;
✦ breast pain / discomfort;
✦ abdominal pain;
✦ and there may be other rare effects, listed by the manufacturer.

According to the latest UK guidance from NICE *(National Institute for Health and Care Excellence)* and the FSRH *(Faculty of Sexual and Reproductive Health)*, there is no association between the use of progestogen-only implant and headaches, weight change, mood change, or reduced libido *(sex drive)*.

Can I have it removed if the side effects become too much?

✦ Yes, of course, you can have it removed if you feel that the side effects become intolerable and given help to find an alternative method.

When does the implant start to work?

✦ It starts to work straight away if put in on the first day of menstruation, otherwise extra protection *(or no sex)* is necessary for 7 days.
✦ As with all hormonal methods of contraception, it takes about three months for the implant to settle and any side effects to improve greatly.

Contraception — Family Planning — Birth Control

Contraception — Family Planning — Birth Control

Will the implant control my periods?

✦ No! No progestogen methods of contraception control menstrual bleeds.
✦ Irregular bleeding / spotting may last for up to six months, occasionally longer.
✦ If this happens to you, return to your healthcare practioner who will guide you about keeping it, suggest using extra hormones, or having it removed.

What will it do to my periods?

✦ Your bleeding pattern may be a little chaotic, with either irregular bleeding, no bleeding or bleeding at the time you would expect if you were not using it.
✦ If you are concerned about your bleeding pattern, speak to your prescriber.

Can anything stop it from working?

✦ The herbal antidepressant called St John's Wort reduces efficacy; and
✦ enzyme inducers. *(These are drugs used to treat a range of conditions such as TB, epliepsy, anxiety and/or depression.)*
✦ If in doubt, you can check a drug's compatibility with your pharmacist.

When should I stop using it?

✦ If you are comfortable using it, there is no reason to stop until you want to get pregnant or use something else.

Will it protect me against pregnancy AND infection?

✦ No, it won't. You will still need to use condoms for protection against sexually acquired infection.
✦ The barrier of mucus, which forms at your cervix, may slow the progress of an infection into your womb and tubes, but it won't prevent you from catching it.

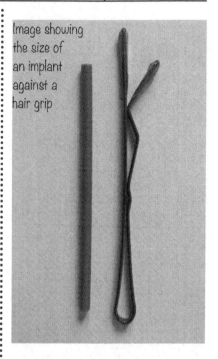

Image showing the size of an implant against a hair grip

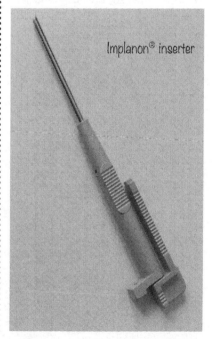

Implanon® inserter

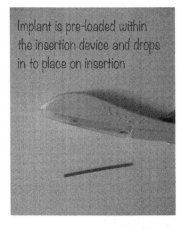

Implant is pre-loaded within the insertion device and drops in to place on insertion

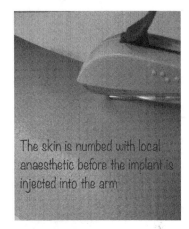

The skin is numbed with local anaesthetic before the implant is injected into the arm

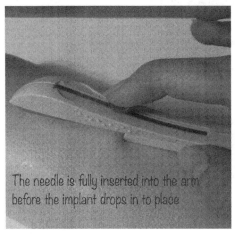

The needle is fully inserted into the arm before the implant drops in to place

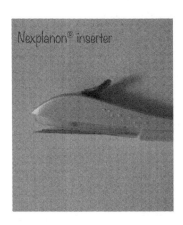

Nexplanon® inserter

Sub-dermal implant

Contraception — Family Planning — Birth Control

IUD / Coil / Copper Coil
Intra-Uterine Contraception (IUC)

Contraception — Family Planning — Birth Control

What is the IUD or copper coil?

✦ IUD means Intra-Uterine Device.
✦ Some people refer to it as the IUCD instead. *(Intra-Uterine Contraceptive Device)*
✦ It is a small device, which is inserted into the womb to prevent pregnancy.
✦ Several different types are available. They're usually made of plastic, contain a small amount of copper and have a small thread, which you can feel at your cervix.
✦ *(Used to check that it's in place correctly and for removal.)*

How does it work?

✦ The copper reduces the number of sperm reaching your fallopian tubes.
✦ It alters the conditions inside your womb and reduces the chance of fertilisation or of a fertilised egg implanting in your womb.

When do I use it?

✦ It must be inserted by a specially trained healthcare practitioner, under aseptic *(sterile)* conditions.
✦ Usually, it's inserted during the first 10 days of a menstrual cycle.
✦ It can be inserted later, as a form of emergency contraception.
✦ It can be inserted at any time as long as the inserter can be sure you are not pregnant.

How do I check that it is still there?

✦ After insertion, you or your partner should check that it's still in place after each period.
✦ You do this by inserting a clean finger into your vagina and feeling for the thread at your cervix.
✦ Your cervix is about a full finger's depth into your vagina – it is around hard muscle which feels like the end of your nose – i.e. it has a dimple in the centre.
✦ If you don't feel the thread, assume it has fallen out. You must then use another method of contraception until you can get it checked by your doctor or nurse.
✦ If you feel something like a matchstick at your cervix, your IUD has slipped and you should not rely on it for contraception until you see your doctor or nurse, who may remove and/or change the device.

How reliable is it?

✦ Very reliable indeed.
✦ *Almost* 100% of pregnancies are prevented for users of the IUD.
✦ It's so good that, today, it's often offered to prevent pregnancy instead of sterilisation.

Who's suitable to use the IUD?

✦ Women in a stable relationship who don't want to use other forms of contraception for several years are the most suitable.

Who's NOT suitable to use it?

Each woman's situation is assessed individually but it is NOT recommended if you have or have had:
1. a sexually acquired infection or pelvic inflammatory disease *(PID)* at the time. After treatment, it may be appropriate to use it as a method;
2. heavy, irregular or painful vaginal bleeding without a known cause;
3. you or your partner have sex with other people and do not use condoms;
4. an allergy to copper.

✦ It's not *usually* the first method of choice for young women who haven't had children, or women who have had an ectopic pregnancy – but if they are keen to use it and are in a stable relationship, where the risk of sexual infection is minimal, it can be used.
✦ Women are assessed individually.

My friend says that the IUD causes infection. Is this true?

✦ No, it is not true.
✦ The IUD is a sterile device.
✦ If you have an existing infection at your cervix at the time of insertion, that can be pushed into your uterus and cause pelvic infection *(PID/pelvic inflammatory disease)*.

For how many years can I use it?

✦ You can use an IUD for between 5-10 years depending on the device inserted; and then have another.
✦ If you want to become pregnant, you can ask for it to be removed earlier.

Will I be tested for anything before I have an IUD fitted?

✦ Many practitioners test for an infection called chlamydia before inserting an IUD.
✦ Some others suggest you're fully screened for infection, at a Sexual Health Clinic, beforehand.
✦ This is a wise precaution, which can help to prevent pelvic infection that could put your fertility at risk.

Are there any benefits from using it, apart from pregnancy prevention?

✦ No, there aren't.

Do diarrhoea, vomiting or antibiotics affect it?

✦ No, they do not affect the IUD.

Must I stop using it and give my body a break?

✦ No, not unless you acquire a sexual infection.

Will it control my periods?

✦ No, it won't.

Will it make my periods heavier or lighter?

✦ Modern IUDs are smaller than their predecessors *(used in the past)* but periods may be longer and heavier.

Do recreational drugs affect its reliability?

✦ No. Not as far as is known.
✦ Drugs can, however, be bad for your long-term physical and mental health and can increase your risk of contracting sexually acquired infections.
✦ If you dehydrate you are more likely to develop thrombosis *(blood clots)*.

Contraception — Family Planning — Birth Control

Contraception — Family Planning — Birth Control

Will the IUD make me put on weight?

✦ No, it won't affect your weight.

Will it protect me from pregnancy AND infection?

✦ No, it won't protect you from infection, only pregnancy.
✦ The only way is to use a condom.

Is it reversible?

✦ Yes, completely, upon removal.

When does it start to work?

✦ It starts to work straight after it has been inserted.
✦ Some people advise the use of extra protection during the first 7-days.

Do I have to have sex to use it?

✦ No, but there's no other reason for having one except for contraception.

Are there any disadvantages to using it?

✦ Yes. If you catch a sexually acquired infection it can pass more easily into your womb than when other methods of contraception are used.
✦ Complications rarely occur but there is a small risk that if pregnancy occurs with an IUD in place that it may be an ectopic *(tubal)* pregnancy. However, there is still less risk of this happening than if you are not using a method of contraception.

Do I need to have a check-up after it's fitted?

✦ Yes, you should have a check-up after six weeks, and then only if you have problems.

Can I use tampons with an IUD?

✦ Yes, you can use tampons but wait and use sanitary towels *(pads)* until after your first period in case the IUD comes out with your first period.
✦ If you use tampons after your first period always check the thread(s) afterwards to make sure the IUD hasn't come out during menstruation.

What should I be aware of if my girlfriend's using an IUD?

✦ Her outward appearance doesn't change when she's using the IUD, so it's up to you to help her check that it's still in place before you have sex. You can do this during foreplay by gently checking that you can feel the threads of the IUD at her cervix.
✦ Diarrhoea, vomiting, antibiotics or other drugs won't put either of you at increased risk of pregnancy.
✦ Remember: your girlfriend's not protected from sexually acquired infections when using the IUD on its own. So, if you're unfaithful to her, you could put her at risk if you don't use a condom.
✦ The only way to protect yourself fully from unplanned pregnancy AND infection is to use a condom during sex, at all times.

Can I use it safely if I smoke?

✦ Yes. But for other reasons, it is not wise to smoke!

What's the difference between an IUD and an IUS?

An IUD just contains copper, on a plastic frame.

An IUS contains the hormone, progestogen, on a plastic frame.

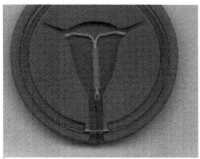

Above: IUS inside demonstrator, showing correct position inside the uterus

What is an IUS?

✦ IUS stands for Intra-Uterine System.
✦ An IUS is a contraceptive device, similar to a coil, with slow release hormone *(progestogen)* on it instead of the copper, used on an IUD.
✦ This relates to the IUS, available worldwide as Mirena® / Levonova ® *(Scandinavia)* ; and the mini-IUS as Jaydess® / Skyla® *(USA)*.

How does it work?

✦ It releases the hormone to the lining of your womb and alters its conditions to prevent you becoming pregnant.
✦ It thickens the mucus at your cervix, which prevents sperm entering your womb.
✦ It prevents some women from ovulating or releasing an egg, although most women still ovulate.

How reliable is it?

✦ Very reliable indeed.
✦ Almost 100% of pregnancies are prevented for users of the IUS.
✦ Mirena® is so good that, today, it's often offered to prevent pregnancy instead of a sterilisation.
✦ Jaydess® delivers 25% of the drug dose of Mirena® and the failure rate is, therefore, slightly higher.

Who's suitable to use the IUS?

✦ Mirena® is particularly suitable for women who've given birth.
✦ Jaydess® is particularly suitable for women who have not given birth.
✦ But, either device can be used by either group of women.
✦ It is sometimes inserted with local anaesthetic, to make insertion more comfortable.

Can it be used for Emergency Contraception like the IUD?

✦ No, it should not be used as a method of emergency contraception.

Who's may not be suitable to use the IUS?

✦ Women who are pregnant must not use it. Women who have or have had:
1. active liver infection or growth;
2. undiagnosed abnormal vaginal bleeding;
3. infection, or at risk of infection;
4. a history of cardiac *(heart)* or circulatory disease.

Are there any benefits from using it apart from preventing pregnancy?

✦ Yes, there are.
✦ It can help some women who get very heavy periods due to fibroids (non-cancerous growths in the uterus) but not all; depending on the fibroid.
✦ Periods are usually less painful, lighter and shorter, or may stop.

How is it fitted?

✦ An IUS is inserted under sterile conditions by a specially trained healthcare professional – usually in the first week of your period although it can be inserted any time, if they can be certain you are not pregnant.

Contraception — Family Planning — Birth Control

IUS / Mirena® / Jaydess®
Intra-Uterine Contaception (IUC)

Contraception — Family Planning — Birth Control

When does it start to work?

✦ It works immediately when fitted within seven days of a period starting.
✦ If fitted after the 7th day of a cycle, a condom should be used for 7-days *(or previous method continued for a week, altermatively, avoid sex the first 7-days)*.

For how many years can I use it?

✦ Mirena® / Levonova® is licensed for five years' use; Jaydess®/Skyla® for three.
✦ It can be removed sooner if you want to get pregnant and another can be inserted after removal if you want to continue with the method.

Do diarrhoea, vomiting, antibiotics or smoking affect it?

✦ No. It is not affected by any of these.

Should I stop using the IUS and give my body a break?

✦ No.

Will it control my periods or make them heavier or lighter?

✦ No. It won't control their timing but your periods will become lighter and less painful, perhaps even stop during use.
✦ You may experience irregular bleeding or spotting in the first few months of use.

What should I be aware of if my girlfriend's using an IUS?

✦ Her outward appearance doesn't change when she's using the IUS, so it's up to you to help her check that it's still in place before you have sex. You can do this during foreplay by gently checking that you can feel the threads of the IUS at her cervix.
✦ Diarrhoea, vomiting antibiotics or other drugs won't put either of you at increased risk of pregnancy.

✦ Remember: your girlfriend's not protected from sexually acquired infections when using the IUS on its own. So, if you're unfaithful to her, you could put her at risk if you don't use a condom. The only way to protect yourself fully from unplanned pregnancy AND infection is to use a condom during sex, at all times.

Can I use tampons with an IUS?

✦ You should use sanitary towels *(pads)* during your first period in case the IUS comes out with your first period.
✦ After that, yes, you can use tampons with an IUS.
✦ Always check the thread*(s)* afterward a period, to make sure the IUS hasn't come out.

Do recreational drugs affect its reliabilty?

✦ No. Not as far as is known.
✦ Drugs can, however, be bad for your long-term physical and mental health and can increase your risk of contracting sexually acquired infections.
✦ If you dehydrate you are more likely to develop thrombosis *(blood clots)*.

Will the IUS make me put on weight?

✦ No, not as far as is known.

Will it protect me from pregnancy AND infection?

✦ No, it won't protect you from infection. You still need to use a condom.

Is it reversible?

✦ Yes, completely, upon removal.

Do I have to have sex to use it?

✦ No – see the list of benefits on the previous page.

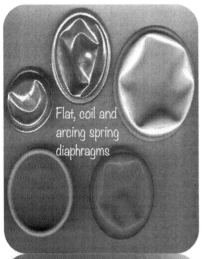

Flat, coil and arcing spring diaphragms

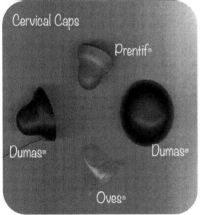

Cervical Caps

Prentif®

Dumas®   Dumas®

Oves®

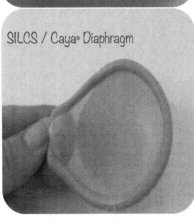

SILCS / Caya® Diaphragm

What are caps and diaphragms?

✦ Diaphragms and caps are domed devices, commonly made of latex or rubber. Shaped to fit over your cervix they act as an intravaginal *(inside the vagina)* barrier method of contraception. There are different types:

✦ The Dutch cap - flat or coil spring diaphragms;

✦ Omniflex® and other arcing spring diaphragms;

✦ Dumas® — vault cap;

✦ Prentif® — cavity rim cervical cap;

✦ Vimule® — cervical cap;

✦ SILCS / Caya® Diaphragm — approved for use in Europe in 2013, this is the latest design, and a 'one size fits *(nearly)* all' device, made of silicone;

✦ The Honey Cap® is available; but not given free at Sexual Health Clinics. It is extremely expensive and not widely recommended.

✦ Oves® cervical cap, in three sizes, is disposable and is made of silicone. It's suitable for some women who get recurrent cystitis. It's not available on the NHS, but can be purchased from a pharmacy or online.

✦ FemCap® and Lea Shield® — soft, silicone devices — best used as a backup method when using a condom, for safer sex.

✦ Contraceptive Sponges — impregnated with spermicide *(chemical that kills sperm)* — are a barrier method that can stay in the vagina for up to 24 hours. Not to be used during a menstrual period. *(See information on The Sponge.)*

Contraception — Family Planning — Birth Control

Contraceptive Caps and Diaphragms
Barrier Contraception

Contraception — Family Planning — Birth Control

How do caps and diaphragms work?

✦ Caps and diaphragms, once inserted in to the vagina correctly, form a barrier between a woman's eggs and a man's sperm, thereby preventing pregnancy.

How reliable are caps and diaphragms?

✦ Used correctly and carefully, they can be extremely reliable.
✦ If you're extremely organised and good about using yours correctly, every single time you have sex, this can be a very good method and can be over 90% effective.
✦ But, they are not as reliable as the injection, the IUS, sterilisation, the combined Pill, patch, vaginal ring, progestogen only, pill *(POP)*, the IUD, IUS or the male condom.
✦ They are more reliable if you put strips of spermicidal cream or gel *(jelly)* on both sides of the cap or diaphragm, before insertion.
✦ It may be more effective if you wait until you are in your mid 20s to 40s; or in a long-term, stable relationship — but good motivation is the main factor as it has to be used carefully, correctly and consistently.

Who's suitable to use this method?

It's suitable for women:
✦ for whom a pregnancy would not be disastrous;
✦ who can't use, or don't want to use, any other method of contraception; or
✦ women who are very organised and for whom sex needs to be planned not spontaneous *(as with pills etc)*.

Who's NOT suitable to use this method?

✦ It's not suitable for women who get recurrent, common cystitis *(inflammation of the bladder)*.
✦ Women who really don't want to be pregnant.
✦ Or, women who are not prepared to touch their genital area.

Are there any non-contracpetive benefits?

✦ Some women use it to contain the menstrual flow and protect their bedding, if they have sex during their period.

How do I use it?

✦ Because vaginas come in different shapes and sizes, a cap or a diaphragm must be fitted individually by a contraception *(Family Planning)* trained doctor or nurse.
✦ You'll be given a practise cap, shown how to use it and allowed to take it home for a week to practice inserting and removing it on your own.
✦ Even when practicing your insertion technique, you should add spermicidal cream or jel, before inserting it.
✦ You shouldn't rely upon it as a method of contraception in that time because the practise device may have a hole in it.

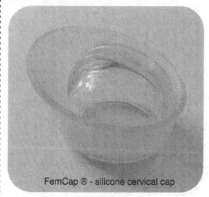

FemCap ® - silicone cervical cap

Contraceptive Caps and Diaphragms
Barrier Contraception

Why would a practice cap have a hole in it?

✦ Holes prevent you from using the method for contraception until the doctor or nurse says you've inserted and removed it correctly.

✦ This gives you time to learn the correct technique of insertion, how to check that it's in the correct position and also to give your partner the opportunity to become familiar with this method of contraception.

✦ Once you've mastered the technique, you'll be given your own, new cap, without holes.

What if I want to have sex with my practice cap in?

✦ If you want to have sex during practise either use a condom or other reliable method of birth control. You can leave your practice cap in place to see how sex feels when it's in place.

Will sex feel different with a cap?

✦ No. Fitted correctly, you shouldn't be aware that you're wearing a cap when you're having sex.

✦ If it's not the right size, nor positioned correctly, you MAY or may not notice a strange sensation.

Will my partner feel it during sex?

✦ No, he shouldn't feel a correctly fitted cap during sex.

✦ Sometimes, the man notices a slight stinging sensation from the spermicide, if he's not using a condom. If he notices this, change spermicides.

How long must I have it in, before I have sex?

✦ You can insert it any time up to three hours before you have sex.

✦ If you exceed *(go over)* this time before having sex, simply put more spermicide into your vagina – or remove, wash and re-insert your cap.

✦ Spermicide in the form of a pessary – solid spermicide which melts at body temperature; or via an applicator – like a syringe without a needle; may be used.

Can I take the cap out straight after I have sex?

✦ No, you can't because of the risk of pregnancy.

✦ After sex you must leave the cap in place for six hours for the spermicide to kill any ejaculated sperm, otherwise you'll just stun them.

What if I want to have sex again, within 6 hours?

✦ If you have sex again in those six hours, you should leave the cap in place AND insert more spermicide into your vagina.

✦ Start counting your six hours again, from the second time after you had sex.

How long can I keep the cap in for and 'top up' the spermicide?

✦ Try not to keep it in for any longer than 30 hours because of the risk of developing Toxic Shock Syndrome (*TSS).

✦ *For more TSS information, see "The Sexplained Column", page 270.*

Contraception — Family Planning — Birth Control

Contraceptive Caps and Diaphragms
Barrier Contraception

Contraception — Family Planning — Birth Control

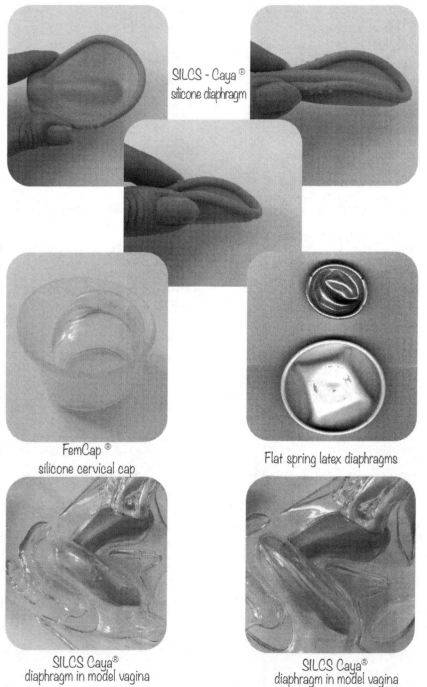

SILCS - Caya ®
silicone diaphragm

FemCap ®
silicone cervical cap

Flat spring latex diaphragms

SILCS Caya®
diaphragm in model vagina

SILCS Caya®
diaphragm in model vagina

How do I take the cap out and what must I do with it?

✦ To take out your cap, simply wash your hand, insert a finger into your vagina, hook the edge of your cap and pull it out.

✦ When you've removed it, just wash it under running water and pat it dry with a towel before replacing it in its carrying box.

✦ You should check it regularly for holes whilst cleaning it.

✦ You should be shown how to look after your cap when you're taught how to use it by the contraception nurse.

For how many years can I use it?

✦ Caps usually have a life span of 12-24 months' use.

✦ However, should you develop a vaginal infection, you should ask for a new cap, to prevent reinfection.

Can anything damage the cap?

✦ Some vaginal medication is oil-based, which can rot the latex of the cap (and condom), so you should avoid sex altogether when being treated.

✦ If in doubt, always ask your local pharmacist or your condom supplier for advice.

✦ For further information about potential interactions, turn to the list of lubricants and vaginal medication on page 219.

Will it control my periods?

✦ No, it won't.

✦ If you have your cap in when your period starts, your blood loss will collect inside your cap.

When does the cap NOT work?

You risk pregnancy:

✦ when it's inserted incorrectly ie. if you don't have your cervix covered;

✦ if you don't use it every time you have sex;

✦ if you use it without spermicide — it's much less reliable;

✦ if you take it out before the 6 hours are up, after sex;

✦ if you fail to top-up with more spermicide and have sex again within your 6 waiting hours.

Is it afected by diarrhoea, vomiting or antibiotics?

✦ No, but it can be affected by some vaginal oil-based medication.

Will it make my periods heavier or lighter?

✦ It won't affect your periods.

What should I be aware of if my girlfriend's using a cap?

✦ You should know how it should feel when it's in her vagina correctly.

✦ You should check, during foreplay, that the latex of the cap covers her cervix.

✦ You will find her cervix approximatley a fingers depth inside her vagina. It feels like a round hard lump with a dimple in the centre — similar to the end of your nose.

✦ If you don't think her cervix is covered, don't enter.

✦ At the fertile time of her cycle, you might feel safer if you use a condom, for extra protection against pregnancy.

✦ Using a condom routinely with the cap would, though, greatly increase the success rate of this method of contraception.

✦ Finally, you may find, as some men do, that having sex when your partner has a diaphragm in place produces an unexpectly pleasurable sensation.

Contraception — Family Planning — Birth Control

Contraception — Family Planning — Birth Control

Do recreational drugs affect its reliability?

✦ No, they don't.
✦ Drugs can, however, be bad for your long-term physical and mental health and can increase your risk of contracting sexually acquired infections.
✦ If you dehydrate you are more likely to develop thrombosis *(blood clots)*.

Will it make me put on weight?

✦ No, but if you lose or gain 7lbs *(3 kg)* or more, you should return to your clinic and have your cap checked for the correct fit.

Will it protect me from pregnancy AND infection?

✦ You gain some protection to your cervix but it doesn't prevent transmission of infection.
✦ In the laboratory spermicide has been found to kill some germs but unless a condom is used, your vaginal surface area is still at risk of infection, as is your external genital area.
✦ Using a condom AND a cap gives better protection against both pregnancy and infection.

Is it reversible?

✦ Yes. As soon as it's removed or; if it's inserted incorrectly, you're at risk of pregnancy.

When does it start to work?

✦ It's effective as soon as it's in the correct position.

Can I use it safely if I smoke?

✦ Yes, you can. But, for other reasons, smoking is not advised!

Do I have to have a check-up after I am fitted with my cap?

✦ Yes, you should return a week after fitting, to see that you're practiced inserting and removing it correctly; and get a new cap *(one without a hole)* if you were not given one at fitting.
✦ Thereafter, many places advise that you don't really need to have a check-up unless you lose or gain 7 lbs or more in weight.
✦ If you do, you should return for a check-up to make sure you are still using the correct size, with a snug fit.

Illustration showing a diaphragm in situ, inside a model vagina.

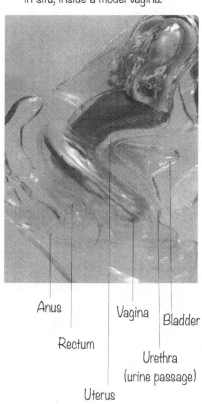

Anus

Rectum

Vagina

Bladder

Urethra
(urine passage)

Uterus

What is the contraceptive sponge?

✦ There are three differnt contraceptive sponge marketed, today. They are called Pharmatex®, Protectaid® and Today®.
✦ They each work in a similar way,
✦ As with caps and diaphrams, a sponge provides protection against pregnancy.
✦ It should not be used during a menstrual period and is not as reliable at preventing pregnancy as most other methods used correctly.
✦ However, at certain times, this can be a good method for a woman to use.

How do I use it?

To use e.g. The Today Sponge®:
✦ thoroughly wetting it with tap water *(approx two tablespoons / 30 mls)*;
✦ insert in to your vagina;
✦ leave in place for six hours after last act of sexual intercourse; and
✦ ensure it is in place each time you have sex.

Pharmatex®, Protectaid® do not need to be activated with water before use. They are already moist, and ready to be used in the same way.

How relaible is it as a method of contraception?

✦ The Today Sponge® manufacturer states that with proper use during every act of intercourse, the efficacy rate is 89% to 91%.
✦ They also state that with sustained use of this method, the efficacy rate increases, suggesting that increased familiarity with the device increases success.

For more information about this method, please visit:
✦ www.TodaySponge.com

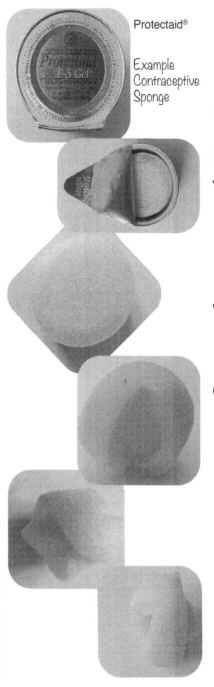

Protectaid®

Example Contraceptive Sponge

Contraception — Family Planning — Birth Control

Contraception — Family Planning — Birth Control

The Male Pill

✦ Much research is under way to develop and market a male pill. However, male fertility is harder to control, since men produce millions of sperm all the time.

✦ Trials have shown that it is possible to control sperm production, but unwanted side effects of the drug combinations must be overcome. Therefore, this method is still some years away from common use.

✦ Although it may be a good idea for men who are well motivated to use it, surveys have shown that many women would be reluctant to trust a man who says he's taken his pill – in case he hasn't and was just saying he had – to get her to agree to his sexual advances!

✦ When, eventually, the male pill becomes widely available, it will only give protection against pregnancy. It won't give any protection against sexually acquired infections.

© Sylvia Rawsthorn 1999

Sterilisation

✦ Sterilisation should be considered permanent surgical intervention to prevent pregnancy.

✦ **In men**, the vas deferens and in women the fallopian tubes are cut, to prevent sperm or eggs from meeting.

✦ Male sterilisation *(vasectomy)* is easy, quick and effective when you've decided you don't want any risk of pregnancy – or have completed your family.

✦ **In women**, sterilisation involves slightly more complicated surgery. Many gynaecologists recommend the IUS while you wait for surgery, as it's so reliable.

✦ Many women decide to keep their Mirena® instead of having surgical sterilisation.

✦ The choice is yours, but you should know that any surgery carries a risk and no method of contraception including sterilisation can guarantee 100% *(except no sex / celibacy).* protection against pregnancy.

✦ However, today the long acting reversible methods of contraception are considered more reliable than female sterilisation.
(e.g. IUS, IUD, Injections, Implant)

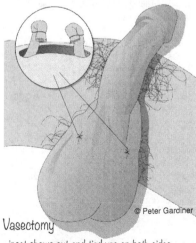

© Peter Gardiner

Vasectomy
- inset shows cut and tied vas on both sides

Female surgical sterilisation

Tubal ligation

✦ This involves cutting or tying a woman's fallopian tubes to prevent a sperm and egg meeting.

✦ It should be considered to be an irreversible *(permanent)* method of contraception / birth control.

✦ There are various surgical options and techniques, all of which involve major surgery.

✦ However, a relatively new form of female sterilisation has been developed, that it is cheaper, quicker, safer and easier, called Essure®.

Essure®

✦ Essure® is a relatively new form of female sterilisation that is minimally invasive, therefore much safer for the woman than undergoing major surgery.

✦ Once the device is inserted into the fallopian tubes, they block, thereby preventing the sperm and egg from meeting.

✦ It does not interfere with natural menstrual cycles and periods should be mostly unaffected by the procedure.

✦ The method should be considered irreversible, so before requesting it, you should be sure you do not want children in the future.

For more information on this method, please see www.essure.co.uk

Other methods being planned:

✦ There are several methods of contraception under development. Most, however, are some years away from general use.

© Sylvia Rawsthorn 1999

Contraception — Family Planning — Birth Control

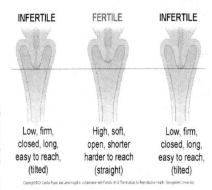

INFERTILE	FERTILE	INFERTILE
Low, firm, closed, long, easy to reach, (tilted)	High, soft, open, shorter harder to reach (straight)	Low, firm, closed, long, easy to reach, (tilted)

Copyright © Dr Cecilia Pyper and Jane Knight in collaboration with Fertility Uk & The Institute for Reproductive Health, Georgetown University

Fertility Awareness Methods (FAMs) or Natural Family Planning (NFP)

✦ FAMs / NFP methods are, simply, the avoidance of or planning of pregnancy by assessment of a women's fertility signals.

✦ Fertility awareness helps young people understand the normal variations in the age in which individuals reach puberty, normal variations in the genitals and breast development, and the normal variation of menstrual cycles. It is also useful for clarifying the difference between a normal physiological discharge caused by cervical secretions and an abnormal discharge caused by a sexually transmitted infection.

✦ It also increases awareness that if sexually transmitted infections are not treated then the woman's fallopian tubes or the man's vas deferens may become damaged, resulting in infertility.

✦ Fertility awareness consultations improve people's understanding about how each method of family planning prevents fertilization taking place and how, if the method is not used correctly, the risk of pregnancy will increase. For example, how the combined oral contraceptive pill prevents ovulation and makes the cervical secretions thick and impenetrable to sperm as well as understanding how fertility can quickly return if pills are not taken as directed. [1]

✦ The effectiveness of FAMs to avoid pregnancy depends on the ability of couples to abstain from intercourse during the fertile time *(natural family planning)* or to use a barrier method consistently during the fertile time *(fertility knowledge with barriers)*.

✦ Research clearly demonstrates that motivated couples can use FAMs effectively. [2]

✦ However, this isn't the first method of choice for a young women whose body is still growing and adjusting; or women who have medical conditions, such as polycystic ovary syndrome *(PCOS)*.

Some period facts that women should know:

✦ The first day of a period is the FIRST day of the menstrual cycle.

✦ A woman will always be asked for the date of the FIRST day of her LAST period when visiting a doctor or nurse for reproductive or sexual health care – so it is helpful to keep a note of the date each period starts.

✦ Period length: count the number of days of bleeding, to find the period duration. Cycle length: count the number of days from the start of a period until the day before the next one starts, to find the cycle length.

✦ Text books commonly state that women have their period every 28 days and that it lasts for 5-days. However it is extremely unlikely:
— that the cycle length will always be the 'text book' 28-days;
— that the period duration will always be 5-days; and
— that ovulation will always be on Day 14 of each cycle. Ovulation normally occurs 10-16 days *(average 14 days)* before the start of the NEXT period, and each woman has her own pattern, with the time from ovulation until next period standard, for her.

If I decide to use this method to avoid or plan a pregnancy, what should I appreciate?

✦ If you want to use this method, there are many elements and you should take time to understand each of them.

✦ FAMs / NFP requires close observation of all your body's fertility signs and symptoms, taken over 6-12 months and it is best understood when taught, on an individual basis, by a specially trained FAMs/NFP teacher.

✦ This is because the menstrual cycle can be complicated to understand and several things can mislead your observations.

✦ Times of abstinence (no sex) are required if you're relying on this method as your sole method of contraception so your partner should also be committed to the method too.

✦ This method can be used well if you are planning to have a baby and this section merely introduces the different elements of FAMs/NFP but cannot offer a full enough explanation about them to be followed as a method of pregnancy prevention.

✦ See the end of this topic for guidance on further reading.

There are many components of Fertility Awareness, which work best in combination.

The main phrases you may hear mentioned when people refer to elements of FAMs / NFP are:

Withdrawal (pulling out)
— NOT recommended
Dates:
— Calendar Method
— The Safe Time
— Rhythm Method
Standard Days Method
— Cycle Beads®
Sympto-thermal Method
— basal body temperature
— changes in the cervix
— cervical mucus consistency
  — Billings Ovulation Method *(BOM)*
  — Creighton Model
    FertilityCare™ System *(CrMS)*
LAM
(Lactationa Amenorrhoea Method)
— breastfeeding
New Technologies:
— Persona®

Contraception — Family Planning — Birth Control

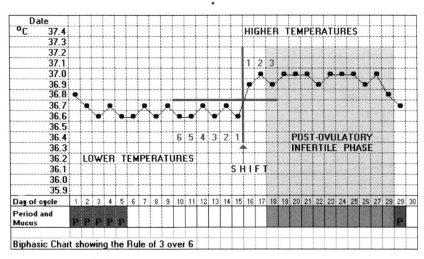

Biphasic Chart showing the Rule of 3 over 6

© Jane Knight / Dr C Pyper / Fertility UK

Withdrawal

✦ NO !
✦ Withdrawal is NOT considered to be a reliable method of contraception or provide protection against sexual infections.
✦ There can be approximately three million sperm *(and sometimes germs)* present in the small amount of fluid at the tip of a man's penis during sexual excitement, so unprotected genital contact should be avoided if a pregnancy is not wanted.

Dates

Calendar Method / Rhythm Method / The Safe Time

✦ Knowing the length of your menstrual cycle is extremely useful.
✦ From the time their periods start, many mothers teach their daughters to record in a diary, on a calendar or mobile phone application (app) the date that each period starts, and the rhythm or frequency of different body changes they notice during their menstrual cycle. This information can then be cross-referenced to understand when the 'ovulation window' occurs or which are the high risk days of a menstrual cycle.
✦ Since sperm can often survive inside the female reproductive tract for five to seven days, but an egg only lives for 24 hours, the Safe Time is calculated to be when there is no risk of ovulation or of sperm penetrating fertile mucus.
✦ The difficult part is knowing which days carry a risk and which don't.

Standard Days Method

✦ The Standard Days Method is simpler to follow than the rhythm method, and is more effective.
✦ Women whose cycles are always between 26 and 32 days in length can use this method.
✦ According to data from the World Health Organization, about 80% of cycles are between 26 and 32 days long and most women have most of their cycles within this range.
✦ So, although this method is not suitable for all women, it is suitable for many.

With this method:

Days 1-7 of a woman's menstrual cycle are considered safe;
Days 8-19 are considered unsafe (unless using the method to plan a pregnancy);
Day 20 until the next period, are considered safe again.

✦ To help women visualise their high and low risk days, a product called CycleBeads® was developed and has been widely adopted in developing countries. There is also an online version available by annual subscription or a smartphone app called iCycleBeads™.
✦ This system can, however, be followed quite easily if the woman keeps a note of the days of her cycle in a diary, so she can visualise the safe and unsafe days.

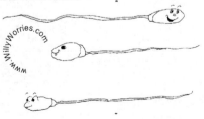

www.WillyWorries.com

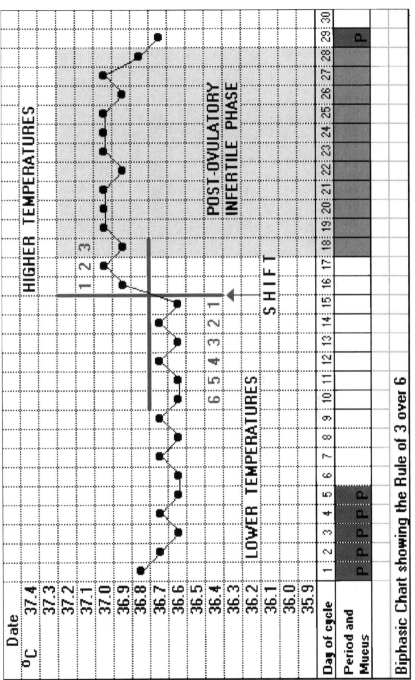

Contraception — Family Planning — Birth Control

Biphasic Chart showing the Rule of 3 over 6

POST-OVULATORY INFERTILE PHASE

HIGHER TEMPERATURES

LOWER TEMPERATURES

SHIFT

Contraception — Family Planning — Birth Control

Sympto-Thermal Method
(symptoms and temperature method)

Basal Body Temperature

✦ A woman's basal body temperature - her temperature first thing in the morning, before she does anything *(even getting up to the toilet)*.

✦ Monitored daily, using a specially graded 'fertility thermometer', a chart of recordings will show when ovulation possibly occurs each month.

✦ It will also show when a woman may not have ovulated in a particular cycle.

✦ Temperature readings cannot be used in isolation, but should only be considered as a component, used in combination with other signs; and can't be relied upon during times of illness.

Changes in the Cervix

This is seldom used alone, and changes are not always easy to detect.

✦ The cervix changes with the onset of the fertile phase and towards ovulation, it softens, opens slightly, is more moist and moves upward in the vagina.

✦ After ovulation, it closes, hardens slightly and lowers again.

A woman can learn to detect these changes by feeling her cervix daily and charting her observations.

Cervical Mucus Consistency

✦ The fertile phase starts at the first sign of any secretions at the vulva *(that is as soon as there is no longer a feeling of dryness)*. At first the cervical mucus is sticky and white, and then it becomes wetter, more transparent and stretchy. The last day the mucus is wet and stretchy is known as peak day. Peak day can only be recognised the day after peak, when the mucus changes back to being thicker, stickier and white again. The fertile time lasts for three full days after the peak day.

✦ Any cervical mucus is potentially fertile.

Cervical mucus varies throughout the menstrual cycle:

✦ Under the influence of oestrogen the ovarian follicles are stimulated to produce an oocyte *(egg)*, and the crypts within the cervix *(neck of the womb)* generates a clear and stretchy, fertile type of mucus, called Spinnbarkeit mucus.

✦ This consists of lush proteins and little channels through which sperm swim to reach the fallopian tubes.

✦ The mucus becomes more stretchy and sticky as ovulation approaches which allows sperm to live in and feed off it whilst waiting for ovulation.

✦ Some women produce fertile mucus for as little as a day, while others produce it for up to seven days.

✦ The duration of mucus production determines the length of time sperm can survive inside a particular woman and also how easily she can become pregnant.

✦ Within four days of ovulation, and under the influence of progesterone, the mucus is thick, clumpy, and impenetrable to sperm again and this effect lasts until the start of the next period / menstrual cycle.

✦ The dry days are considered as safe days, upon which pregnancy won't occur while days where there is ANY mucus are fertile. This is sometimes called 'the mucus method', but it is also referred to as either the:
— The Billings Ovulation Method; or
— Creighton Model Fertility Care™ System

Observation of cervical mucus consistency is a simple method that can be used by any woman from puberty to menopause, and also during breastfeeding.
✦ It can be used to achieve or avoid pregnancy and cycles don't have to be regular.

You must learn to use this method from a properly trained teacher, but it is always more reliable to combine more than one fertility sign *(e.g. temperature and mucus).*

NOTE:
✦ A woman cannot learn this method when she is using hormonal contraception or if she is using a barrier method.
✦ Women using an IUD *(intrauterine contraceptive device / copper coil)* can learn to start recording changes in cervical mucus.

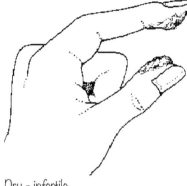

Dry - infertile

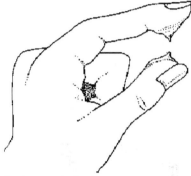

Sticky - early fertile mucus

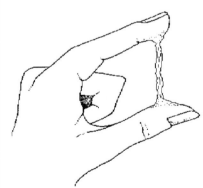

Clear, stretchy Spinnbarkeit fertile mucus

© Jane Knight / Dr C Pyper / Fertility UK

Contraception — Family Planning — Birth Control

Contraction — Family Planning — Birth Control

Lactational Amenorrhoea Method (LAM)

Women who fully breastfeed their baby delay the return of ovulation and menstruation and this physiological effect can be used as a method of contraception, which is up to 98% effective, **as long as all three of these conditions apply**:

There must be:
— no bleeding;
— she must be fully breastfeeding; and
— baby must be younger than six months.

✦ If any of these conditions change, protection against pregnancy reduces and additional contraception is advised.
✦ This is sometimes called 'the breastfeeding method' by women.

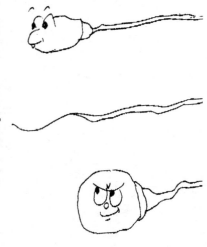

New Technologies

Persona®

This was the first of, now, several different types of electronic device that analyse different hormone levels in specimens of urine and work out whether a woman is at the fertile time of her cycle but it only works for women who have regular menstrual cycles of between 23 and 35 days in length.
✦ It's easy to use but not suitable for all women, especially young women whose bodies are still developing or women who have an irregular menstrual cycle.
✦ It's not recommended for women who are breast feeding, using hormonal medication that can affect their menstrual cycle, have liver or kidney disease, are experiencing menopausal symptoms or who have the common gynaecological condition called polycystic ovary syndrome (PCOS).
✦ It's also not recommended for women taking the antibiotic tetracycline, or using fertility treatment.
✦ It gives no protection against HIV or other sexually acquired infections.
✦ However, there are no side effects and the instructions must be followed carefully.
✦ It offers an alternative method of Fertility Awareness / Natural Family Planning and many women use it successfully every month.

NOTE: For much more detailed guidance on the safety and complexities of using different Fertility Awareness Methods / Natural Family Planning and to find a local teacher, please see:
www.FertilityUK.org
www.Glowm.com
www.cyclebeads.com

Ref: (1)(2) Pyper, C, Knight, J, Glob. libr. women's med., (ISSN: 1756-2228) 2008; DOI 10.3843/GLOWM.10384

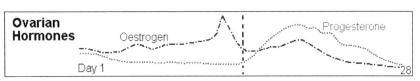

Ovarian Hormones

Oestrogen

Progesterone

Day 1

28

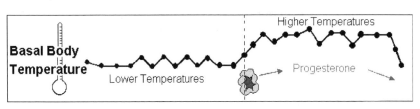

Basal Body Temperature

Higher Temperatures

Lower Temperatures

Progesterone

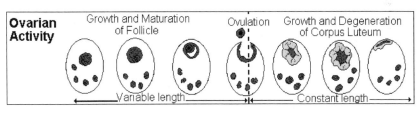

Ovarian Activity

Growth and Maturation of Follicle

Ovulation

Growth and Degeneration of Corpus Luteum

Variable length

Constant length

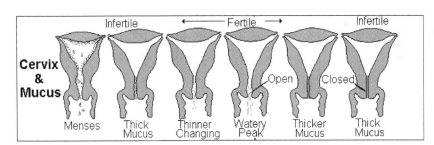

Cervix & Mucus

Infertile

Fertile

Infertile

Open

Closed

Menses

Thick Mucus

Thinner Changing

Watery Peak

Thicker Mucus

Thick Mucus

INFERTILE

Low, firm,
closed, long,
easy to reach,
(tilted)

FERTILE

High, soft,
open, shorter
harder to reach,
(straight)

INFERTILE

Low, firm,
closed, long,
easy to reach,
(tilted)

Copyright © Dr Cecilia Pyper and Jane Knight in collaboration with Fertility UK & The Institute for Reproductive Health, Georgetown University

Contraception — Family Planning — Birth Control

Contraception — Family Planning — Birth Control

C	O	M	B	I	N	E	D	O	R	A	L	S	F	V	P	A	D	G
O	C	Z	P	G	A	S	E	A	E	O	U	Y	A	Z	L	P	I	P
N	B	L	A	F	T	R	V	I	C	Q	B	S	M	T	A	H	B	M
T	D	R	P	L	U	T	I	N	J	E	C	T	I	O	N	E	J	K
R	V	T	A	M	R	S	C	O	C	A	T	E	L	T	N	O	N	E
A	L	F	V	M	A	L	E	A	A	T	E	M	Y	H	I	V	I	R
C	O	I	L	U	L	G	C	X	R	O	M	A	N	C	N	B	U	T
E	M	E	R	G	E	N	C	Y	G	E	J	C	E	H	G	F	M	A
P	O	P	S	T	E	R	I	L	I	S	A	T	I	O	N	B	D	F
T	H	E	C	A	P	A	C	O	N	D	O	M	C	R	U	M	B	A
I	N	T	R	A	U	T	E	R	I	N	E	S	Y	S	T	E	M	S
V	C	E	L	I	B	A	C	Y	U	M	T	Y	N	R	E	T	R	O
E	F	E	M	A	L	E	Y	O	D	I	A	P	H	R	A	G	M	G
P	R	O	G	E	S	T	O	G	E	N	O	N	L	Y	P	I	L	L
I	M	P	L	A	N	T	P	A	T	C	H	T	I	C	R	U	E	S
L	T	I	T	C	H	P	S	F	R	A	B	R	L	O	M	S	T	A
L	O	V	E	R	S	Y	S	E	X	P	L	A	I	N	E	D	H	K

combined pill

contraceptive pill

the cap

intrauterine

injection

system *x2

device

COC

pop

IUD

IUS

progestogen only pill

implant

diaphragm

natural

family

planning

sterilisation

condom

emergency

patch

female

male

no

celibacy

lover

sexplained

coil

pad

titch

Answers page 273

Growing Up
&
New Experiences

Why do people say they have sex?

Why do people have sex?

Why do people have sex if they want a cuddle?

If someone wants to have sex with me, does it mean that they love me?

My partner says that if I love him/her, I'd have sex with him/her...

My boyfriend says he'll leave me if I don't do what he wants.

How do young men masturbate?

How do young women masturbate?

What does it feel like to have an orgasm?

It's so complicated!

What's heavy petting / foreplay?

For both sexes

For Young Women

For Young Men

Love and sex - What's the difference and why?

How soon should we have sex?

What about sex outside marriage?

My boyfriend says he needs to have sex...

I feel left out. Should I ... just do it?

What does French kissing mean?

I think I love someone... Sometimes I fancy two people at one time. Is this common?

Do erect nipples mean we want sex?

I don't know what to do with my partner so how do I become the best at sex?

I've heard boys talk about a fanny fart. What's that?

Does or should sex hurt a woman?

Do love-bites hurt and can they cause disease or harm?

Why do I just want to have sex without any commitment?

Why didn't my partner want to know me after we had sex?

Is sex addictive?

Am I really able to get pregnancy BEFORE my first period?

Can I get pregnant if my boyfriend kisses me?

Do I have to have sex to get pregnant?

How can I get pregnant without having sex, then?

If I'm a virgin, can I get pregnant without having sex?

Can I get pregnant the first time I have sex?

Can I get pregnant without having an orgasm?

Can I get pregnant standing up?

Can I get pregnant by heavy petting or fingering?

My friend used heroin and her periods stopped. Can she still get pregnant?

When can I have a pregnancy test?

Where can I have a pregnancy test?

What if I find out I'm pregnant and don't know what to do or where to turn for help?

What about my partner?

I've heard I won't be able to have a baby in the future if I have a termination. Is this true?

Men make sperm all the time but can I run out of eggs if I have too much sex?

I don't want to be like my Mum and have a baby when I'm a teenager, so what can I do?

Do women have erections?

I've heard that women make something called smegma. What is that?

Should I get pain after sex?

If a pregnant woman has sex with someone who has VD will the baby be affected?

As a young woman, is it dangerous for my health if I have sex under the age of 16?

Can I reduce these risks if I do have sex under the age of 16?

Is it normal to bleed between my periods?

I've heard that it can cause vaginal infections if I douche (squirt water in to my vagina to wash it out) use bubble bath, vaginal deodorants, scented soap, etc. Is this true?

I want my parents to know I'm sexually active and grown up enough to take precautions. But, I don't know how to tell them without them getting angry with me, as they probably won't approve.

My parents get embarrassed when I ask about sex. Why, when they must have *done it* for me to be here?

Who else can I ask because I'm too embarrassed to ask my parents about sex?

Is it OK for me to have sex under the age of 16?

Why don't parents mind boys having sex, but they mind girls having it? Surely this is unfair?

Why do my parents still have sex?

If this is so, why do my parents mind my grandparents having sex?

I worry that I'm different from other young people. How can I tell if I'm gay, and who can I turn to for support?

Willius Floppius Variagata

Commonly called 'The Willy Plant'

Sex is never compulsory. You should never do anything just to please someone, particularly if you feel uncomfortable or because of peer pressure.

I thought sex meant male or female, so why do people say they have sex?

✦ It's short for have sexual intercourse.

Why do people have sex?

People have sex because:
✦ it makes you feel nice;
✦ to have babies;
✦ to feel close to another person;
✦ to feel loved for a short while;
✦ to get a cuddle;
✦ sometimes they feel pressure from friends that they should do it;
✦ some people have sex to make money.

Why do people have sex if they want a cuddle?

✦ Some people find it hard to admit they simply want a cuddle, so they use having sex as a way to feel physically close to another person.
✦ Others fear being rejected by their partner if they say they don't want to have sex, so carry on in the hope of getting their cuddle afterwards.

If someone wants to have sex with me, does it mean that they love me?

✦ Not necessarily.
✦ It may be lust or just physical attraction.
✦ If you've taken time to get to know each other well, you'll probably feel closer and may even feel as if you're in love.

My partner says that if I love him/her, I'd have sex with him/her. S/he just doesn't understand that I'm not ready to have sex. Why do they do this and what should I do?

✦ Tell them to grow up.
✦ This statement is old as time itself! It's a trick and usually backfires on whoever tells you such rubbish. It's unfair emotional pressure which aims to get you to give in.
✦ If you feel you don't want sex – listen to your heart.
✦ You always have the right to say NO.
✦ Don't have sex with anyone until you're ready and are sure YOU want to do it.
✦ It's easy to confuse having sex with being in love. Don't let anyone make you feel bad about your decision not to have sex.
✦ It doesn't mean you don't care for your partner – just that you're not ready for – or don't want this type of relationship yet.
✦ If s/he really cares about you they'll stop pestering you and stay friends.
✦ If they don't stop they're silly and will risk you going right off them. A nicer person's probably waiting round the corner!
✦ Remember: 'there are plenty more fish in the sea'!

Growing Up & New Experiences

Growing Up & New Experiences

My boyfriend says he'll leave me if I don't do what he wants.

✦ Some boyfriend! Let him leave, if that's his attitude towards you!

✦ If you give in to his unfair, immature bullying he'll only try some other way to get his own way.

✦ However nice, good looking, charming, sexy or anything else that he may be when he wants something, he's trying to coerce *(manipulate)* you into doing something against your will.

✦ If he doesn't change his tune, he'll probably lose you anyway with such a childish attitude.

✦ He doesn't sound worthy of your affection. This sort of attitude is more likely to be a complete turn off to you, anyway.

✦ Don't fall for his sweet talk. It's designed to get your clothing off. He's just shown you that he doesn't reall care about how you feel, so do you really need someone like this in your life?

How do young men masturbate?

✦ If you stroke the sensitive area at the head of your penis and think of something sexy, you'll probably have an erection.

✦ Make a fist around the shaft of your penis and move this up and down its length – slowly, at first but faster as the pleasurable feelings increase and you near orgasm.

✦ After ejaculation your penis goes soft *(flaccid)* as you relax.

✦ As you explore your body more, and with practice, you'll develop your own masturbation technique.

✦ Like women, you may get pleasure from massaging areas of your body called erogenous zones – eg. your nipples or another area you find sensitive and pleasurable.

How do young women masturbate?

✦ When you're sexually aroused – either by thought or sensation – your vagina produces a welcoming fluid (lubricant) to make insertion of a penis more comfortable.

✦ Your clitoris is extremely sensitive and when rubbed gently it enlarges and erects.

✦ Gently massaging or rubbing it can feel very nice and gradually give you intense pleasure.

✦ You might also use a finger from your other hand to copy the movement a penis makes during sex – moving in and out of your vagina, gently.

✦ Some women use sex toys such as vibrators, dildo's or similar shaped objects to mimic the size or shape of a penis instead of their finger.

✦ Masturbation is similar to the heavy petting of foreplay performed by your partner.

✦ As with men, you may get pleasure from massaging areas of your body called erotic zones such eg. your nipples or another area you find sensitive and pleasurable.

What does it feel like to have an orgasm?

Different people feel different strengths of sensation.

For both man and women

✦ The largest part of sex is in your mind and your body reacts physically to its stimulation.

✦ Orgasm doesn't happen, automatically, every time you have sex especially if you try too hard for one or if you're not really in the mood.

✦ Some people get terribly upset and feel it's the man's duty to give a woman her orgasm. This isn't true.

✦ Orgasm is more likely to happen when you're totally relaxed. It may be because you want purely physical sex or because you're making love together.

✦ With some practice, you can think yourself into and out of orgasm mode, control it and decide when you want to come/cum.

✦ You'll breathe more rapidly. Your pulse and heart rate will rise.

✦ You may feel a warm glow throughout your body and sweat slightly before breaking out in a rash (sex flush) after you reach orgasm.

For Young Men

✦ It's more obvious than for young women, because you ejaculate. This gives you intense pleasure as the semen and sperm are forced out of your penis by muscular contractions.

✦ After ejaculation your penis softens as you relax.

For Young Women

✦ The centre for orgasm is your clitoris, which swells during sexual arousal *(just like a penis)* and your vagina, which produces a lubricant so that a penis can slip in and out easily.

✦ There's a gradual build up of pleasurable sensation, your breathing becomes deeper and more rapid, your heart beats faster and your vagina may go into involuntary spasm as you reach orgasm, with your body becoming tense all over.

✦ After orgasm it relaxes and you feel a warm glow throughout your body and you may notice a rash *(sex flush)* all over.

It's so complicated!

✦ Yes, it is complicated. That's why taking time to get to know someone well, and talking openly about what you both want or don't want, is the best way to understand what's happening.

✦ Today, virginity, monogamy *(staying with just one sexual partner)* and celibacy *(not having sex)* are actually quite trendy.

✦ Along with the temporary physical pleasure from sex, there can be considerable emotional pain.

✦ It's better to wait until you're more mature and in a stable/settled friendship before starting a sexual relationship.

✦ Once you give away your virginity you can't get it back.

✦ Also, for young women, sex before you're physically mature *(approx. 23 years of age)* can increase the risk of damage to your cervix *(neck of the womb)* – especially if you smoke cigarettes and/or have sex with someone who's had or who carries a sexually acquired infection such as HPV *(human papilloma virus)*. There is a vaccine against HPV and it would be wise to have it..

✦ Furthermore, you risk infertility or difficulty getting pregnant if you catch gonorrhoea or chlamydia and don't get it treated quickly.

✦ Many books are available about sex, which you could read with your partner when you feel ready to learn more about the subject.

Growing Up & New Experiences

What's heavy petting / foreplay?

For both sexes

✦ First, always be clear about how far you are prepared to go and what you're prepared to allow. If you change your mind, and don't want to go further with foreplay, make your wishes clear. Try to do this without hurting your partner's feelings to enable their arousal to subside.

✦ There are generally two types of foreplay.

1– Psychological foreplay *(in your mind)* – eg. talking seductively to each other, dressing in a particular fashion *(sexy underwear),* watching films together or listening to soft music to set the mood or scene – and lots more.

2– Physical foreplay *(intimate play before sex)* is similar to masturbation and usually takes place before or perhaps instead of penetration.

✦ You may go as far as reaching orgasm *(climax / coming)* during foreplay, but penetration doesn't take place at this stage.

✦ Women can sometimes have multiple orgasms; men usually ejaculate only once then need a bit of a rest before starting again.

✦ Some men can control themselves very well, delay orgasm and make sex last a long time.

✦ Other men aren't able to control themselves very well and reach orgasm within minutes *(or seconds)* of penetration.

For Young Women

✦ Generally you'll get physically turned on *(aroused)* when your breasts or your clitoris are gently rubbed or massaged.

✦ Clitoral arousal, in particular, stimulates your vagina to make a lubricant or welcoming fluid.

✦ You may then allow your partner to go a bit further, to the stage commonly called fingering.

✦ This is when they gently insert one or two fingers into your vagina to simulate the movement a penis makes during sex.

✦ At the same time, they continue to rub your clitoris gently.

✦ Before long, if you're relaxed, you'll start to have an orgasm.

✦ You may, however, reach orgasm without any finger penetration but from breast or clitoral stimulation, alone.

✦ With some practice, you'll be able to learn to control your orgasm – ie. to have it as and when you decide. But, if you're not relaxed or feeling safe, you're unlikely to reach orgasm.

✦ If you're unable to masturbate to orgasm and are worried about it, your doctor or Sexual Health Clinic can advise you.

For Young Men

✦ This is when your partner masturbates your penis with their hand. *(Commonly known as a wank, hand job or hand relief.)*

✦ They gently squeeze and massage along the shaft and/or tip of your penis which, when you're relaxed, stimulates and gives pleasure.

✦ If you're unable to masturbate to orgasm on your own and are worried about it, your doctor or Contraception Clinic can advise you or refer you if you would like help.

Some people say that boys want sex but girls want to make love. What's the difference and why?

✦ To many people, making love sounds more emotionally involved, it's usually more planned, slower and more tender.

✦ Having sex is generally considered to be just a physical thing – relatively quick and without much emotion.

✦ Men and women can have sex without any emotions becoming involved; so, it's not just a male thing.

How soon should we have sex?

✦ It's becoming trendy to be able to say you're still a virgin, so there's no rush at all to start having sex.

✦ It's best to wait until you're both absolutely sure that the time is right and until you're safely protected from the risk of unplanned pregnancy and/or infection. You have the rest of your life to enjoy it.

✦ Sometimes you might not want to do something but feel you should go along with your partner out of fear of rejection if you don't agree.

✦ Communication is the key, so talk to each other to see what you both like, want to do, or don't want to do.

✦ Don't be scared to speak out. You are probably just as nervous as each other.

✦ There's really no rush to have sex.

✦ You'll need practise if you use condoms. The Double Dutch method is widely advised these days – ie. being on The Pill *(or other contraceptive method)* AND using condoms, even if you're both virgins.

What about sex outside marriage?

✦ Many cultures and religions still frown upon sex outside marriage. However, millions of people the world over are sexually active without being married *(fornicate)*.

✦ No one can dictate how you live your life once you reach the legal age of consent.

✦ It's your choice whether you wait until marriage or have sex outside it.

✦ Many people don't want to marry but choose to stay in long-term committed and faithful relationships, for a variety of reasons.

✦ Being made to feel guilty for having sex without being married can cause long-term psychological problems for some people.

✦ The desire to have sex is an animal instinct and it's not helpful to damn others for their choice or circumstances.

✦ Sexual abuse, rape or sexual assault outside or within marriage is an entirely different matter. They're illegal and frowned upon by most religions or cultures around the world – some to a greater extent than others.

✦ If you're married and have sex outside it *(commit adultery)*, that's a matter for your conscience. It can, however, lead to numerous emotional, financial, legal or physical problems. This may include pregnancy and/or sexually acquired infection.

✦ Unless you're forced to have sex, the choice is yours and yours alone.

Growing Up & New Experiences

Growing Up & New Experiences

My boyfriend says he needs to have sex with me.

✦ This is selfish rubbish and typical emotional pressure to make you give in.
✦ He doesn't **need** to have sex, he **wants** to have sex.
✦ He won't die if you don't give in to him, whatever he says or thinks!
✦ He can always relieve himself by masturbation!
✦ It won't make him blind, deaf or dumb. His penis belongs to him, so he'll come to no harm if he masturbates instead.
✦ Let him sulk, if he's that childish – but don't give in unless YOU want to have sex, too.

I'm still a virgin but all the other kids at school boast about how many times they've had sex and how many partners they've had. I feel left out. Should I find someone and just *do it*?

✦ No, you shouldn't just do it.
✦ They may be making it up!
✦ Today, it seems more sensible to be able to boast about still being a virgin!
✦ Studies show that the majority of young women who choose to have sex early, regret it later and wish they'd waited until they were older.
✦ A lot of young men also wish they'd waited until they were older.
✦ Let sex happen when it feels right for you and you're sure it's what you want.
✦ Having sex is not always what it's cracked up to be, so don't panic and do it just to tell your friends you've done it.
✦ Sex can be lovely when it's part of a caring, loving relationship but it's only part of any relationship.
✦ Being good pals with your partner is more important in the long run.

What does French kissing mean?

✦ French kissing is when, during lip to lip kissing, your partner slips their tongue into your mouth and feels your tongue.
✦ They may suck your tongue gently and you can suck theirs.
✦ It's also called deep or wet kissing.
✦ You don't have to be in France or kissing a French person to French kiss!

I think I love someone, they're gorgeous, then it goes and I fancy someone else. Sometimes I fancy two people at one time. Is this common?

✦ Yes, it's very common and it's all part of growing up.
✦ These fleeting feelings are usually called a crush.
✦ You'll probably find you experience these same feelings again as you get older.

Do erect nipples mean we want sex?

✦ They could mean you're sexually aroused – there again, you could be cold!
✦ The cold makes the muscles around your nipples contract *(shorten)* so they're more obvious.
✦ By the way, this happens to men and women.

I don't know what to do with my partner so how do I become *the best at sex*?

✦ There's no such thing as becoming the best at sex. Each person has his or her own opinion of what good sex is and their own technique.

✦ It's most important to be able to talk to each other; and to listen to what your partner says they'd like to do or would like you to do.

✦ You should then be honest with each other, not just go along with what they say they'd like, for two reasons:

(a) They may not really want to do it but think you want them to try or ask.

(b) You should never let anyone persuade you to do or try anything, just to keep him/her happy and not yourself.

✦ It can take a lot of time, patience, understanding, practice and romance – plus a lot of genuine care, to improve your skill as a lover.

✦ Always treat your partner with respect and as you'd like to be treated.

✦ Sometimes, being honest with yourself and then someone else about sex is quite difficult but it's the best way forward.

I've heard boys talk about a *fanny fart*. What's that?

✦ The word *fanny* is a UK nickname for the vagina.

✦ Since there's only one entrance / exit to your vagina, air can get trapped in it when you have sex in certain positions.

✦ This sometimes escapes noisily – but it doesn't smell!

✦ It's common and harmless.

(In the USA: fanny is backside / bum.)

Does or should sex hurt a woman?

✦ No, sex between two consenting partners shouldn't hurt.

✦ During foreplay and sex you should be gentle and not appear in an obvious hurry.

✦ Listen to what your partner wants.

✦ It's usually wise to spend the length of time they want on foreplay, so that they can relax and get in the mood, rather than just spend a minute or two and think that's long enough! Nobody would thank you for that!

✦ If you're in a hurry or pressure your female partner into having sex, there won't be sufficient time for her body to make the special welcoming fluid in her vagina for your penis to slip in easily.

✦ If she's dry or tense, sex is likely to be uncomfortable for both of you.

✦ If there's pain during sex, you should stop.

✦ If your partner wants you to continue you may find that a different position may help. Some sexually acquired infections cause pain during sex.

✦ If the problem is not from dryness or from the position you're in, visit your Sexual Health Clinic or your doctor for advice.

✦ Sex will, however, hurt women who have been genitally mutilated *(circumcised)*, who are raped or anyone who is forced to have anal sex *(buggered / sodomised)*.

✦ This is not sex between two caring and consenting partners.

✦ Never force yourself on anyone.

✦ If you're told to stop, then you must stop; otherwise you'll be committing a criminal offence.

✦ *For further information on The Law & Sex, see Section 6, page 149.*

Do love-bites hurt and can they cause disease or harm?

✦ Love-bites can be uncomfortable.

✦ They cause bruising when blood is drawn to the surface levels underneath your skin by the pressure of sucking required to produce them.

✦ They cause embarrassment rather than any real harm or disease and they can look unattractive, especially when they begin to wear off.

✦ Tip – Smearing toothpaste over them can sometimes help love-bites wear off a bit quicker!

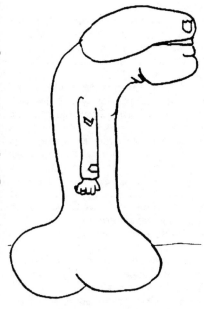

Why do I just want to have sex without any commitment?

✦ There could be many reasons why you don't want commitment.

✦ Only you know the answer but being honest with yourself may be quite difficult.

✦ If you tell the person with whom you're having sex how you feel before you just use them, you may find they feel the same way.

✦ You may be young and don't want to tie yourself down yet.

✦ You may be older and have been through a traumatic emotional experience. Therefore don't want to allow someone else to get to know you well enough to get hurt again.

✦ Perhaps you enjoy the chase and conquest rather than ongoing relationships.

✦ You may be scared to risk being let down by another person. Therefore, hold yourself back from loving and being loved in return.

✦ Perhaps you're scared of someone being dependent upon you and don't want that kind of responsibility.

✦ Always be honest rather than lead someone else on.

✦ If you know another reason and want help to resolve *(sort out)* your feelings but don't know where to start, contact your doctor or Sexual Health Clinic.

Why didn't my partner want to know me after we had sex?

✦ Unfortunately this is quite common and may be due to several reasons.
✦ Wanting to have sex is an animal instinct.
✦ People don't always plan this, but it's commonly known as a one-night stand.
✦ Sometimes people simply want casual sex. Many people don't realise until afterwards that all the sweet talk has been used to make them feel wanted and desirable enough to agree.
✦ Even when you've known each other for a while, your emotions can change after you've had sex.
✦ These are not just a male thing. Women can want casual sex without any further commitment, too. It could be for the better – or for the worse!
✦ Sometimes the chase seems more exciting than catching your partner!
✦ Sex often gets better the more time you spend together, as your relationship gets stronger, and as your care and respect for each other grows into a loving relationship.
✦ That's a good reason to wait.

Is sex addictive?

✦ For some people it can become addictive.
✦ Sex between two consenting partners improves with time, and becomes a deeply satisfying part of their lives.
✦ Some people, however, do feel they're obsessed with sex.
✦ If you feel this way, ask your doctor or Sexual Health Clinic to refer you to a specialist in psychosexual medicine.

Am I really able to get pregnant BEFORE my first period?

✦ Yes, you may.
✦ Although many girls don't ovulate as they start their periods, some do and it's not possible to tell if you are one of them, so don't take risks!

Can I get pregnant if my boyfriend kisses me?

✦ No, kissing, alone, can't make you pregnant.

Do I have to have sex to get pregnant?

✦ No, it's possible to get pregnant without having sex.
✦ A virgin can get pregnant and remain, technically, a virgin.
✦ Expensive fertility treatments, surgery etc. are not the only ways to get pregnant without having sex!

How can I get pregnant without having sex, then?

✦ Pregnancy can occur without sexual intercourse occurring because the ejaculation of sperm is not always necessary to create a pregnancy. Many people – adults included – get this fact wrong!
✦ When a young man gets an erection there are about 3,000,000 sperm in the drop of clear fluid which appears at the tip of his penis.
✦ That's enough sperm to populate the whole of the Central American country of Honduras!
✦ If he just rubs his erection around the entrance to your vagina *(without putting it inside you)*, sperm could get into the fertile mucus you make before ovulation *(egg release)* and travel up to your fallopian tubes.
✦ If they meet an egg, hey presto, one unplanned pregnancy!

If I'm a virgin, can I get pregnant without having sex?

✦ Yes, you can, as just answered.

Can I get pregnant the first time I have sex?

✦ Yes, you can and many girls do.
✦ There's about a one in three chance of pregnancy each time you have unprotected sex at the fertile time of the month.
✦ You MAY get away with it, but many don't.

Can I get pregnant without having an orgasm?

✦ Yes, you can.
✦ Orgasm and fertility are unrelated.
✦ Orgasm has nothing to do with egg release.

Can I get pregnant standing up?

✦ Yes and many women have become pregnant in this position.
✦ The position in which you have sex makes no difference whatsoever.
✦ As long as sperm get into your fertile mucus (*the special fluid you make before egg release*) there's a chance of pregnancy.

Can I get pregnant by heavy petting or fingering?

✦ Generally, no.
✦ Not unless there are sperm on the fingers which get into your fertile mucus.
✦ In practice, this is a very low, but not no risk activity.
✦ If you do this and are worried, seek emergency contraception.

My friend used heroin and her periods stopped. Can she still get pregnant?

✦ Yes, she is still at risk of pregnancy if she has unprotected sex.
✦ Even though she hasn't got regular periods, it doesn't mean she isn't ovulating.
✦ She must use Double Dutch protection – ie. use a condom AND other reliable method of birth control – at all times.
✦ Her risk of contracting hepatitis and/or HIV is greater than a non-drug user – particularly if she injects the heroin.
✦ *For further information on contraception see Section 4, page 71.*

When can I have a pregnancy test?

✦ A test cannot tell if you may become pregnant the day after unprotected sex or even the next week since it takes an average of 9 days (between 6 to 12 days) for a fertilised egg to implant. It's only after implantation that the hormone a pregnancy test detects starts to show in your urine (*HCG/ human chorionic gonadotrophin*).
✦ Therefore, you will have to wait at least two, ideally three weeks after unprotected sex until there is enough HCG to detect.

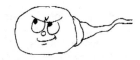

Generally, you can have a pregnancy test if:

(a) you miss a period after having sex, whether you were using contraception including condoms or were not using contraception or protection;

(b) you have a light period after having sex;

(c) you have a light period after taking Emergency Contraception;

(d) you have a light period after an abortion or miscarriage;

(e) you're using the combined Pill and not getting withdrawal bleeds *(periods)*;

(f) you want to put your mind at rest if you're worried for another reason.

Where can I have a pregnancy test?

✦ You can take a specimen of your urine to a Contraception or Sexual Health Clinic, they will test it and give you the result immediately.

✦ Your doctor can send a sample of your urine to the laboratory. In this case you have to wait for the result.

✦ You can buy a home pregnancy testing kit at a pharmacy and do your own test.

What if I find out I'm pregnant and don't know what to do or where to turn for help?

✦ Your doctor or Contraception / Sexual Health Clinic can help or refer you for advice on antenatal care, adoption or, for termination of the pregnancy *(abortion)*.

✦ Sometimes sitting down quietly on your own and writing a list of all the reasons for or against each option is helpful.

✦ You'll have to be totally honest with yourself to do this and probably, it won't be easy.

✦ Whatever you decide you'll have to live with your decision. You may need a lot of emotional support in the future.

✦ Don't be afraid to admit you feel scared. Let your tears come out and don't try to be brave about it all.

✦ Your decision will be right for you if you're strong enough to be honest with yourself. Although you may feel sad, look ahead and try to make something positive come out of what you may feel is a negative situation.

✦ If you decide to keep your baby, focus on being the best Mum in the world. You'll need lots of support and it'll be very hard work at times.

✦ If you decide to terminate or have the baby adopted, try to aim for something which you wouldn't have been able to do had you kept the baby; then go for it and do it really well.

✦ You may spend time going through a natural grieving process of anger, guilt, frustration, resentment and, finally, acceptance.

✦ Sometimes, it helps to talk your feelings through with someone; at other times, just writing down all your feelings, being very honest with yourself as you write, can be particularly helpful and healing, too.

✦ It takes some women a long time, others only a short time, to recover emotionally after terminating their pregnancy or giving their baby up for adoption. It depends on the circumstances surrounding your decision.

✦ Whatever course of action you decide upon, you will find that a lot of help is available, if you ask for it. Don't feel pressured into taking a particular decision.

Growing Up & New Experiences

What about my partner?

✦ Your partner will also have emotions about it, if you've told him you're pregnant.
✦ Encourage him to talk, rather than bottle up his feelings.
✦ He may be confused, feel guilty and not know how to talk to you honestly, from fear of upsetting you.
✦ He may want you to terminate the pregnancy but not know how to tell you.
✦ He may want you to keep the baby – but, again, not know how to tell you.
✦ He may rant and rave and try to make you do the opposite of what you really want to do.
✦ He may, of course, be extremely supportive and, like you, may not know what he really wants you to do.
✦ He needs to be able to talk to someone, just as you do but, most men don't share their feelings as openly or easily as women.
✦ For him, too, the technique of writing all his feelings down, honestly and openly, may help.
✦ If he bottles up his feelings it could lead to emotional or physical problems eg. impotence and other sexual difficulties.
✦ Don't deny him his feelings. Even though he can't force you to do what you don't want with the pregnancy, it can be as emotionally traumatic for him as it is for you.
✦ This is a difficult decision but it must be yours and yours alone.
✦ For further support he could visit his Contraception Clinic or GP for referral to a psychosexual therapist if there is not a Well Man Clinic in the area or nearby access to other counselling services.

I've heard I won't be able to have a baby in the future if I have a termination. Is this true?

✦ A legal, surgical or medical termination *(abortion)* should not prevent you getting pregnant again.
✦ The greatest risk of infection/infertility after termination is from an existing infection eg. chlamydia – which you are suffering from at the time of your operation. This could be pushed further into your body during surgery.
✦ Most reputable clinics now offer a test for chlamydia before surgery and some recommend that you go for an additional SAI check up at a Sexual Health Clinic, to prevent complications after an operation.

Men make sperm all the time but can I run out of eggs if I have too much sex?

✦ No, you can't run out of eggs this way.
✦ You're born with your lifetime's supply of potential eggs in your ovaries.
✦ You gradually run out of them as you get older.
✦ Becoming pregnant can get more difficult as your age increases.
✦ Most women remain fertile until their menopause, which is usually around 50 years of age, when their periods stop.

I don't want to be like my Mum and have a baby when I'm a teenager, so what can I do?

✦ There's no need for you to repeat what happened to your mother.
✦ Wait until you're ready to bring a baby into the world.
✦ *For further information on contraception, see Section 4, page 71.*

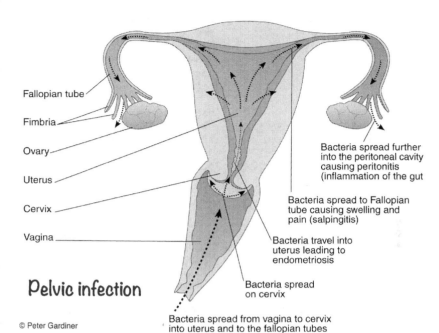

Fallopian tube

Fimbria

Ovary

Uterus

Cervix

Vagina

Bacteria spread further into the peritoneal cavity causing peritonitis (inflammation of the gut

Bacteria spread to Fallopian tube causing swelling and pain (salpingitis)

Bacteria travel into uterus leading to endometriosis

Bacteria spread on cervix

Pelvic infection

© Peter Gardiner

Bacteria spread from vagina to cervix into uterus and to the fallopian tubes

Do women have erections?

✦ Yes, your clitoris becomes erect when you're sexually aroused, as does the area on either side of the entrance to the vagina.

I've heard that women make something called smegma. What is that?

✦ Smegma is a natural lubricant and, just as men make it in the tiny glands under their foreskin, you make it to keep the area around your clitoris comfortable.
✦ That's a good reason why it's important to wash your genital area and wear clean underwear every day.

Should I get pain after sex?

✦ No, you shouldn't get pain after, or during, sex.
✦ If you get pain, which doesn't go if you change your sexual position, there could be a number of reasons.
✦ It's advisable to seek medical advice to make sure you don't have a pelvic infection eg. from chlamydia and/or gonorrhoea, in particular. They're infections *(SAIs)* which can lead to pelvic inflammatory disease which can cause painful sex and lead to infertility – ie. being unable to get pregnant naturally.

If a pregnant woman has sex with someone who has VD might the baby be affected?

✦ VD *(venereal disease)* means sexually transmitted disease or infection. So yes, the baby may be at risk of infection.

Growing Up & New Experiences

Growing Up & New Experiences

As a young woman, is it dangerous for my health if I have sex under the age of 16?

✦ You could become pregnant – which carries many risks.

✦ There's a high risk of infertility *(being unable to have a baby)* if you catch sexually acquired infections *(SAIs)*, such as gonorrhoea or chlamydia and develop pelvic inflammatory disease *(PID)*.

✦ The neck of your womb *(cervix)* doesn't mature until you're about 23 years of age. Sometimes its delicate covering can be affected when not fully mature or developed – particularly if you catch certain varieties of the genital wart virus *(HPV/human papilloma virus)* from a partner or if you smoke.

✦ Both are thought to increase your risk of developing pre-cervical cancer.

Can I reduce these risks if I do have sex under the age of 16?

✦ If a condom or other barrier form of contraception – eg. a diaphragm /cap or female condom – is used properly each time, it can protect your cervix.

✦ It's better to wait until you're older and always use condoms.

Is it normal to bleed between my periods?

✦ No, bleeding on days when you wouldn't normally expect to bleed is not normal.

✦ If you're taking The COC Pill, check if you've forgotten any, had medication, diarrhoea or vomiting, all of which can interfere with the effect of The COC Pill.

✦ If you've had sex with a new partner in the last three months, or you're not sure if your partner is faithful to you, seek medical advice.

✦ You may have caught an infection called chlamydia, have an abnormality at your cervix, or another medical condition which should be diagnosed properly.

I've heard that it can cause vaginal infections if I douche *(squirt water in to my vagina to wash it out)* use bubble bath, vaginal deodorants, scented soap, etc. Is this true?

✦ Yes, douching is not advisable. Your vagina is a self-cleansing area which doesn't need to be washed out.

✦ It's OK to use scented soaps or bubble-baths occasionally but don't overdo it.

✦ Vaginal deodorants aren't necessary and can cause irritation.

✦ Don't soak for too long in a very soapy bath because you could upset the normal acid conditions of your vagina and develop thrush or bacterial vaginosis.

✦ Just wash and dry yourself with mild soap and water externally *(outside)* rinse well, then towel dry.

✦ Wash daily or twice daily as preferred.

✦ Don't put talcum powder in your genital area either. It can get sweaty, sticky or smelly and isn't necessary.

I want my parents to know I'm sexually active and grown up enough to take precautions. But, I don't know how to tell them without them getting angry with me, as they probably won't approve.

✦ Just because you've had sex it doesn't necessarily mean you're grown up. Your parents love you and after they get over any initial shock, they'll realise you're being responsible seeking advice about contraception and/or infection.

✦ Some young people broach the subject by leaving contraception and safer sex leaflets lying around for their parents to find.

✦ That way, they can mention the subject to you instead and you can start talking about it together.

✦ Once any initial shock wears off, your parents might actually surprise you and be very supportive.

✦ You don't have to tell them about visiting your doctor or Contraception / Sexual Health Clinic but some people suggest you do.

✦ Generally, they won't tell anyone without your permission, whatever your age.

✦ This type of service is confidential.

My parents get embarrassed when I ask about sex. Why, when they must have *done it* for me to be here?

✦ Not all parents feel comfortable talking about sex to their children.

✦ Sometimes parents find it difficult to accept that their children are growing up and developing their sexuality *(sexual preference)*.

✦ For many people talking about sex is still a taboo *(forbidden)* subject.

✦ Some adults simply don't know how to answer questions about sex properly. They avoid answering you to try and hide their embarrassment or ignorance!

Who else can I ask because I'm too embarrassed to ask my parents about sex?

✦ You can ask you Contraception / Sexual Health Clinic doctor or nurse, your school nurse, own doctor or practice nurse, teacher, youth worker, the FPA helpline or Childline.

✦ You may find it less embarrassing to talk to an aunt, uncle or another adult if you know they will answer you honestly.

✦ In the UK, apart from health authority Sexual Health Clinics and specialist young people's services, the charity called Brook runs contraception and advice sessions for young people.

✦ If the answer to your question isn't in this book – and you have access to the Internet – you can get confidential online Contraception and Sexual Health advice by visiting the Sexplained® website: :
http://www.sexplained.com

✦ Books and magazines are another popular source of information for many young people, too.

Is it OK for me to have sex under the age of 16?

✦ In the UK and most other countries, it's illegal for a male to have sex with a female who is a minor and is under the legal age to give consent *(permission)*.

✦ It is classified as unlawful sexual intercourse *(USI)* and/or rape.

✦ In the UK, the age of consent is 16.

✦ *For further information on The Law & Sex: see Section 6, page 149.*

Why do parents not mind boys having sex, but they do mind girls having it? Surely this is unfair?

✦ It's unfair but it's universally accepted.
✦ Adults tend to be protective towards their daughters and feel that sons can look after their physical safety.
✦ A young man needs an erection to have sex, which he can learn to control.
✦ A young woman can get pregnant. She can also be forced, bullied or persuaded to have sex and is much more vulnerable.
✦ Unless a young woman has an abortion, or has the baby adopted, this often leaves Mum holding the baby while her daughter goes back to school to finish her education; or the young woman's life is put on hold until her baby goes to school etc.
✦ Most parents want their children to experience many things in life before becoming parents.
✦ Unfortunately, many young fathers are irresponsible and don't stay around for very long after their baby is born. They prefer their freedom!

Why do my parents still have sex?

✦ Presumably because they still love each other and enjoy the physical side of love and an active sex life together.
✦ It often goes hand in hand with having a happy relationship, so you should be pleased they still want to enjoy each other in this way.
✦ Having sex doesn't have to stop when you reach a 'certain age'.
✦ Believe it or not, you'll probably still want to have sex yourself when you are as old as they are!

If this is so, why do my parents mind my grandparents having sex?

✦ Just as you find it difficult to think of your parents still having sex, they may think the same way about *their* parents!
✦ Once they think it through, they'll realise there's nothing wrong with their parents making love and expressing their affection for each other in this way.

© Sylvia Rawsthorn 1999

I worry that I'm different from other young people. How can I tell if I'm gay, and who can I turn to for support?

✦ Generally, growing up is a very confusing time. It's complicated by sexual feelings and wonderings.
✦ Sexuality is not something anyone can tell by looking at you. Most people have wondered about theirs at some stage in their life – if they're honest.
✦ Some, live in great fear of what they don't want to admit to themselves; and others who wonder only briefly about their sexual preference.

The Law
&
Sex

Terminology

Consent occurs when...

Lack of consent may be

demonstrated by...

Age of Consent

Rape

Assault by penetration

Sexual assault

USI - Unlawful sexual intercourse

Child Sexual Offences

Sexual activity with a child

Abuse of position of trust

Familial child sex offences

Offences against persons with a

mental disorder impeding choice

Indecent photographs

Indecent images

Revenge porn

Paying for sexual services of a child

Other child sexual offences

Interpretation / Definitions

Preparatory offences

Administering a substance with intent

Committing an offence with intent

to commit a sexual offence

Trafficking

Sex with an adult relative

Other offences

Exposure

Voyeurism

Sexual activity in a public lavatory

Offences outside the UK

Forced and Arranged Marriage

Female Genital Mutilation / Cutting

(FGM/C)

Child Marriage

Girl-child Beading

Obstetric Fistulae

Plus: many common situational

questions and answers

This section quotes others:
UN Convention on the Rights of the Child
http://www.unicef.org.uk

Sexual Offences Act 2003
http://www.legislation.gov.uk/ukpga/2003/42/contents; and
Sentencing Council - Sexual Offences Definitive Guide
http://sentencingcouncil.judiciary.gov.uk/docs/Final_Sexual_Offences_Definitive_Guideline_content_(web).pdf

Crown Copyright material used under Open Licence:
http://www.nationalarchives.gov.uk/doc/open-government-licence/version/2/
Licence Accessed 26/8/2014

The UN Convention on the
Rights of the Child

The United Nations Convention on the Rights of the Child (CRC) was written by the UN in 1989, signed by almost every country in the world, and states that every child and young person under the age of 18 has rights and responsibilities. These are protected by the United Nations Convention on the Rights of the Child (CRC), which contains 54 Articles.

These are:

Article 1
Everyone under the age of 18 has the rights of this Convention.

Article 2
The Convention applies to everyone, whatever their race, religion, abilities, whatever they think or say, no matter what type of family they come from.

Article 3
All organisations concerned with children should work towards what is best for the child.

Article 4
Governments should make these rights available to children.

Article 5
Governments should respect the rights and responsibilities of families to direct and guide their children so that, as they grow, they learn to use their rights properly.

Article 6
Children have the right to life. Governments should ensure that children survive and develop as healthily as possible.

Article 7
Children have the right to a legally registered name and nationality. Children also have the right to know and, as far as possible, to be cared for by their parents.

Article 8
Governments should respect children's right to a name, a nationality and family ties.

Article 9
Children should not be separated from their parents unless it is for their own good – for example, if a parent is mistreating or neglecting them. If parents are separated, the child has the right to stay in contact with both parents, unless this might be harmful.

Article 10
Families who live in different countries should be allowed to move between those countries so that parents and children can stay in contact or get back together as a family.

Article 11
Governments should take steps to stop children being taken out of their own country illegally.

Article 12
Children have the right to say what they think should happen when adults are making decisions that affect them, and to have their opinions taken into account.

Article 13
Children have the right to get, and to share, information as long as the information is not damaging to themselves or others.

Article 14
Children have the right to think and believe what they want and to practise their religion, as long as they are not stopping other people from enjoying their rights. Parents should guide children on these matters.

Article 15
Children have the right to meet with other children and young people and to join groups and organisations, as long as this does not stop other people from enjoying their rights.

Article 16
Children have the right to privacy. The law should protect children from attacks against their way of life, their good name, their family and their home.

Article 17
Children have the right to reliable information from the mass media. Television, radio, and newspapers should provide information that children can understand, and should not promote materials that could harm them.

Article 18
Both parents share responsibility for bringing up their children, and should always consider what is best for each child. Governments should help parents by providing services to support them, especially if both parents work.

Article 19
Governments should ensure that children are properly cared for, and protect them from violence, abuse and neglect by their parents or anyone else who looks after them.

Article 20
If a child cannot be looked after by their own family, they must be looked after properly, by people who respect your religion, culture and language.

The Law & Sex - UN Convention

Article 21
If a child is adopted, the first concern must be what is best for the child. The same rules should apply whether the adoption takes place in the country where they were born or if they move to another country.

Article 22
If a child has come in to a country as a refugee, they should have the same rights as children born in that country.

Article 23
If a child has a disability, they should receive special care and support so that they can live a full and independent life.

Article 24
Children have the right to good quality healthcare and to clean water, nutritious food and a clean environment so that they can stay healthy. Rich countries should help poorer countries achieve this.

Article 25
If a child is looked after by their local authority rather than their parents, they should have their situation reviewed regularly.

Article 26
The government should provide extra money for the children of families in need.

Article 27
Children have the right to a standard of living that is good enough to meet their physical and mental needs. The government should help families who cannot afford to provide this.

Article 28
Children have the right to an education. Discipline in schools should respect children's human dignity. Primary education should be free. Wealthy countries should help poorer countries achieve this.

Article 29
Education should develop the child's personality and talents to the full. It should encourage the child to respect their parents, their own and other cultures.

Article 30
Children have a right to learn and use the language and customs of their family whether or not these are shared by the majority of the people in the country in which they live.

Article 31
Children have the right to relax, play and join in a wide range of activities.

Article 32
The government should protect children from work that is dangerous or might harm their health or education.

Article 33
The government should provide ways of protecting children from dangerous drugs.

Article 34
The government should protect children from sexual abuse.

Article 35
The government should ensure that children are not abducted or sold.

Article 36
Children should be protected from any activities that could harm their development.

Article 37
If children break the law, they should not be treated cruelly. They should not be put in a prison with adults and they should be able to keep in contact with their family.

Article 38
Governments should not allow children under 16 to join the army. In war zones, children should receive special protection.

Article 39
If a child has been neglected or abused, they should receive special help to restore their self-respect.

Article 40
If a child is accused of breaking the law, they should receive legal help. Prison sentences for children should only be used for the most serious offences.

Article 41
If the laws of a particular country protect a child better than the articles of the Convention, then those laws should stay.

Article 42
The government should make the Convention known to all parents and children.

Articles 43 – 54
These are about how adults and governments should work together to make sure all children get all their rights.

(Ref: UNICEF.org)

All UN member states except for the United States and Somalia have approved the Convention.

The UK signed it on 19 April 1990 and ratified it on 16 December 1991. It came into force in the UK on 15 January 1992.

The US and Somalia signed it in 1995 and 2002 respectively, but are yet to ratify it (make it legally valid).

(Ref https://treaties.un.org - accessed 18th July 2014)

The Law & Sex - UN Convention

Prison Service

Segregation Unit

Real Men Don't Rape!

No ALWAYS Means No

Consent is Definite Not Just Implied

This is meant as a thought provoking guide based on the *Sexual Offences Act 2003*. It is an awareness raiser, ONLY and this is NOT a substitute for qualified legal advice and should not be used in isolation.

This section describes and explains some important legal points that are not always obvious. It relates to the laws of England, Wales and Northern Ireland. Scottish and other laws are mentioned, with reference; and joint UK law is mentioned when appropriate. Other countries have similar laws.

Terminology:
— defendant / perpetrator (A) - the person accused of the offence or crime;
— complainant (B) - the person making the complaint (the victim);

Extracts from the *Sexual Offences Acts 1956 and 2003*, state that it is an offence for a man to rape a woman or another man; and there are many other sexual offences, some of which may not seem as obvious. Consent is vital, as this explains.

Consent occurs when:

A person consents if he agrees by choice, and has the freedom and capacity to make that choice. Consent cannot be given if the following circumstances occur.

The circumstances are that —
(a) any person was, at the time of the relevant act or immediately before it began, using violence against the complainant or causing the complainant to fear that immediate violence would be used against him;
(b) any person was, at the time of the relevant act or immediately before it began, causing the complainant to fear that violence was being used, or that immediate violence would be used, against another person;
(c) the complainant was, and the defendant was not, unlawfully detained at the time of the relevant act; (held against their will);

(d) the complainant was asleep or otherwise unconscious at the time of the relevant act;
(e) because of the complainant's physical disability, the complainant would not have been able, at the time of the relevant act, to communicate to the defendant whether the complainant consented;
(f) any person had administered to or caused to be taken by the complainant, without the complainant's consent, a substance which, having regard to when it was administered or taken, was capable of causing or enabling the complainant to be stupefied or overpowered at the time of the act (e.g. being drugged / drug rape).

Lack of consent may be demonstrated by:

— the complainant's assertion of force or threats;
— evidence that by reason of drink, drugs, sleep, age or mental disability the complainant was unaware of what was occurring and / or incapable of giving valid consent; or
— evidence that the complainant was deceived as to the identity of the person with whom (s)he had intercourse.

A boy or girl under the age of 16 cannot consent in law.   *(Archbold 2004, 20-152)*

Consent should be carefully considered when deciding not only what offence to charge but also whether it is in the public interest to prosecute. Sometimes consent is given, or appears to be given, but the law does not treat it as effective consent.

The law does not allow a person's consent to sexual activity to have effect in the following situations:
— where the person giving consent did not understand what was happening and so could not give informed consent, for example in the case of a child or someone suffering from a severe mental disability;
— where the person giving consent was under the relevant age of consent.

Where the victim has consented in fact, but not in law, alternative offences may be appropriate.

Examples include incest or unlawful sexual intercourse *(USI) (in the case of a female victim)* or, where consensual intercourse with a male under the age of consent, the offence of buggery.

The Act sets out the offences requiring the prosecution to prove absence of consent.

They are:
— rape;
— assault by penetration;
— sexual assault; and
— causing a person to engage in sexual activity.

In relation to these offences a person

(A)*(the perpetrator)* is guilty of an offence if she/he:
— acts intentionally;
— (B) *(the other person / the complainant)* does not consent to the act; and
— (A) does not reasonably believe that (B) consents.

In relation to many other offences there is no requirement to prove an absence of consent.

Only the act itself and the age of the victim or other criteria need to be proved.

They include:
— rape of a child under 13;
— assault by penetration of a child under 13;
— sexual assault of a child under 13; and
— inciting or causing a person to engage in sexual activity with a child under 13;
— child sexual offences involving children under 16;
— children under 18 having sexual relations with persons in a position of trust;
— children under 18 involved with family members over 18;
— persons with a mental disorder impeding choice;
— persons with a mental disorder who are induced, threatened or deceived;
— persons with a mental disorder who have sexual relations with care workers.

This section mainly relates to the offences of:
— rape;
— unlawful sexual intercourse (USI); and
— sexual assault.

Age of Consent

✦ In the UK, the age of consent for heterosexual and homosexual sex is 16.
✦ The age of consent and the Law varies in other countries and states.
✦ In Europe, for example, the lowest age of consent, at 13, is in Spain and the highest, at 18, is in Malta and Turkey; but all other European countries set theirs between 14 and 17 years of age.

The following pages provide definitions of and contain extracts from the *Sexual Offences Act 2003,* and related documents.

Rape

A person (A) commits an offence if:
(1) he intentionally penetrates the vagina, anus or mouth of another person (B) with his penis;
(2) B does not consent to the penetration; and
(3) A does not reasonably believe that B consents.
✦ The maximum sentence for this offence is imprisonment for life.

Assault by penetration

A person (A) commits an offence if—
(a) he intentionally penetrates the vagina or anus of another person (B) with a part of his body or anything else;
(b) the penetration is sexual;
(c) B does not consent to the penetration; and
(d) A does not reasonably believe that B consents.
✦ The maximum sentence for this offence is imprisonment for life.

Sexual assault

A person (A) commits an offence if—
(a) he intentionally touches another person (B);
(b) the touching is sexual;
(c) B does not consent to the touching; and
(d) A does not reasonably believe that B consents.
✦ The maximum sentence for this offence is imprisonment for 10 years.

Buggery / sodomy means:

✦ Anal penetration with a penis.

USI
✦ Unlawful sexual intercourse

Causing a person to engage in sexual activity without consent

A person (A) commits an offence if—
(a) he intentionally *causes* another person (B) to engage in an activity;
(b) the activity is sexual;
(c) B does not consent to engaging in the activity; and
(d) A does not reasonably believe that B consents.
✦ The maximum sentence for this offence is imprisonment for 10 years.
(No penetration)

A person is guilty of an offence under this section, if *the activity caused* involved—
(a) penetration of B's anus or vagina;
(b) penetration of B's mouth with a person's penis;
(c) penetration of a person's anus or vagina with a part of B's body or by B with anything else; or
(d) penetration of a person's mouth with B's penis.
✦ The maximum sentence for this offence is imprisonment for life. *(With penetration)*

The Law & Sex

Rape and other offences against children under 13

Rape of a child under 13 OR Assault of a child under 13 by penetration

A person commits an offence if—
(a) he intentionally penetrates the vagina, anus or mouth of another person with his penis; and
(b) the other person is under 13.
✦ The maximum sentence for this offence is imprisonment for life.

Sexual assault of a child under 13

A person commits an offence if—
(a) he intentionally touches another person;
(b) the touching is sexual; and
(c) the other person is under 13.
✦ The maximum sentence for this offence is 14 years.

Causing or inciting a child under 13 to engage in sexual activity

Section 1
A person commits an offence if—
(a) he intentionally causes or incites (persuades) another person (B) to engage in an activity;
(b) the activity is sexual; and
(c) B is under 13.
✦ The maximum sentence for this offence is imprisonment 14 years.

Section 2
A person is guilty of an offence under this section, if the activity caused or incited involved—
(a) penetration of B's anus or vagina;
(b) penetration of B's mouth with a person's penis;
(c) penetration of a person's anus or vagina with a part of B's body or by B with anything else; or
(d) penetration of a person's mouth with B's penis.

If Section 1 and Section 2 occur:
✦ the maximum sentence is imprisonment for life.

Child Sexual Offences

Sexual activity with a child

Subsection 1
A person aged 18 or over (A) commits an offence if—
(a) he intentionally touches another person (B),
(b) the touching is sexual, and
(c) either—
— **(i)** B is under 16 and A does not reasonably believe that B is 16 or over, or
— **(ii)** B is under 13.

Subsection 2
A person guilty of an offence under this section, if the touching involved—
(a) penetration of B's anus or vagina with a part of A's body or anything else,
(b) penetration of B's mouth with A's penis,
(c) penetration of A's anus or vagina with a part of B's body, or
(d) penetration of A's mouth with B's penis.
✦ The maximum sentence is 14 years.

Child sex offences committed by children or young persons

A person under 18 commits an offence if he does anything which would be an offence if he were aged 18 or over.
✦ The maximum sentence is 5 years.

Arranging or facilitating commission of a child sex offence

A person commits an offence if—
(a) he intentionally arranges or facilitates something that he intends to do, intends another person to do, or believes that another person will do, in any part of the world; and
(b) doing it will involve the commission of an offence under any of Sections 9 to 13.
✦ The maximum sentence is 14 years.

Meeting a child following sexual grooming etc.

A person aged 18 or over (A) commits an offence if—

(a) having met or communicated with another person (B) on at least two earlier occasions, he—
— **(i)** intentionally meets B, or
— **(ii)** travels with the intention of meeting B in any part of the world,
(b) at the time, he intends to do anything to or in respect of B, during or after the meeting and in any part of the world, which if done will involve the commission by A of a relevant offence,
(c) B is under 16, and
(d) A does not reasonably believe that B is 16 or over.
✦ The maximum sentence is 10 years.

A person aged 18 or over can also be found guilty of many other sexual offences, some are:

Sexual activity with a child.
✦ The maximum sentence is 14 years.

Causing or inciting a child to engage in sexual activity.
✦ The maximum sentence is 14 years.

Engaging in sexual activity in the presence of a child.
✦ The maximum sentence is 10 years.

Causing a child to watch a sexual act.
✦ The maximum sentence is 10 years.

Arranging or facilitating the commission of a child sex offence.
✦ The maximum sentence is 14 years.

Abuse of position of trust

Any of the above sexual offences in relation to an "abuse of postion of trust".
✦ The maximum sentence is 5 yrs *(separate charge)*.

The Law & Sex

Familial child sex offences

Sexual activity with a child family member.
✦ The maximum sentence is 14 years.

Inciting a child family member to engage in sexual activity.
✦ The maximum sentence is 14 years.

What counts as a family relationship?

The relation of one person (A) to another (B) is within this section if—
(a) one of them is the other's parent, grandparent, brother, sister, halfbrother, half-sister, aunt or uncle; or
(b) A is or has been B's foster parent.

The relation of A to B is within this subsection if—
A and B live or have lived in the same household, or A is or has been regularly involved in caring for, training, supervising or being in sole charge of B, and:
(a) one of them is or has been the other's step-parent;
(b) A and B are cousins;
(c) one of them is or has been the other's stepbrother or stepsister; or
(d) the parent or present or former foster parent of one of them is or has been the other's foster parent.

The relation of A to B is within this subsection if—
(a) A and B live in the same household, and
(b) A is regularly involved in caring for, training, supervising or being in sole charge of B.

For the purposes of this section—
(a) "aunt" means the sister or half-sister of a person's parent, and "uncle" has a corresponding meaning;
(b) "cousin" means the child of an aunt or uncle;
(c) a person is a child's foster parent if—
— **(i)** he is a person with whom the child has been placed; or
— **(ii)** he fosters the child privately;
(d) a person is another's partner *(whether they are of different sexes or the same sex)* if they live together as partners in an enduring family relationship; and
(e) "step-parent" includes a parent's partner and "stepbrother" and "stepsister" include the child of a parent's partner.

Offences against persons with a mental disorder impeding choice

Sexual activity with a person with a mental disorder impeding choice.
✦ The maximum sentence is life imprisonment *(if penetration involved)*, — otherwise 14 years.

Causing or inciting a person, with a mental disorder impeding choice, to engage in sexual activity.
✦ The maximum sentence is life imprisonment *(if penetration involved)*, — otherwise 14 years.

Engaging in sexual activity in the presence of a person with a mental disorder impeding choice.
✦ The maximum sentence is 10 years.

Causing a person, with a mental disorder impeding choice, to watch a sexual act.
✦ The maximum sentence is 10 years.

Inducements etc. to persons with a mental disorder

Inducement, threat or deception to procure sexual activity with a person with a mental disorder.
✦ The maximum sentence is 14 years.

Causing a person with a mental disorder to engage in or agree to engage in sexual activity by inducement, threat or deception.
✦ The maximum sentence is 14 years.

Engaging in sexual activity in the presence, procured by inducement, threat or deception, of a person with a mental disorder.
✦ The maximum sentence is 10 years.

Causing a person with a mental disorder to watch a sexual act by inducement, threat or deception.
✦ The maximum sentence is 10 years.

Care workers for persons with a mental disorder

Sexual activity with a person with a mental disorder
(1) A person (A) commits an offence if—
(a) he intentionally touches another person (B);
(b) the touching is sexual;
(c) B has a mental disorder;
(d) A knows or could reasonably be expected to know that B has a mental disorder; and
(e) A is involved in B's care in a way that falls within section 42.

(2) Where in proceedings for an offence under this section it is proved that the other person had a mental disorder, it is to be taken that the defendant knew or could reasonably have been expected to know that that person had a mental disorder unless sufficient evidence is adduced to raise an issue as to whether he knew or could reasonably have been expected to know it.

(3) A person guilty of an offence under this section, if the touching involved—
(a) penetration of B's anus or vagina with a part of A's body or anything else;
(b) penetration of B's mouth with A's penis;
(c) penetration of A's anus or vagina with a part of B's body; or
(d) penetration of A's mouth with B's penis.
✦ The maximum sentence is 14 years *(if penetration involved)*,
— otherwise 10 years.

Further offences in this section are:

(1) Causing or inciting sexual activity.
✦ The maximum sentence is 14 years *(if penetration involved)*,
— otherwise 10 years.

(2) Sexual activity in the presence of a person with a mental disorder; and
(3) Causing a person with a mental disorder to watch a sexual act.
✦ The maximum sentence is (2&3) 7 yrs.

The Law & Sex

Indecent photographs of children under the age of 18

Indecent photographs of persons aged 16 or 17.

(1) Apart from when photographs are required for legal reasons, it is illegal for anyone to take indecent photographs of a young person aged 16 or 17 unless the defendant can prove that at the time of the offence, they:
(a) were married, or
(b) lived together as partners in an enduring family relationship.

This section applies whether the photograph showed the child alone or with the defendant.

The defendant is guilty of the offence if it is proved that the child did not consent to the photography and that the defendant did not reasonably believe that the child so consented.

If the defendant shows or distributes the picture(s) to others, the question of consent is paramount.

Indecent photographs of children under 16.

Apart from when photographs are required for legal reasons, it is illegal for anyone to take indecent photographs of a child under the age of 16.
✦ The maximum sentence is 10 years.

Indecent image

The word 'indecent' has not been defined by the *Protection of Children Act 1978*, but case law has said that it is for the jury to decide based on the recognised standards of propriety.

Prohibited images

Possession of Prohibited Images of children

Section 62 of the *Coroners and Justice Act 2009 ('the Act')* creates a new offence of possession of a prohibited image of a child, punishable by up to three years' imprisonment. This offence, came into force on the 6 April 2010.

Possession of a prohibited image is an either way offence.
✦ The maximum penalty is 5 years' imprisonment, a fine, or both.

What is a pornographic image?

The Act defines a 'pornographic image' as one which must reasonably be assumed to have been produced solely or principally for the purpose of sexual arousal.

Ref: CPS.gov.uk

The offence is targeted at non-photographic images *(this includes computer generated images (CGI's), cartoons, manga images and drawings)* and therefore specifically excludes indecent photographs, or pseudo-photographs of children, as well as tracings or derivatives of photographs and pseudo-photographs.

What is "revenge porn" *(pornography)*?

Revenge porn is the distribution of a private sexual image (photograph or video) of someone without their consent and with the intention of causing them distress.
Sending images of this kind may, depending on the circumstances, be an offence under the Communications Act 2003 or the Malicious Communications Act 1988. Behaviour of this kind, if repeated, may also amount to an offence of harassment under the Protection from Harassment Act 1997.

✦ The maximum sentence is 14 years imprisonment.

The Law & Sex

In order for an image to be a "prohibited image", there are 3 elements that must be satisfied. An image must meet all 3 of the elements which are:

1. that the image is pornographic;
2. that the image is grossly offensive, disgusting, or otherwise of an obscene character; and
3. that the image focuses solely or principally on a child's genitals or anal region, or portrays any of the following acts:

✦ the performance by a person of an act of intercourse or oral sex with or in the presence of a child;
✦ an act of masturbation by, of, involving or in the presence of a child;
✦ an act which involves penetration of the vagina or anus of a child with a part of a person's body or with anything else;
✦ an act of penetration, in the presence of a child, of the vagina or anus of a person with a part of a person's body or with anything else;
✦ the performance by a child of an act of intercourse or oral sex with an animal (whether dead or alive or imaginary);
✦ the performance by a person of an act of intercourse or oral sex with an animal (whether dead or alive or imaginary) in the presence of a child.

Prohibited images of children

Related to prohibited images, this was amended on 1st April 2014 to:
✦ **category A** – images involving penetrative sexual activity, sexual activity with an animal or sadism;
✦ **category B** – images involving non-penetrative sexual activity; and
✦ **category C** – other indecent images not falling within categories A or B.

Criminal charges relate to either:
✦ possession;
✦ distribution; or
✦ production of such images.
✦ The maximum sentence is 10 years.

Child Prostitution - Sexual Exploitation

Paying for sexual services of a child

(1) A person (A) commits an offence if—
(a) he intentionally obtains for himself the sexual services of another person (B);
(b) before obtaining those services, he has made or promised payment for those services to B or a third person, or knows that another person has made or promised such a payment; and
(c) either—
— (i) B is under 18, and A does not reasonably believe that B is 18 or over; or
— (ii) B is under 13.

(2) In this section, "payment" means any financial advantage, including the discharge of an obligation to pay or the provision of goods or services (including sexual services) gratuitously or at a discount.

Ages:

If the victim is under the age of 13.
✦ The maximum sentence is life in prison *(with penetration)*; 14 years without.

If the victim is aged 13-15.
✦ The maximum sentence is 14 years.

If the victim is aged 16-17.
✦ The maximum sentence is 7 years.

Other child sexual offences include:

Causing or inciting child prostitution or pornography.
✦ The maximum sentence is 14 years.

Controlling a child prostitute or a child involved in pornography.
✦ The maximum sentence is 14 years.

Arranging or facilitating child prostitution or pornography.
✦ The maximum sentence is 14 years.

The Law & Sex

Interpretation / Definitions

(1) "Pornography"

Section 63 of the *Criminal Justice and Immigration Act 2008* describes an image "of such a nature that it must reasonably be assumed to have been produced solely or principally for the purpose of sexual arousal"

(2) "Extreme pornography"

Section 63 of the *Criminal Justice and Immigration Act 2008* creates a new offence of possessing "an extreme pornographic image."

An image is deemed to be extreme if it "is grossly offensive, disgusting or otherwise of an obscene character" and "it portrays, in an explicit and realistic way, any of the following—
(a) an act which threatens a person's life;
(b) an act which results, or is likely to result, in serious injury to a person's anus, breasts or genitals;
(c) an act which involves sexual interference with a human corpse; or
(d) a person performing an act of intercourse or oral sex with an animal *(whether dead or alive)*, and a reasonable person looking at the image would think that any such person or animal was real."

✦ Where (a) or (b) apply, the maximum sentence is 3 years; otherwise the maximum is 2 years.

Those sentenced to at least two years will be placed on the Violent and Sex Offender Register *(ViSOR)*.

(2) "Prostitute" means—
a person (A) who, on at least one occasion and whether or not compelled to do so, offers or provides sexual services to another person in return for payment or a promise of payment to A or a third person; and "prostitution" is to be interpreted accordingly.

(3) "Payment" means—
any financial advantage, including the discharge of an obligation to pay or the provision of goods or services *(including sexual services)* gratuitously or at a discount.

(4) "Gain" means—
— **(a)** any financial advantage, including the discharge of an obligation to pay or the provision of goods or services *(including sexual services)* gratuitously or at a discount; or
— **(b)** the goodwill of any person which is or appears likely, in time, to bring financial advantage.

Exploitation of prostitution

Causing or inciting prostitution for gain

A person commits an offence if—
(a) he intentionally causes or incites another person to become a prostitute in any part of the world; and
(b) he does so for or in the expectation of gain for himself or a third person.
✦ The maximum sentence is 7 years.

Controlling prostitution for gain

A person commits an offence if—
(a) he intentionally controls any of the activities of another person relating to that person's prostitution in any part of the world; and
(b) he does so for or in the expectation of gain for himself or a third person.
✦ The maximum sentence is 7 years.

Keeping a brothel used for prostitution
✦ The maximum sentence is 7 years.

Preparatory offences

Administering a substance with intent

A person commits an offence if he intentionally administers a substance to, or causes a substance to be taken by, another person (B)—
(a) knowing that B does not consent, and
(b) with the intention of stupefying or overpowering B, so as to enable any person to engage in a sexual activity that involves B.
✦ The maximum sentence is 10 years.

Other preparatory offences:

Committing an offence with intent to commit a sexual offence.
✦ If the offence involves kidnapping or false imprisonment - life imprisonment;
— otherwise 10 years

Trespass with intent to commit a sexual offence.
✦ The maximum sentence is 10 years.

Trafficking

Trafficking into the UK for sexual exploitation

A person commits an offence if he intentionally arranges or facilitates the arrival in the United Kingdom of another person (B) and either—
(a) he intends to do anything to or in respect of B, after B's arrival but in any part of the world, which if done will involve the commission of a relevant offence, or
(b) he believes that another person is likely to do something to or in respect of B, after B's arrival but in any part of the world, which if done will involve the commission of a relevant offence.
✦ The maximum sentence is 14 years.

Other trafficking offences:

Trafficking within the UK for sexual exploitation.
✦ The maximum sentence is 14 years.

Trafficking out of the UK for sexual exploitation.
✦ The maximum sentence is 14 years.

Adapted from the Sexual Offences Act 2003 - Crown Copyright - used through Open Government Licence (OGL) V1-0 and reference to Sentencing Council - Sexual Offences Definitive Guide - April 2014

The Law & Sex

Sex with an adult relative

Sex with an adult relative: penetration

(1) A person aged 16 or over (A) commits an offence if—
(a) he intentionally penetrates another person's vagina or anus with a part of his body or anything else, or penetrates another person's mouth with his penis;
(b) the penetration is sexual;
(c) the other person (B) is aged 18 or over;
(d) A is related to B in a way mentioned in subsection (2); and
(e) A knows or could reasonably be expected to know that he is related to B in that way.

(2) The ways that A may be related to B are as parent, grandparent, child, grandchild, brother, sister, half-brother, half-sister, uncle, aunt, nephew or niece.

(3) In subsection (2)—
(a) "uncle" means the brother of a person's parent, and "aunt" has a corresponding meaning;
(b) "nephew" means the child of a person's brother or sister, and "niece" has a corresponding meaning.

(4) Where in proceedings for an offence under this section it is proved that the defendant was related to the other person in any of those ways, it is to be taken that the defendant knew or could reasonably have been expected to know that he was related in that way unless sufficient evidence is adduced to raise an issue as to whether he knew or could reasonably have been expected to know that he was.
✦ The maximum sentence is 2 years.

Sex with an adult relative: consenting to penetration

As above but when A consents to the penetration.
✦ The maximum sentence is 2 years.

Other offences

Exposure

(1) A person commits an offence if—
(a) he intentionally exposes his genitals; and
(b) he intends that someone will see them and be caused alarm or distress.
✦ The maximum sentence is 2 years.

Sexual activity in a public lavatory

(1) A person commits an offence if—

(a) he is in a lavatory to which the public or a section of the public has or is permitted to have access, whether on payment or otherwise,
(b) he intentionally engages in an activity, and,
(c) the activity is sexual.

(2) For the purposes of this section, an activity is sexual if a reasonable person would, in all the circumstances but regardless of any person's purpose, consider it to be sexual.

(3) A person guilty of an offence under this section is liable on summary conviction, to imprisonment for a term not exceeding 6 months or a fine not exceeding level 5 on the standard scale or both.

The Law & Sex

Voyeurism

(1) A person commits an offence if—

(a) for the purpose of obtaining sexual gratification, he observes another person doing a private act; and
(b) he knows that the other person does not consent to being observed for his sexual gratification.
(2) A person commits an offence if—
(a) he operates equipment with the intention of enabling another person to observe, for the purpose of obtaining sexual gratification, a third person (B) doing a private act; and
(b) he knows that B does not consent to his operating equipment with that intention.
(3) A person commits an offence if—
(a) he records another person (B) doing a private act;
(b) he does so with the intention that he or a third person will, for the purpose of obtaining sexual gratification, look at an image of B doing the act; and
(c) he knows that B does not consent to his recording the act with that intention.
(4) A person commits an offence if he instals equipment, or constructs or adapts a structure or part of a structure, with the intention of enabling himself or another person to commit an offence under subsection.

Voyeurism cont.: A private act

A person is doing a private act if the person is in a place which, in the circumstances, would reasonably be expected to provide privacy, and—
(a) the person's genitals, buttocks or breasts are exposed or covered only with underwear;
(b) the person is using a lavatory; or
(c) the person is doing a sexual act that is not of a kind ordinarily done in public.
(2) A "structure" includes a tent, vehicle or vessel or other temporary or movable structure.
✦ The maximum sentence is 2 years.

Intercourse with an animal

(1) A person commits an offence if—
(a) he intentionally performs an act of penetration with his penis;
(b) what is penetrated is the vagina or anus of a living animal; and
(c) he knows that, or is reckless as to whether, that is what is penetrated.

(2) A person (A) commits an offence if—
(a) A intentionally causes, or allows, A's vagina or anus to be penetrated;
(b) the penetration is by the penis of a living animal; and
(c) A knows that, or is reckless as to whether, that is what A is being penetrated by.
✦ The maximum sentence is 2 years.

Other offences

Sexual penetration of a corpse
✦ The maximum sentence is 2 years.

Why are exposure and voyeurism important ?

Exposure *(commonly described as someone flashing his genitals at passers by)* and voyeurism *(commonly described as someone being a 'peeping Tom')* are important because large numbers of convicted rapists and paedophiles started their criminal activity in this way.

Increasingly children are being groomed by voyeuristic paedophiles who target them for online abuse. Because the perpetrator is acting remotely *(at a distance and without physical contact)*, it doesn't mean that the long-term consequences of such betrayal of trust are less for their victim than if they had met them in person. Trusting strangers online can have unwanted side effects.
(See Social Media - page 231)

Why is intercourse with an animal important?

Zoophilia means *'abnormal human sexual attraction to animals'* and zoophilia pornography is widely and highly illegal. Sex with animals *(bestiality)* is illegal in many states and countries *(including the UK)* but it is not yet illegal in all. There appears to be a growth in 'animal brothels' in countries where it is legal, frequented by men who seek sex with animals.

The Law & Sex

Offences outside the United Kingdom

(1) Subject to subsection (2), any act done by a person in a country or territory outside the United Kingdom which—
(a) constituted an offence under the law in force in that country or territory; and
(b) would constitute a sexual offence to which this section applies if it had been done in England and Wales or in Northern Ireland, constitutes that sexual offence under the law of that part of the United Kingdom.

(2) Proceedings by virtue of this section may be brought only against a person who was on 1st September 1997, or has since become, a British citizen or resident in the United Kingdom.

(3) An act punishable under the law in force in any country or territory constitutes an offence under that law for the purposes of this section, however it is described in that law.

(4) Subject to subsection **(5)**, the condition in subsection (1)(a) is to be taken to be met unless, not later than rules of court may provide, the defendant serves on the prosecution a notice—
(a) stating that, on the facts as alleged with respect to the act in question, the condition is not in his opinion met;
(b) showing his grounds for that opinion; and
(c) requiring the prosecution to prove that it is met.

(5) The court, if it thinks fit, may permit the defendant to require the prosecution to prove that the condition is met without service of a notice under subsection **(4)**.

> For information about the
> FMU (Forced Marriage Unit),
> UK Home Office and
> Foreign & Commonwealthy Office see:
> www.fco.gov.uk/forcedmarriage

Forced and Arranged Marriage

The United Nations views forced marriage as a form of human rights abuse, since it violates the principle of the freedom and autonomy of individuals. *The Universal Declaration of Human Rights* states that a woman's right to choose a spouse and enter freely into marriage is central to her life and dignity, and equality as a human being.

A forced marriage is where one or both people do not *(or in cases of people with learning disabilities, cannot)* consent to the marriage and pressure or abuse is used. It is an appalling and indefensible practice and is recognised in the UK as a form of violence against women and men, domestic / child abuse and a serious abuse of human rights.

The pressure put on people to marry against their will can be physical *(including threats, actual physical violence and sexual violence)* or emotional and psychological *(e.g. when someone is made to feel like they're bringing shame on their family)*. Financial abuse *(taking your wages or not giving you any money)* can also be a factor.

Forced marriage is a violation of human rights and is contrary to UK law, including the Matrimonial Causes Act 1973, which states that a marriage shall be voidable if: "either party to the marriage did not validly consent to it, whether in consequence of duress, mistake, unsoundness of mind or otherwise."

Force marriage offences
Forced marriage became illegal in England and Wales on 16th June, 2014, and includes: taking a British national overseas to force them to marry *(whether or not the marriage takes place)*; marrying someone who lacks the mental capacity to consent to marriage (whether they're pressured to or not).
✦ Forcing someone to marry can result in a sentence of up to 7 years in prison.

Ref: www.gov.uk (7/8/2014)

The April 2014 Final Sexual Offences Definitive Guideline on sentencing, states:

Rape and assault offences:

Rape
+ life imprisonment

Assault by penetration
+ life imprisonment

Sexual assault
+ 10 years' custody

Causing a person to engage in sexual activity without consent
+ life imprisonment *(if penetration involved)*
— otherwise 10 years

Offences where the victim is a child:

Rape of a child under 13
+ life imprisonment

Assault of a child under 13 by penetration
+ life imprisonment

Sexual assault of a child under 13
+ 14 years' custody

Causing or inciting a child under 13 to engage in sexual activity
+ life imprisonment *(if penetration involved)*
— otherwise 14 years

Sexual activity with a child
+ 14 years' custody

Causing or inciting a child to engage in sexual activity
+ 14 years' custody

Sexual activity with a child family member
+ 14 years' custody

Inciting a child family member to engage in sexual activity
+ 14 years' custody

Engaging in sexual activity in the presence of a child
+ 10 years' custody

Causing a child to watch a sex act
+ 10 years' custody

Arranging or facilitating the commission of a child sex offence
+ 14 years' custody

Meeting a child following sexual grooming
+ 10 years' custody

Abuse of position of trust:

Sexual activity with a child
+ 5 years' custody

Causing or inciting a child to engage in sexual activity *(This guidline also applies to offences committed remotely/online.)*
+ 5 years' custody

Sexual activity in the presence of a child
+ 5 years' custody

Causing a child to watch a sexual act
+ 5 years' custody

Indecent images of children:

Possession of indecent photograph of child
+ 5 years' custody

Indecent photographs of children
+ 10 years' custody

Exploitation offences:

Causing or inciting prostitution for gain
+ 7 years' custody

Controlling prostitution for gain
+ 7 years' custody

Keeping a brothel used for prostitution
+ 7 years' custody

Causing or inciting child prostitution or pornography
+ 14 years' custody

Controlling a child prostitute or child involved in pornography
+ 14 years' custody

Arranging or facilitating child prostitution or pornography
+ 14 years' custody
(For offences that involve wide scale commercial and/or international activity sentences above the category range may be appropriate.)

Paying for sexual services of a child:

Victim under 13 *(penetration)*
+ life imprisonment

Victim under 13 *(non-penetrative)*
+ 14 years' custody

Victim 13-15
+ 14 years' custody

Victim 16-17
+ 7 years' custody

The Law & Sex

Adapted from the Sexual Offences Act 2003 - Crown Copyright - used through Open Government Licence (OGL) V1-0 and reference to Sentencing Council - Sexual Offences Definitive Guide - April 2014

The Law & Sex

Trafficking people for sexual exploitation
- ✦ 14 years' custody

Offences against those with a mental disorder

Sexual activity with a person with a mental disorder impeding choice
- ✦ life imprisonment *(if penetration involved)*
- — otherwise 14 years

Causing or inciting a person, with a mental disorder impeding choice, to engage in sexual activity
- ✦ life imprisonment *(if penetration involved)*
- — otherwise 14 years

Engaging in sexual activity in the presence of a person with mental disorder impeding choice
- ✦ 10 years' custody

Causing a person, with a mental disorder impeding choice, to watch a sexual act
- ✦ 10 years' custody

Inducement, threat or deception to procure sexual activity with a person with a mental disorder
- ✦ Life imprisonment *(if penetration involved)*
- — otherwise 14 years' custody

Causing a person with a mental disorder to engage in or agree to engage in sexual activity by inducement, threat or deception
- ✦ Life imprisonment *(if penetration involved)*
- — otherwise 14 years' custody

Engage in in sexual activity in the presence, procured by inducement, threat or deception, of a person with a mental disorder
- ✦ 10 years' custody

Causing a person with a mental disorder to watch a sexual act by inducement, threat or deception
- ✦ 10 years' custody

Care workers

Sexual activity with a person with a mental disorder:
- ✦ 14 years *(if penetration involved)*
- — otherwise 10 years

Causing or inciting sexual activity
- ✦ 14 years *(if penetration involved)*
- — otherwise 10 years

Sexual activity in the presence of a person with a mental disorder
- ✦ 7 years' custody

Causing a person with a mental disorder to watch a sexual act
- ✦ 7 years' custody

Other sexual offences:

Exposure
- ✦ 2 years' custody

Voyeurism
- ✦ 2 years' custody

Sex with an adult relative: penetration
- ✦ 2 years' custody

Sex with an adult relative: consenting to penetration
- ✦ 2 years' custody

Administering a substance with intent
- ✦ 10 years' custody

Committing an offence with intent to commit a sexual offence
- ✦ life imprisonment *(if kidnapping or false imprisonment committed)*
- — otherwise 10 years

Trespass with intent to commit a sexual offence
- ✦ 10 years' custody

Offences committed by offenders under the age of 18

Child sex offences committed by children or young persons *(offender under 18)*
- ✦ 5 years' custody

Sexual activity with a child family member *(offender under 18)*
- ✦ 5 years' custody

Inciting a child family member to engage in sexual activity *(offender under 18)*
- ✦ 5 years' custody

The Law & Sex

Gillick Competency Ruling:

In 1985 the House of Lords and the Law Lords *(Lord Scarman, Lord Fraser and Lord Bridge)* ruled that in medical settings:

✦ "...whether or not a child is capable of giving the necessary consent will depend on the child's maturity and understanding and the nature of the consent required.

✦ The child must be capable of making a reasonable assessment of the advantages and disadvantages of the treatment proposed, so the consent, if given, can be properly and fairly described as true consent."

Therefore, parental consent is not mandatory for young people under the age of 16.

Fraser Guidelines

Referring to guidelines set out by Lord Fraser in his judgement of the Gillick case *(above)* in the House of Lords *(1985)*, which apply specifically to contraceptive advice:

✦ "...a doctor could proceed to give advice and treatment provided he is satisfied in the following criteria:

(1) that the girl *(although under the age of 16 years of age)* will understand his advice;

(2) that he cannot persuade her to inform her parents or to allow him to inform the parents that she is seeking contraceptive advice;

(3) that she is very likely to continue having sexual intercourse with or without contraceptive treatment;

(4) that unless she receives contraceptive advice or treatment her physical or mental health or both are likely to suffer;

(5) that her best interests require him to give her contraceptive advice, treatment or both without the parental consent."

The girl looked older

✦ In defence of having sex with a minor, some men state that the girl looked older — but they may end up in trouble with the Law if she's under 16.

✦ Although the Law is clear, in practice, because of the Children And Families Act 1989 and 2014, Gillick Competency Ruling and Fraser Guidelines, sex with young people can be a complicated area.

✦ If a male, over the age of 24 has sex with a female under 13, he faces a sentence of life in prison for unlawful sexual intercourse *(USI)*. The question of consent does not arise and without consent it is rape.

✦ If a male is over 24 and the female 14-16 it is rape without consent or USI with consent. He faces a maximum sentence of life in prison for rape or 2 years for USI.

✦ If a male is under the age of 24 and the female is between 14 and 16 years of age, it is unlawful sexual intercourse *(USI)* or rape. Age is sometimes used as an excuse unless he's been charged with a similar offence before.

Two teenagers having sex together

✦ If a 14 or 15 year old male and female have sex together, by mutual agreement, it's illegal but in practice is deemed *(considered)* to be a less serious offence.

✦ It's not wise though and something they may regret later.

✦ The young man is at risk of being charged with a sexual offence, for which he could be placed on the Violent and Sex Offender Register *(ViSOR)* and have to report to the Police.

Threats

✦ It is an offence for a person to procure *(obtain)* a female, by threats or intimidation, to have sexual intercourse.

Drug rape

✦ The question of capacity to consent is particularly relevant when a complainant is intoxicated by alcohol or affected by drugs.

✦ It is an offence for a person to apply or administer to, or cause to be taken by another any drug, matter or thing with intent to stupefy *(confuse)* or overpower her so as thereby to enable any man to have unlawful sexual intercourse with her.

✦ If a male has sex with a female who is asleep naturally or under the influence of alcohol or other drug*(s)* it is rape, for she is unconscious *(not awake)* and unable, therefore, to give valid consent.

✦ The maximum sentence for date rape is life in prison.

Other people present

✦ Although she cannot commit rape, a female – or another male who is present at the time of a rape, commits an offence – and may be charged with aiding and abetting him to rape.

✦ It is legal for two people over the age of consent to have sex – but, if ther is a 3rd party *(another person or people)* present, it is a criminal offence, whether the group is heterosexual or homosexual.

✦ It is a criminal offence to have sex in a public place – or a private place if a 3rd party is present *(heterosexual OR homosexual)*.

Lesbian offence

✦ Since a female under 16 cannot give consent, another female having lesbian sex with her commits indecent assault.

✦ The maximum sentence is 10 years.

Property offence

✦ It is an offence for a property owner or occupier to allow his or her premises to be used for someone to have sex with a minor. If the female is under 13, he or she faces a maximum sentence of life in prison. If the female is under 16, he or she faces 2 years in prison.

At what age can I marry?

✦ In England, Wales and Northern Ireland a young person can marry from the age of 16 to 18 with parental consent and from 18 without parental consent.

✦ In Scotland young people can marry from the age of 16 without parental consent.

✦ The age of consent to marriage varies in other parts of the world, from 12 to 21 years of age.

Anal sex or sodomy / buggery

(a) Anal sex, in the UK, between a consenting heterosexual OR homosexual couple, over the age of 16, is legal.

(b) Anal sex with a person – male or female – under the age of 16 or an older male or female without consent is illegal and carries a maximum sentence of life in prison.

(c) Anal sex under the age of 16, whether receiving or giving with agreement, the couple are both guilty in law and it carries a prison sentence.

Bestiality means:

✦ Bestiality means sex with an animal. It is illegal and carried a maximum sentence of 2 years in prison.

Therefore:

✦ It's far safer to wait until you're older before having sex.

✦ It's better for a man to wait until there's no doubt whatsoever about a young woman's age before trying to have sex with her – with her agreement.

✦ Sometimes a young girl lies about her age when they fancy an older man. Being questioned by the Police about underage sex could be damaging to a man's reputation.

✦ There's no legal age of consent for heterosexual boys but it's illegal for a woman over 16 to have sex with or interfere with a young man under the age of 16.

✦ She can be prosecuted for indecent assault and faces a maximum sentence of 10 years in prison, the same as men.

What is abuse?

✦ Actual or threatened violence or abuse is usually by one person against another or others, as a quest for power over them and to make their victim do what they want.

✦ This may be by an adult against a child, a child against another child, adult to adult, child to adult or group/gang bullying.

✦ It can be male against male, male against female or female against male or female.

Abuse comes in many forms, and is not just physical

✦ **Emotional abuse** – eg. constantly ridiculing *(poking fun at or belittling)* someone, instilling fear in or criticising them with or without the threat of using physical violence against them.

✦ **Physical abuse** – eg. hitting, punching, poking, slapping or pushing someone about.

✦ **Sexual abuse** – eg. rape; being forced to participate in humiliating sex acts; being shown or having access to pornographic material beyond your understanding; or being touched in a private place in a way which makes you feel uncomfortable.

✦ **Neglect** – eg. where you're left unattended, unfed and/or feel unloved.

✦ **Financial abuse** – eg. depriving someone of any money or refusing to pay bills, so that they're in fear of the gas or electricity being cut off or of going hungry.

✦ **Bullying** – eg. by other pupils at school is also abuse, as is having to watch domestic violence or be forced into any of these abuses, at home.

Note: Where domestic violence occurs in households where children live, social services may become involved to protect the children from either physical or emotional harm.

Which, to you, is more sexy?

Condom King
The Partner Pleaser

Bad Boy Dip 'n' Run
The Safety Teaser

www.WillyWorries.com

Some of that has happened to me but I am too terrified to tell anyone. I'm scared they won't believe me and I'm scared I'll get in to trouble if I tell. I can't stop having nightmares about what's happened. Where can I get help?

✦ As long as you don't ask the person abusing you, be brave enough to ask anyone else for help. SPEAK OUT.
✦ If the first person you turn to doesn't help you in the way you want, KEEP ASKING UNTIL YOU GET THE HELP YOU NEED TO FEEL SAFE.
✦ If the trouble is at home, tell someone outside the home, ie. your teacher – but if the trouble is from outside your home, tell your parents, trusted aunts, uncles or grandparents.

Other people to ask for help include:

Other people to ask for help include:
✦ a neighbour you know well;
✦ a youth worker;
✦ the Police or social worker;
✦ Health Visitor, Doctor, Practice Nurse or School Nurse;
✦ Childline or the Samaritans;
✦ NSPCC, Barnardos or Rape Crisis;
✦ your best friend, older cousin, brother, sister or someone else that you trust to help you;
✦ you may find that another member of your family is also a victim of abuse and equally scared to speak out, but with your help they may feel able to do so.

If a girl or woman says NO, does she really mean NO — or does she mean Yes?

✦ She means NO and don't think otherwise.
✦ If you say No do you mean Yes?
✦ By saying NO a girl or woman is stating that she does NOT give consent *(permission)* for whatever happens next.
✦ By taking no notice and carrying on, you're breaking the Law, acting recklessly and without due regard or care for your partner.
✦ If you don't stop you're committing a sexual offence.

But some girls say they mean YES when they say NO. It's very confusing.

✦ As confusing as it may be, it's best and safest not to listen to them and simply accept that NO means NO, and stop.
✦ Even if you're about to ejaculate, STOP, otherwise you could get into serious legal trouble.
✦ It may not seem fair to have to stop – and it may even seem impossible but it could prevent you from ruining your life by going to prison and/or getting a criminal record with all the associated stigma attached to sex related crime. All for something you didn't mean to do!
✦ Sex by consent can be very enjoyable. Sex without consent is miserable and degrading.
✦ Stopping may make you feel confused, grumpy, annoyed, frustrated etc. but it could keep you safe and out of prison.
✦ This goes for all men, not just for young men embarking on a sexual journey.
✦ You could be charged with rape if you misread the signals.
✦ No man is immune, however much you may think *"it couldn't happen to me."*

✦ Take time to get to know someone very well before you have sex together. Be clear about what your partner will or won't allow, before you start.

✦ If you change your mind during foreplay, state clearly that you don't want penetration. If you allow penetration, it's not rape for that individual incident.

✦ If, however, you/they get up, leave the room and return, it's a separate incident and you must not assume that you have permission to touch or have sex again, without consent.

✦ To do so, would be sexual assault or rape since it's a different incident from the first.

Recreational drugs, alcohol and taking advantage

✦ Young men, in particular, should be aware that it's a criminal offence to give alcohol or other drug to someone with the intention of having sex with them later.

✦ You risk being accused of rape or another sexual offence, should they later state that they didn't want to have sex with you.

✦ Whilst under the influence of alcohol or mind-altering drugs, inhibitions are likely to be reduced and casual, unprotected sex more than likely.

✦ This brings with it the serious risk of (a) pregnancy and (b) sexually acquired infections.

✦ Remember that emergency contraception is available.

✦ A Sexual Health Clinic can help diagnose/treat the infections you may worry about. However, they can not always clear up some viral infections from your system.

I fancy my teacher *(youth worker or other adult I look up to)* **and think I'm in love with him or her. Is this OK?**

✦ Many young people get a crush on, or fancy, a teacher or another significant adult of either sex, whom they admire and can't imagine life without them around.

✦ In some ways it's a compliment you're paying that person.

✦ The teacher or other adult may realise you have a crush on them and should try to understand your feelings.

✦ They may be rather embarrassed when they realise how you feel but they should find a gentle way to discourage you from developing your feelings further, even if you'd like them to act differently towards you.

✦ They know more about the rights and wrongs of the world and until you're physically and emotionally mature and independent, they shouldn't do or say anything to let your crush lead any further – or take advantage of your feelings.

✦ They know they'd be breaking the Law if they developed the relationship in a physical way, if you're under 16 years of age.

✦ Most teachers are aware that this can happen and try their best not to hurt their pupils' feelings. At the same time, they keep a potentially troublesome situation from developing.

✦ As hard as it may sound, you have come into their life as part of their job, not as part of their family.

✦ They've been placed in a position of trust by your parents or guardians and have a responsibility towards you.

✦ They're not employed to love you, to lead your feelings on in any way, or make you feel that they could ever be more than a friend to you, in the adult role they hold.

✦ With time, these feelings fade and are diverted towards someone nearer your own age, with whom you can develop a more appropriate relationship.

✦ They'll may well remain as a cherished memory, reminding you of happier times at that particular school, and you will look back on their support as a best friend upon whom you could count for help and advice.

If an older guy wants to have sex with me but I'm under age and not ready, what should I do?

✦ Don't do it. It's illegal.

✦ Tell him you're under age and what he's suggesting is illegal.

✦ It's true and may make him realise the trouble he could get into with the police.

✦ He could end up in jail on a rape charge, since you're under the legal age to give consent.

✦ In law, a male having sex with a male or a female under the age of consent is committing unlawful sexual intercourse, and because you're under the age of consent, it's rape.

✦ It's no joke for a man to go to prison on a rape charge and it could be very dangerous for him.

✦ He'll be terrified of other prisoners finding out why he's there, since few people like child molesters – i.e. someone who has sex with a minor.

✦ He should keep his penis in his pants and keep away from you until you're older and you can give your consent legally.

✦ Don't allow him to make you feel pressured.

✦ If he doesn't accept that, ask yourself whether you really want or need him in your life. It's obvious that what he really wants is sex; he doesn't care about you – just your body and his wants.

What if the person trying to have sex with me is a member of my own family?

✦ Sex with a member of your own family is called incest and it's against the Law *(illegal)*.

✦ If pregnancy occurs where there are blood ties between sexual partners it's genetically dangerous.

✦ Therefore, a man must not knowingly have sex with his mother, sister, daughter or grand-daughter. If the female is under 13, he faces life in prison. If the female is over 13 he faces 7 years in prison. There is NO question of consent in this case.

✦ A woman over 16 must not knowingly ALLOW her son, brother, father, grand or great-grand father to have sex with her. To do so is illegal and could result in a prison sentence of 7 years. There is NO question of consent in this case.

✦ Although not incest, step-parents or other relatives have also been known to abuse young people. This is wrong so you must speak out about that, too.

✦ The Law is there to protect you, so get help from the Police, or a reliable adult, who will take it further for you. Speak out to end the distress.

✦ By speaking out, when you feel ready and safe, you may be able to protect other family members from a similar kind of abuse.

✦ If the older person tells you to keep it a secret – or says that bad things will happen to you if you tell anyone – again, raise the alarm. This is a common way that the abuser terrifies in order to keep their victim under their control.

✦ Use the Law, get help and fight back, however scared you feel.

✦ If you're open and honest with the Police, you'll get lots of support. They won't force you to go to court if you're too scared, even though your attacker should be locked away to prevent them hurting someone else. They do have powers to make you go ahead, but your safety is their top priority.

✦ It's also important for them to try and protect other people from harm, too.

✦ They're on YOUR side, so do talk to them.

If I'm going out with an older person should I tell my parents?

✦ Yes, you should tell your parents.

✦ You may not want to but it's better to tell them than let them find out some other way.

✦ If you feel they'll disapprove, try telling them gradually and let them get to know your friend.

✦ If they get to know him or her, they might not feel as uncomfortable about it as you expect or tell you not to continue the relationship.

✦ They're not really out to stop you having fun, just looking out for your safety, however hard this may be to accept.

✦ They probably realise that telling you not to do something is the best way to push you to do it and if they disapprove strongly, it would probably backfire on them and make you more determined to continue!

✦ Your parents know about many things that can happen when older people are involved that you're innocent about.

✦ How would you feel if your child hid the truth from you?

✦ If you can't tell them, ask yourself why, then ask yourself if you should really be doing whatever it is. The chances are that you shouldn't; so ask yourself why you're doing it and be honest with your answers.

All my friends go to parties and have sex with other people. I don't want to have sex, but my friends put pressure on me. I feel left out because I haven't done it yet. What should I do?

✦ Check out any venue where you don't know the host/ess. If you feel uncomfortable, don't go in.

✦ It is illegal for people to have sex
(a) in a public place; and/or
(b) if a third party is present.

✦ If you find yourself in a club – or at a party where people are having sex – don't feel you have to have sex just because your friends do – or because you are there.

✦ Having sex is neither compulsory nor a kind of competition.

✦ Don't allow anyone to pressurise you into having sex.

✦ Secretly, your friends might be jealous that you still have your virginity and want to save it for later.

✦ Studies show that the majority of young people who have sex wish they'd waited until they were older before they started.

✦ Listen to your heart, not the bullies!

She's a tease, look how she dresses, she's asking for it (sex).

✦ If she hasn't verbally requested sex, to assume any woman wants sex, just from the way she dresses, is ignorant and dangerous.

✦ It's absolute nonsense and commonly thrown as a defence by men who've failed to realise that there's a huge difference between look – but don't touch and the clearly spoken permission to touch.

✦ Whatever anyone chooses to wear is up to her/him.

✦ Although someone may dress in a provocative or sexy style, at no time does that give you the right to assume they're willing, or ready, to have sex with you.

✦ Nor does it give you the right to cross the boundary of good manners and decency towards them.

✦ A man is in complete control of his hands and his penis, what he does with them and where he puts them.

✦ Neither is it sufficient defense to cast aspurtions (make bad comment) on the way someone chooses to dress.

✦ To step from looking with admiration at someone to touching, assaulting or raping her/him because of how they're dressed is totally unacceptable.

✦ It's a criminal offence, punishable in Law.

I was abused when I was younger. Will I still be able to have a baby?

✦ Your chance of getting pregnant is unlikely to have been damaged.

✦ Don't assume you can't get pregnant. It's always wise to use a reliable method of contraception until you're ready to get pregnant.

✦ If, however, you were given a sexually acquired infection – eg. chlamydia or gonorrhoea – which led to pelvic inflammatory disease (PID) you may need to see a gynaecologist for specialist advice.

✦ PID can lead to infertility but there really is no difference between you and a girl who wasn't abused but who caught these infections.

✦ Not all adults are monsters, but of course, it's quite understandable that your trust in those who should have been protecting you has been damaged.

✦ It's important not to bottle your feelings up or harm yourself – especially when you did nothing wrong. Try to find someone with whom you can share those painful feelings and start to rebuild your life in a positive way.

✦ If the abuser was a relative or family friend, it's very important to tell the Police what's happened, even if it's off the record. You can, of course, tell them when you are older and feel more able to cope.

✦ If you then decide not to press charges against your abuser the Police will, at least, know about a possible abuser. But, you can, however, press charges later. By speaking out, you may help them protect another victim.

✦ Most abusers are known to their victim and family.

✦ You may not be emotionally relaxed or feel comfortable talking about or having sex. If you'd like help from a specially trained psychosexual counsellor, your Sexual Health Clinic or your doctor can refer you.

The Law & Sex

Since I was abused, I've hated myself. I don't trust other people or feel I'm worth loving, but I really want someone to love me. Am I normal?

✦ Wanting to be loved is perfectly normal; everyone wants to be loved.

✦ For those who have been abused, it's natural to find it hard to trust other people.

✦ First, you have to learn to love yourself.

✦ You ARE worthy of love.

✦ When you start to believe this, you'll find that other people will respond to you in a more friendly way. Don't confuse sex with love. Sex and love can be totally separate requirements for many people.

✦ Be careful not to destroy yourself because of what someone did to you when you were younger.

✦ Learn to be in control of your feelings and fears. Don't let them rule you any longer.

✦ You CAN be happy again.

✦ Your doctor, Contraception or Sexual Health Clinic can refer you to a specialist psychosexual counsellor who can give you time and help you work through your feelings.

I want someone to love me, so I have sex and lots of one night stands, with lots of people. Is this OK?

✦ Simply having sex with someone doesn't mean they love you.

✦ After a while, you'll probably feel used or abused if you continue to search for love in this way.

✦ You may get a temporary ego boost when you feel that someone finds you attractive enough to have sex – but not much more.

✦ Except that, the more people you have sex with, the greater your risk of catching a sexually acquired infection.

✦ Take time to get to know someone

very well before you have sex. It's safer and, in many ways, healthier for you physically and emotionally than just having sex to get affection.

✦ Don't confuse the act of sex, with the act of love.

If I have a baby, I'll have someone to love and someone who needs me, but they say I'm too young. Why do adults think like this?

✦ The adults probably say this because they've got the experience and are able to advise you from situations they've been in over the years.

✦ Your dream may seem wonderful but the reality is often less bright.

✦ Many young mothers wish they'd waited until they were older, although many do say they were glad they had their baby at that age.

✦ Having a baby is not a decision to make lightly. Your life will change forever.

✦ Not all men are reliable enough to provide for their partner and child.

✦ Your partner may walk away and leave you to cope alone. So don't assume he'll stay – you will need to plan accordingly.

✦ It's a fact of life that a man may promise to stick by you during pregnancy or when the baby's born. Promises may evaporate when your child becomes more demanding, when another woman comes along without the tie of a baby; or when he wants to have some fun without responsibility.

✦ If you don't have close family or friends with babies nearby, child care for times you want or need to go out alone can be very expensive.

✦ Don't rush into pregnancy; wait until you are sure of the support you'll receive.

✦ You should also consider the impact a baby will have on your education. Obtaining the necessary qualifications from school or college will put you in a better position to find employment. This will provide your baby with the security which he/she needs in addition to your love.

✦ It's very difficult to return to studying once you leave full-time education – particularly if you've been used to having some money in your pocket.

✦ Test your maternal instincts. Look after a friend's baby 24 hours a day, 7-days a week – then see how you feel.

✦ Alternatively, some educators have access to computerised teaching babies which behave, and display demands, just like those of a real baby. You may be able to borrow a teaching baby for a trial period so that you can see what it's like to have to respond to all its demands. But, unlike a real baby, you will be able to hand it back when you've had enough!

✦ A baby is a minimum 18 year commitment; expensive; hard physical and emotional work and not something to have for novelty value.

✦ When you're older, you will want a stable relationship. A partner might not be so attracted to someone who attracts the stigma of being a single parent on welfare.

✦ You cannot guarantee that your baby/child will be healthy all its life. This doesn't mean you'll love him/her any less but life can be extremely tough as a young parent under stress.

✦ Think very carefully before planning a baby. If you still decide to go ahead and have a baby, your life will change forever. Let's hope all your dreams come true.

If you decide to have a baby, you need to look after yourself. Think of this question. What does a gardener do when planting seeds?

✦ A gardener plans ahead and takes time to nurture and prepare the area in which his seeds will grow.

✦ He waters and feeds the tiny plants and he works long and hard to ensure that they have the best chance of survival.

✦ After they grow, he still tends to their needs, protecting them from infection and harm.

✦ A baby deserves as much planning and forethought because you're planning the life of another human being, not just a plant.

✦ If, after careful planning and a lot of saving you still think this is what you want to do, then seek medical advice about pre-conceptual *(pre-pregnancy)* care.

✦ You'll need to be healthy during the first three months of your pregnancy, have vaccinations to protect your baby from miscarriage, blindness or deafness etc. – in case you come into contact with someone who has rubella *(German measles)*.

✦ You'll need pre-natal care throughout your pregnancy to check that the baby is growing well and is healthy. This is particularly important if you have a medical condition that could be made worse by pregnancy.

✦ You'll also be advised to take folic acid tablets regularly before and during pregnancy.

What does sexual exploitation mean?

The Oxford Dictionary definition of exploitation is *'the action or fact of treating someone unfairly in order to benefit from their work'*.
✦ When that work involves sex, it becomes sexual exploitation.
✦ Sexual exploitation happens to people of any age, although the phrase most commonly relates to exploitation of children and young people, both male and female.

What is child sexual exploitation?

✦ Child sexual exploitation involves children and/or young people being pursuaded, by someone who has power over them, to exchange sex or sexual acts for money, cigarettes and/or drugs, food, somewhere to stay, affection, protection, new clothes or shoes, cinema or concert tickets, meals out, gifts and/or other basics of life.
✦ It also includes that person involving them in the creation of pornographic, sexually explicit films/ images and/or websites;
✦ and it can happen through the use of mobile phone as well as webcam technology.

If the police or social services find out that young people are accessing porn material online, on television, or via magazines, films or other digital media, it can raise Child Protection / Safeguarding concerns and problems for their parents / guardians.

Pornography (Porn)

The Oxford Dictionaries' definition of pornography *(porn)* is: *"Printed or visual material containing the explicit description or display of sexual organs or activity, intended to stimulate sexual excitement."*

✦ It is illegal for young people, under the age of 18 to access pornographic material.
✦ Some of the images shown in porn films and photographs are not as genuine as they appear and it is illegal for porn actors to be or look under the age of 18.
✦ Participants may negotiate the use of rules and 'safe words', which, if said during filming, ensure the activity stops.
✦ Participants are acting a part and to improve sales photographic tricks are sometimes used by the producers during filming to make things appear more exciting.

Why is porn dangerous for young people to watch?

The danger caused by viewing porn at a young age, when you are sexually inexperienced, is that you could assume that this is what real sexual relationships are all about, and what you're meant to do to each other, when it isn't.
✦ The scenes in professionally made films are all agreed before filming starts and the actors have contracts, stating what they will or won't do or allow.
✦ As described in the *Sexual Offences Act, 2003*, there are different levels of porn, which grow increasingly violent towards women.
✦ If this is all a young man learns, he is not learning about love, care and respect for someone else in the healthy way that he should.

The Law & Sex

Amateur pornography *(filming or photographing yourself and your partner having sex)* then uploading it to the Internet

✦ Even if you both think taking a film whilst having sex is a fun thing to do, putting sexy material on the Internet can have long-lasting consequences and may be illegal.
✦ Professional film producers follow guidelines and actors have regular health checks.
✦ Safety is ensured and there are legal sanctions if the law is not followed.
✦ If either of you is or looks as if you are under 18 and film yourselves this would be illegal, and the images may be considered to be pornographic.
✦ Amateur photographers may not realise the difference between hard and soft core pornography.
✦ If sexually explicit pictures are taken without consent and distributed via digital media, this is illegal.
✦ Seek legal advice if this has happened to you or if you are worried about an image someone has posted of you on the Internet.
✦ It may seem like fun to take and upload images or post offensive material online but this is considered to be publishing material, just as if you were printing a book or a magazlne, for which there are rules.
✦ Would you circulate the same material in print format? Would you like your parents or other family members to see what you want to circulate? If not, think twice before rushing to upload material to the Internet, or other digital platforms.
✦ *There is a big difference between having sex and making love. Just having sex in various ways is all that porn films portray. They don't explain anything about the enjoyable feelings that are involved within a loving, caring sexual relationship; or that it's important to learn about healthy and unhealthy relationships; respect; and care for someone else as you mature.*

When is a child described as a young person?

✦ Legally, a child is anyone under the age of majority, which is when someone is treated as an adult.
✦ In the UK, the 'age of majority' changed from 21 to 18 in 1971.
✦ In practice, this definition is further broken down by description, with:
— a child described as anyone under the age of 14;
— a young person, as anyone between the age of 14 and 18;
— and a young adult, as anyone who is aged between 18 and 25 years.

What's the difference between a young person and a youth?

Definitions of the specific age range that constitutes youth vary.
✦ For example, the United Nations define youth as *'persons between the ages of 15 and 24'*;
✦ while the African Youth Charter states that 'youth' means *'every person between the ages of 15 and 35 years'.*
✦ But whichever definitions is followed, 'youth' often means the time between childhood and adulthood *(maturity).*
✦ In practice, terms such as youth and young person can be used interchangeably with terms, such as kid, teenager, and adolescent.
✦ Youth also refers to the looks and behaviour of someone who is young.
✦ Young person, therefore relates to a person who is young, in age, or who is in their youth.

What does the term 'vulnerable person' mean?

✦ The Oxford Dictionary describes the word vulnerable as *'exposed to the possibility of being attacked or harmed, either physically or emotionally.'*
✦ Related to people, it describes *'someone in need of special care, support, or protection because of age, disability, or risk of abuse or neglect'.*
✦ Someone can be vulnerable at any age but the term is most commonly used to refer to young people and elderly adults, although it also refers to people of any age, who have physical, emotional or learning diffculties and people with mental health problems.
✦ The term also relates to other people, who find themselves in a vulnerable situation.

Vulnerable Adults and Young People

Vulnerable people are at risk because of physical disability, their age, mental or other health problems, and they may find it difficult to protect themselves from abuse or abusers.

Sadly, many different kinds of people abuse others at risk. Some include:
✦ people who deliberately target others, at risk;
✦ members of the person's own family or their friends;
✦ sometimes professionals who are closely involved in the person's life or with their finances; and
✦ sometimes tired and stressed people become abusive.

However, it's important to report these situations, as Social Services can help to reduce pressure on stressed carers and make life better for them, as well as the person they are caring for. It can be hard work and very stressful caring for someone else, just as it can be upsetting and stressful for the person needing help.

Social Services may, for example, offer 'respite care' whereby the person being cared for has alternative care for a while, which allows their carer the opportunity of having a rest, or taking a holiday.

Signs of abuse include but are not limited to: the person looking dirty, unkempt or not dressed properly; never seeming to have money of their own; being frightened, withdrawn or sometimes injured without a good explanation about why.
✦ If you worry that someone is not getting good care, you should follow your heart and report your concerns to the police or social services. It is better to do that than to ignore something and leave someone in danger.

What is meant by the term learning disability?

Learning disability is the term that the UK's Department of Health uses within its policy and practice documents. They describe learning disability as:

✦ *'a significantly reduced ability to understand new or complex information, to learn new skills; and*

✦ *starting before adulthood, with lasting effects on development, a reduced ability to cope'.*

The US National Council for Learning Disability *(LD)* states that:

✦ *'LD is more than a 'difference' or 'difficulty' with learning — it's a neurological disorder that affects the brain's ability to receive, process, store and respond to information.*

✦ *LD will vary in how it impacts each individual child, adolescent and adult.'*

MENCAP, a UK charity that supports people with mental health problems, states that:

✦ *"some people with a learning disability also have other physical and emotional conditions, and may receive more than one diagnosis. This could have an impact on the kind of support they and their families need in their day-to-day life".*

✦ People with learning disabilities are considered to be more vulnerable than other people, making them more at risk of harm and exploitation.

✦ Reasons and/or conditions behind someone's learning disability vary greatly and this is a specialist area of health and social care; too big to cover adequately in this book.

✦ More information about conditions associated with learning disability and leaning difficulty can be found by visiting example websites, such as:

— www.ncld.org

— www.mencap.org.uk

Sex and learning disability

If someone with *learning disability or difficulty* wants to have sex, who is over the age of consent; they have the right to do so, but the legality of this hinges on their ability to give their consent.

✦ A clinical judgement about the individual's ability to give their consent to sex is important.

✦ Without consent, any physical contact would be considered assault, or sexual touching, and a crime, under the *Sexual Offences Act, 2003*.

✦ People with a mild learning disabilities or difficulties may understand the implications of their actions.

✦ People with severe learning disabilities or difficulties, may not.

✦ Each case must be assessed individually and as with other people, safer sex should be employed when sexual activity occurs.

Sex and *physical* disability

If someone has a *physical* disability; is over the age of consent; and can legally give their consent to have sex, there is no reason why they should not enjoy a healthy, active sex life.

✦ If they don't have a partner but want sex, there are support organisations that link people together, some of whom are sex workers, experienced in helping disabled people enjoy having a safe, happy and active sex life.

✦ Disabled men and women should consider the risk of pregnancy and sexual infection, just like anyone else, and ensure that protection is used.

✦ For more information about sex and disability, see the Outsiders Trust website. They are a respectful and well respected UK charitable organisation that supports the sexual health needs of disabled people.

— www.outsiders.org.uk

Sexting
— Texts, Pictures and Video

Sexting is a made up word,which combines the words sex and texting. It usually involves storing, sending nude or sexually suggestive / explicit images and / or sexually explicit text messages between mobile phones and/or other electronic communication devices. This may also involve e-mail; video web chat systems - e.g. Skype or ooVoo; social networking sites - e.g. Facebook, MySpace, Bebo,Twitter etc.; instant message systems e.g. WhatsApp, Messenger or via Bluetooth.

Whichever system is used, there is a real risk of long term legal, personal and emotional consequences for the person featured in the image, and also for those who receive, store or pass on *(share)* the image with others.

✦ Any sexy image of a person under 18 may be considered child pornography by a court.

✦ Once such images are in cyber space they can not be removed easily.

✦ They can be transmitted around the world in a matter of minutes.

✦ Possession and distribution constitute a criminal offence.

(See previous pages.)

✦ Therefore, from something that may have started as an innocent game, dare or joke, you could end up in serious trouble with the Law, lead to a criminal conviction and your name being placed on the Violent and Sex Offender Register *(ViSOR)* for a period of up to five years; all for just possessing such images on your phone, computer, iPad, notebook etc.

✦ In addition to that, and the stigma of having a criminal record, the collateral consequences of criminal charges could prevent you from getting a job, travelling to various countries, getting a loan or even emigrating in the future.

✦ Is it really worth it?

The Internet
— Online Grooming and Safer Use

The Internet is a fabulous resource but there are some important things to be aware of whilst using it.

✦ Sadly, people are not always honest, nor who or what they present themselves to be, especially online.

✦ It is safest not to talk to strangers in online chat programs and social networking sites.

✦ If you do, keep your wits about you and, just as you would offline, take great care getting to know a new person.

✦ Don't trust too quickly. Don't give out your home, school, college or email address; your mobile or landline phone number to online friends.

✦ Although they may be genuine, paedophiles *(people who sexually abuse children)* often appear in chat environments as if they are another young person, before getting a young person to do or show them things, meet up or do other things they shouldn't.

✦ Do talk to others about what you are doing, including a trusted adult, and tell them who you're speaking to.

✦ If you can't talk to them about something, perhaps you shouldn't really be doing it!

✦ They won't want to stop you enjoying yourself but they are acutely aware of how some adults pretend to be young people online and lull others in to a false sense of security, so that they will be prepared to meet up one day.

✦ It's safest not to meet online friends in person but if you do, don't meet them on your own. Take an older person with you and meet in a public place.

✦ Keep your personal information personal!

✦ Be careful of the sort of websites you visit and if anything you see or read online worries you, tell a trusted adult about it.

✦ Few people need a frienship based on lies or deception.

Cyber Bullying

Just as in real life, there are some nasty bullies who lurk online.

✦ Every time a web page, email, text or other message is sent or placed, background information about the user's activity is logged.

✦ Bullies think that because they can't be seen, that they can't be traced by the police. But they are wrong.

✦ Online bullying comes in a variety of ways to frighten and intimidate people. Sadly, some of the bullies are people who wouldn't have the nerve or be nasty enough to be a bully offline and, not always, but occasionally they may even turn out to be a victim's jealous 'friend' in real life!

✦ They post comments, images or videos to intimadate the person and make them feel upset, worried or frightened.

✦ Some even manage to 'hack in' (break in) to someones online account(s) and cause problems from within a user's profile settings.

✦ Bullies are people who behave in a very nasty way towards others.

✦ It's not nice and they wouldn't want it to happen to them.

✦ If it happens to you, tell someone.

✦ Change your passwords.

✦ Stop using social media sites for a while and report it to the police.

✦ The bully's identity CAN be traced and they can be prosecuted.

✦ Let the police guide you further.

**Note re Sexting
to Parents/Guardians**

If a child's mobile phone is on a contract for which you pay, and it is found to have been used for taking, sending or receiving sexual images of or by the user or of other young people under the age of 18, you could find yourself in trouble with the Law, as well as them.

Stalking

In the UK, the *Protection of Freedoms Act 2012* created two new offences of stalking and it states the following.

This list is not exhaustive but gives an indication of the types of behaviour that may be displayed in a stalking offence. The listed behaviours are:
(a) following a person;
(b) contacting, or attempting to contact, a person by any means;
(c) publishing any statement or other material relating or purporting to relate to a person, or purporting to originate from a person;
(d) monitoring the use by a person of the internet, email or any other form of electronic communication;
(e) loitering in any place *(whether public or private)*;
(f) interfering with any property in the possession of a person;
(g) watching or spying on a person.

✦ The effect of such behaviour is to curtail *(limit)* someone's freedom, leaving them feeling that they have to be careful all of the time.

✦ In many cases, the conduct might appear innocent *(if it were to be taken in isolation)*, but when carried out repeatedly so as to amount to a course of conduct, it may then cause significant alarm, harassment or distress to the victim.

Online stalking most often involves women and girls, often harrassed by an ex-partner who cannot accept that their relationship is over:

✦ it may also occur if an online friendship becomes uncomfortable;

✦ and it may even begin entirely at random, by one online stranger towards another, if, for example, they don't like a comment someone makes in an online conversation chain.

✦ DO report this crime to the police.

Domestic and Intimate Partner Violence

The Government's definition of domestic violence (DV) is: *"any incident of threatening behaviour, violence or abuse (psychological, physical, sexual, financial or emotional) between adults who are or have been intimate partners or family members, regardless of gender or sexuality."*

✦ Domestic violence is a serious crime, which happens across all communities, faiths and cultures. Most often, it is committed by men against women, although the reverse is also true.
✦ It happens in straight, gay, lesbian bisexual and transgender relationships, although other family members may be involved.
✦ Pregnant women are at increased risk and as many as one in four women, and one in six men experience some form of domestic violence at some time in their life.
✦ Violence rarely happens just once. It usually gets worse the longer it carries on and it is well recognised that it often takes several dozen incidents before the victim musters the courage to leave their abuser and get help to save their life.
✦ After leaving, many abusers continue to stalk their victim and cause further problems because they, quite simply, can't accept the loss of power and control over someone, or accept that they should just let someone go when they don't love them any more.
✦ DV is one of the most dangerous crimes because the attacker has a key to the front door and it takes great courage to break free. It also takes great courage, love and support from others to help keep someone away.

Please see 'Abuse' on oage 171 for sugges-tions on how to get help and to keep safe if you are worried about your situation.

Honour Based Violence

The Crown Prosecution Service and the Association of Chief Police Officers have a common definition of honour based violence and state:

"Honour based violence" is a crime or incident, which has or may have been committed to protect or defend the honour of the family and/or community".

But any "Honour Based Violence" is a fundamental abuse of Human Rights.

In certain communities, some people live in fear incase they fall in love with 'the wrong person', have sex outside marriage, are homosexual *(gay or lesbian)* or are considered to have embarrassed the family or 'the community' in some other way. If they break an 'honour code' they fear that great violence will be meted out upon them *(or even their family)*, unless they can escape their situation.

They fear being murdered or receiving threats to kill; being made to commit suicide; being raped; kidnapped; falsely imprisoned; forced in to marriage; forced to have an abortion; and many other 'punishments', which involve violence in the name of so-called honour.

Perpetrators believe that they have the right to control, usually female autonomy and sexuality, but there is no 'honour' in any of these crimes. These practices, are used to control behaviour within families or other social groups, to supposedly protect perceived cultural and religious beliefs and / or honour.

Even today, such crimes cut across all cultures, nationalities, faith groups and communities as well as national and international boundaries. This, and other violence against women, is a global problem.   (Ref: CPS.gov.uk)

Protection and Safeguarding

The Care Quality Commission's (CQC) definition of safeguarding is: *"protecting people's health, wellbeing and human rights, and enabling them to live free from harm, abuse and neglect. It is fundamental to creating high-quality health and social care."*

✦ Health, education, youth and social services, police and other adults in a position of authority and / or care have a legal obligation.
✦ They must carry out certain checks and report certain situations relating to children and vulnerable adults to the authorities for further investigation, assistance and care.
✦ The aim is to protect vulnerable people, of all ages, not, as many people fear, to break up families or cause anyone undue upset; although this may be the initial outcome.
✦ The authorities can offer temporary or permanent support, working with those affected, as well as those causing the problem.
✦ Mistakes happen. Life is stressful.
✦ People need help but don't always realise, or want to accept it, but social services can be viewed as societies' safety net.
✦ If, children are living in a home where DV (domestic violence) occurs, even if the children are not physically hurt, they witness what happens and are psychologically upset by it.
✦ This is a Child Safeguarding issue and professionals have a duty of care to the children and look after them.
✦ This may be by removing the children from the situation and placing them temporarily in to foster care, children's homes, with relatives or in some cases, by supporting the parent(s) to end the abuse and/or violence.
✦ The long term aim is to support families, not to break them up.

Gangs

The Oxford Dictionary definition of a gang is *"a group of people, especially young people, who regularly associate together."* but it also states that it is *"a group of young people involved in petty crime or violence".*

According to the Metropolitan Police *(London),* the difference between the two is that they are unlikely to be interested in the first, peaceful peer group of friends meeting up, but they *are* likely to be in the membership and activities of the second.

Gangs have always exsited, where young people would meet up and spend their free time together. Many joined youth and social clubs and enjoyed a happy, healthy time, without fear. Indeed, many young people still do this, quite safely.

In general, young people either gravitate towards similar young people, with whom their parents are happy for them to spend time, or they rebel from what they know and think an alternative lifestyle looks more glamorous and exciting.

Before long, many of the young people who rebel are out of their depth and involved in something they didn't anticipate, don't want to be involved with, and are now scared but feel they are unable to escape from the gang, easily.

By the time many want out, they have probably committed several criminal acts and the gang has a hold over them. They're trapped, unhappy and feel it's too late to turn back.

It may be hard to leave a gang but it is possible, and there is help available to do so if it's looked for.

The Law & Sex

Why do parents worry about their children joining a gang?

Each parent brought their children into this world, with hopes and dreams for their future.

✦ Most parents envisage a good life for their offspring, in which they hope they will do better than them at school and become happy, healthy, loved and successful people.

✦ Very few, if any, parents hope that their new baby will grow up to be a violent criminal who spends their life terrorising other people, and wastes large periods of their life in prison, where they may, in turn, become terrorised by even more violent criminals.

✦ But, that sometimes happens and parents'/siblings' lives are affected by the behaviour of such children when they join a gang and get sucked in to a world they find difficult to leave.

Why do young people join a gang?

✦ In a rush to grow up, most young people admire older people, whose lifestyle looks exciting and they want to be part of that group or gang.

✦ Flattered by group members who invite them to hang around with them, they sometimes join a gang instead of a group, and are drawn in to a world that they know little about, which is where trouble often starts.

Gang culture

Police advice includes but is not limited to the fact that:

✦ *Gangs operate under their own rules, often requiring aspiring members to undertake initiation tests to show their loyalty towards the gang and / or its leader(s).*

✦ *This can range from something minor but risky, which is not a criminal offence to something quite serious, with legal consequences if they're caught.*

✦ *Violence and disrespectful behaviour feature highly within gang culture; as do drugs, theft, territorial and partner disputes;* plus other bullying and unkind behaviour.

Gangs have always existed but the level of violence and criminal activity between rival gangs has not always existed to the extent that it does today.

The other side of gang culture

There are a few things your friends might NOT tell you about the 'benefits' of being part of a gang but:

✦ *gang leaders want you to run errands for them, becoming one of their 'soldiers' or, if female, be used as a a 'link', or someone to have casual sex with;*

✦ *most gang members never really earn much money, if they say they do, they're probably lying or are committing crime;*

✦ *you are more likely to be seriously hurt if you belong to a gang; and*

✦ *you won't earn respect from those that matter the most to you — your loved ones — by getting arrested and you may grow increasingly frightened about what you've been made to do in the name of the gang.*

Gang rivalry

Gangs tend to have rivals and retaliation / payback, is a common reason given for gang violence, but:

✦ *if gangs keep retaliating, violence escalates;*

✦ *if staying in the area, members who don't want to participate may never feel safe again;*

✦ *but, there are people who can help members to get out.*

Wherever you live, for guidance about gangs and how to leave one safely, please check the Metropolitan Police Website: http://safe.met.police.uk

The Law & Sex

Violence and The Law

Violence is against the law, is a police matter and according to the Metropolitan Police *(London)* research shows that members of a gang *(with a name and a territory)* are far more likely to:

✦ be victims of crime;

✦ carry weapons, e.g. knives / guns;

✦ commit a serious offence;

✦ break the law repeatedly;

✦ have complaints made about them for rude or noisy behaviour;

✦ use illegal drugs;

✦ get involved in alcohol-related incidents.

Joint Enterprise — the serious risk of just being part of a gang

"Joint enterprise" is when you can be found guilty of a crime if, for example.:

✦ *you are part of a gang and someone in that group commits murder with a weapon or by some other means (this also includes attacks where the victim is punched, kicked, raped etc.);*

✦ *if you realised that the person was going to use violence or you knew that they were carrying a weapon and even though you didn't agree to the attack or use of the weapon you remained as part of that gang.*

✦ *But, to avoid liability under "joint enterprise" you would need to tell all the other members of the group that you were no longer part of the group (gang) or stop the attack by physical intervention; or by calling the police.*

✦ *However it is very difficult to prove that you had communicated your withdrawal from the gang, and the only effective means of avoiding liability would be by not being part of the group (gang) in the first place.*

✦ *Furthermore, committing any crime as part of a gang may lead to a longer prison sentence when a case goes to court.*

Ref: www.CPS.gov.uk

The Law and Same Sex Relationships

Same sex relationships are also called homosexual relationships.

✦ Homo comes from the Greek word homos or same.

✦ Homosexual people are physically, sexually and emotionally attracted to people of the same sex.

✦ Male homosexuals are commonly called *gay men.*

✦ Female homosexuals are commonly called *lesbian.*

✦ In the UK, same sex marriage became legal on 29th March, 2014 and has exactly the same legal status as marriage between opposite sex partners.

Same sex relationships are, however, stigmatised and illegal in many parts of the world, and carry considerable risk.

If you are confused or scared about the feelings you may have towards someone of the same sex, see Section 5, p129 called *"Growing Up and New Experiences".*

If someone feels trapped in the body of the opposite gender, and they have a sex change, does it mean that they are gay / lesbian?

✦ No. This is a complicated topic, but when someone feels they are transgender *(cross gender)* or intersex, it is not the same as feeling that they are gay / lesbian.

✦ Our gender identity is about how we see ourselves and which gender we associate ourselves with.

✦ Our sexual identity is about our sexual orientation or how we are attracted to other people.

✦ Because sexual orientation is a different thing from gender identity, a transgender person can be straight, gay, bisexual or intersex— just like anyone else.

✦ For further information - see page 272.

✦ Also see http://kidshealth.org

What is prostitution?

In addition to what has been stated on earlier pages, from the *Sexual Offences Act 2003*, The Oxford Dictionary defines prostitution as *'the practice or occupation of engaging in sexual activity with someone for payment'*; which is often described as commercial sex work.

✦ At present, prostitution is LEGAL *(UK)* as long as the prostitute is over the age of 18 and not being exploited by someone else, even though the age of consent is 16 for non-commercial sex.

✦ However, a number of related activities are illegal, e.g. soliciting in a public place, kerb crawling, owning or managing a brothel, pimping etc.

What do prostitutes prefer to be called?

✦ A respectful phrase that many prostitutes prefer is 'sex worker'.
✦ They may also be described as a commercial sex worker.

What are some of the other names that prostitutes are called?

Example names include:
✦ working girl; working boy;
✦ brass; hooker; whore;
✦ high class hooker/whore;
✦ escort; sugar babe;
✦ call girl; sauna girl; and/or
✦ common prostitute.

What does soliciting mean?

The Oxford Dictionary definition of soliciting is to: *"Accost someone and offer one's or someone else's services as a prostitute"*.

Suggested websites for more information about prostitution and sexual assault can be found at www.sexplained.com

How many people visit sex workers?

✦ Nobody can answer this question because using the services of sex workers is not something that many people talk about openly. However, there are estimated to be over 40 million sex workers, globally. *(BusinessInsider.com)*
✦ The U.K is a major sex trafficking destination with many people trafficked from developing countries.
✦ In 2004, the Home Office estimated that there were around 80,000 commercial sex workers in the U.K. with 730 off-street sites selling sex in London, alone. *(Dickson 2004)*
✦ Today's statistics will be higher.

The "oldest profession in the world"

✦ Commonly called this, sex work can be a very dangerous occupation but other times it can be safer, and as if being paid for sex by an acquaintance.
✦ Many people choose to work in the industry for their own financial reasons but many others, both male and female, don't get to choose and are forced in to it by a third party *(a pimp / gang or, sometimes, a parent)*, which is wrong.
✦ The police are trying hard to stop such sexual exploitation.

Will prostitutes do anything sexual?

No. Prostitutes who work freely decide what they will consent to and what they won't. Some consent to activities that others don't, which must ALWAYS be respected.
✦ Remember: Sex without consent is ALWAYS a crime.

Remember:

Each sex worker is someone's son or daughter, brother or sister. Don't judge them. Think twice before using unkind or offensive language about somoene who is earning their living this way.

Male Circumcision

✦ Male circumcision is legal and is almost always carried out during the first two months of life when a baby boy is too young to remember what's happened.

✦ The foreskin *(prepuce)* or loose skin which covers the glans penis, is surgically removed; perhaps under local anaesthetic.

✦ It is widely practised in Jewish and Moslem communities for religious reasons; and it may be medically indicated later in life if the foreskin becomes inflamed and difficult to retract *(pull back)*. This is called phimosis and is often caused by poor genital hygiene.

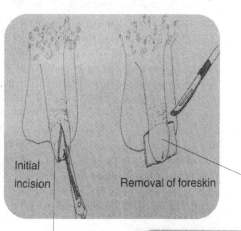

Initial incision

Removal of foreskin

Foreskin or prepuce

Left:
steps taken during circumcision

Below:
suturing may be required following removal of prepuce

Glans penis

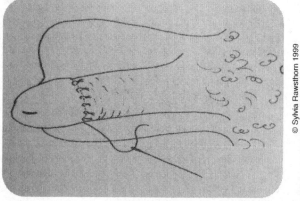

© Sylvia Rawsthorn 1999

Female Genital Mutilation / FGM
Female Genital Cutting / FGC
(previously called Female Circumcision)

✦ In the West, FGM/C is viewed as cruel and as a form of child abuse, as well as GBH *(grievous bodily harm)*.

✦ It is illegal to perform it in the UK *(and many other countries)* and it is illegal to take a UK national from the UK to have this done to them in another country.

✦ The maximum UK sentence is 14 years imprisonment for those found guilty of performing or facilitating *(enabling)* FGM/C.

✦ However, it is still carried out, today, in over 28 countries, mostly in Africa, parts of the Middle East and Asia.

✦ And, to a lesser extent by the Aboriginal community in Australia.

Why is it called FGM/C?

✦ This practice used to be called 'female circumcision' but that term is no longer used and can be confused with male circumcision - which is quite different.

✦ In 1996 WHO *(the World Health Organisation)* defined FGM as any procedure which involves partial or total removal of, or injury to, the external genitalia, whether for cultural or other non-therapeutic *(medical)* reasons.

✦ FGC describes the practice of female genital cutting and many women refer to it as having been 'cut'.

✦ It is also termed 'initiation' but there are over 20 local terms for it across the communities in which it is practiced.

When is FGM/C performed?

✦ When it is performed depends on local custom and practice.

✦ UNICEF states that the age of the girls varies, usually from weeks after birth to puberty; in half the countries for which figures were available in 2013, most girls were cut before the age of five.

✦ However, in some cases, it is carried out shortly before a young women marries or even during, or following, her first pregnancy.

What happens during FGM/FGC?

✦ Although, nowadays, safer, surgical FGM/C is performed by doctors in some countries, with which anaesthetic is used, traditional FGM/C is still widely practiced and can involve removal of the prepuce *(skin covering the clitoris)* or removal of the clitoris, called clitaroidectomy, *without anaesthetic*.

✦ Quite often the labia minora *(inner vaginal lips)* are also cut off.

✦ In Type 3 FGM/C the damage is so severe that almost all of the young woman's external genitalia is removed and the raw areas sewn together, allowing only a small hole for urine and menstrual blood to leave the body.

✦ This is called 'infibulation'.

Why is FGM/C done?

Although the rate of FGM/C is slowing down in some countries, some reasons that supporters give for performing FGM/C include that:

✦ it's a way to make a woman socially acceptable, particularly for marriage; and that by keeping her from wanting to have sex, preserve her virginity and reduce her temptation to have sex with anyone except her husband;

✦ it's performed to maintain her cultural identity; as a rite of passage and to give her status in her community;

✦ it's believed that women who have had FGM/C appear more attractive, cosmetically, than women who have not had it done;

✦ it cleanses and purifies her, helping her to be clean and hygenic; and

✦ it's a way to uphold family honour and there is still social pressure to do it..

The Law & Sex - FGM/C

The World Health Organisation classifies FGM/C into four major types.

Type 1. Clitoridectomy:
✦ partial or total removal of the clitoris (a small, sensitive and erectile part of the female genitals) and, in very rare cases, only the prepuce (the fold of skin surrounding the clitoris, also called the clitoral 'hood').

Type 2. Excision:
✦ partial or total removal of the clitoris and the labia minora, with or without excision of the labia majora (the labia are "the lips" that surround the vagina).

Type 3. Infibulation:
✦ narrowing of the vaginal opening through the creation of a covering seal. The seal is formed by cutting and repositioning the inner, or outer, labia, with or without removal of the clitoris.
(Oxford Dictionary definition of infibulation: the practice of excising the clitoris and labia of a girl or woman and stitching together the edges of the vulva to prevent sexual intercourse.)

Type 4. Other:
✦ all other harmful procedures to the female genitalia for non-medical purposes, e.g. pricking, piercing, incising, scraping and cauterizing the genital area.

Why remove the clitoris?

✦ The clitoris consists of erectile tissue, similar to that in the man's penis and it is an area which, when touched gently, gives a woman significant sexual pleasure.
✦ This encourages the vagina to lubricate, which enables comfortable penetration and greater pleasure.
✦ By removing the clitoris the woman will not enjoy sexual pleasure in the way she would if it was left intact, and in theory if she doesn't get 'turned on' sexually or enjoy sexual intercourse, she won't look for men and will either remain a virgin or be faithful to her husband. (See 'clitoris' on page 47)

Which types of FGM/C are most commonly performed?

✦ Type 1 and Type 2 account for the large majority of all FGM/C.
✦ Type 3 is most commonly performed is eleven of the African countries that practice the procedure.
✦ Type 4 is all other forms of female genital mutilation - see page 197.

Who does the cutting?

✦ Traditionally, it's performed by older women from within the community, who have had it done to them and who believe in it. This may even be the young girl's grandmother.
✦ The 'cutter' is supported by supposedly loving parents, family and friends who hold the girl's legs and arms down whilst it is carried out, so she can't struggle or get away.
✦ This commonly leaves the girl feeling vulnerable, and frightened by the people who are supposed to love and care for her most.

How do male circumcision and FGM/C compare?

✦ In men, only the prepuce (skin of the foreskin) which covers the glans penis (head of penis) is removed during circumcision. (See page 190.)
✦ In women, considerably more tissue is removed.
✦ By removing the prepuce (covering or hood of the clitoris) the clitoris becomes extremely sensitive, and the area becomes very painful.
✦ To reduce this, the small raised bud of erectile tissue, called the clitoris, is usually, though not always, removed.
✦ The open edges are sewn, dressed or left, for the wound to heal; although they may be held together by sharp twigs.

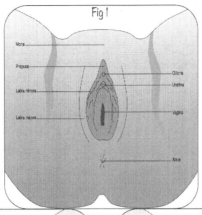

Left:
Normal female
genitalia

© Peter Gardiner

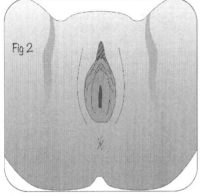

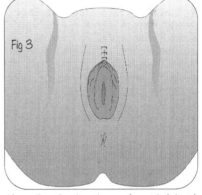

Above: Type 1 - removal of clitoris and / or clitoral hood (prepuce) - also called sunna or traditonal circumcision
Below: Type 3 - Infibulation - vulva after cutting - also called pharaonic circumcision

Above: Type 2 - clitaroidectomy *(removal of clitoris)*

Below: Type 3 - vulva sewn up - infibulation

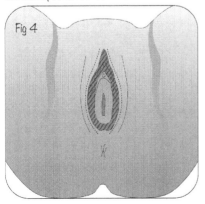

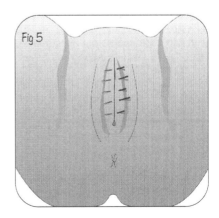

The Law & Sex - FGM/C

The Law & Sex - FGM/FGC

Does the woman choose her husband or is he chosen for her?

✦ In many cases, a young woman's husband is chosen for her by her family.
✦ He may be a lot older, may have other wives and she may be forced to marry him.
✦ Forced marriage is illegal in the UK and many other countries — but it still happens.

Does FGM/C ensure faithfulness?

✦ No. FGM/C does not always ensure faithfulness.
✦ It can backfire because depending on the type of mutilation the young woman has endured, she may find sex very painful and unpleasurable Then, if she has heard that sex can be enjoyable, she may want to try having sex with someone different.
✦ She may grow to believe that her husband is a poor lover and that someone else would be more gentle, loving and caring of her sexual needs!

FGM/C seems very dangerous.

✦ Yes. FGM/C is very dangerous and incredibly painful.
✦ It carries potentially serious consequences, including risk to life.
✦ In traditional settings, girls / young women may bleed to death from the procedure or from septicaemia (blood poisoning) caused by the dirty, shared instruments and / or technique used to perform the 'cutting'.
✦ In countries where it is practiced widely, it is increasingly carried out in hospitals or clinics by qualified medical practitioners, in a more hygenic way.
✦ There are many potential complications of FGM/C.

For how long has FGM/C been practiced?

✦ The short answer, 'a long time'!
✦ Some historians state that FGM/C has been performed since the time of the Pharoahs, in Ancient Egypt.
✦ Others, that it's been practiced for over 2000 years; the exact origin of which is unclear.
✦ Differently, the Romans are said to have fastened a fibula or brooch across the outer labia of female slaves to stop them having sex — thought to be the origin of the term infibulation.

Is there a religious requirement for FGM/C to be performed?

✦ No. There is absolutely no religion that reqires FGM/C to be carried out.
✦ The practice predates Islam as well as Christianity and Judaism
✦ The fact that Islamic words are used to describe the practice is misleading (e.g. sunna circumcision).
✦ Indeed, followers of the Islam are taught to do no harm to themselves or to others.

What sort of complications can occur through FGM/C?

Immediate problems of FGM/C include but are not limited to:
✦ Intense pain and / or severe bleeding, which can lead to shock and / or collapse, both during and / or after the procedure.
✦ Anaemia, from severe bleeding.
✦ Wound infections, including tetanus.
✦ Nearby organs can be damaged by the blunt, dirty instruments that are often used.
✦ Swollen or blocked urine passage - causing retention of urine (being unable to pass urine).
✦ These are classified as medical emergencies, which require urgent attention to preserve life.

Long-term complications of FGM/C include, but are not limited to:

✦ Infertility, due to infections following complications of procedural technique.
✦ Difficulty passing urine or menstrual blood, from which urinary and pelvic infections may occur.
✦ Sex can be very painful and women may not want to endure intercourse.
✦ Childbirth can be excruciatingly painful, and dangerous, with the risk of tearing, bleeding, infection and even death of the baby and / or the mother.
✦ Delayed 2nd stage delivery can deprive the baby of oxygen and lead to brain damage.
✦ Women often have 'flashbacks' and re-live the terror of the procedure, for life.
✦ Abscesses may occur *(pus filled sacs of infected matter)*.
✦ Dermoid cysts — which are usually non-cancerous growths.
✦ Keloid — hardened scar tissue.
✦ Recurrent urinary tract infections because the bladder may not empty properly and / or urine may stagnate in the area of infibulation.
✦ Painful or blocked periods, in which there is build up of menstrual blood loss, which is unable to escape from the vagina normally.
✦ Fistula formation — an abnormal opening or passage between the vagina and the bladder or the vagina and the rectum - leads to incontinence and/ or infection (*not being able to hold on to urine and / or faeces (poo)*) with body waste escaping through the fistula channels. *(See page 201)*
✦ Anxiety, depression and / or shame, either at the time or in the future.
✦ Behavioural change, self harm and/ or substance abuse.
✦ Increased risk of HIV, Hepatitis B, C, and other communicable infections - most commonly because the same equipment *(razor or knife)* is used to 'cut' up to as many as 30 girls at a time and it is not sterilised between them.

✦ The majority of women require medical attention at some point in the future, for physical and psychological conditions resulting from the procedure.

Will the practice of FGM/C ever end?

✦ FGM/C may end or be abandoned, one day, but sufficient disapproval of the practice needs to come from within each community that supports it, rather than external sources telling them that it shouldn't be performed.
✦ If disapproval doesn't develop this way, it will never end.
✦ Thankfully, the issue of FGM/C is being highlighted politically, on an international scale and, now, there are campaigns to stop FGM/C, and other forms of violence against women and girls.
✦ Furthermore, many young men within affected communities, as well as young women, plus mothers of young girls who were themselves 'cut', are vocalising their disapproval.
✦ Hopefully further momentum will gather against the practice of FGM/C.

If a woman has undergone Type 3 FGM/C (infibulation), how does she have a baby without bleeding to death?

✦ Women who have had infibulation need their episiotomy incision to be made in the opposite direction.
✦ Others require an operation, a Caesarian section, to deliver the baby safely and protect the mother's life.
✦ Sadly, and especially in areas where this is practiced, many women die in childbirth due to complications of obstructed labour — as do their babies.
✦ In the West, so that a woman won't tear and the baby won't be restricted during delivery, some women require an episiotomy *(an incision or cut in the perineum, the area between the vagina and the anus)*, performed hygenically by midwives or doctors during delivery.

Can FGM/C be reversed?

✦ Yes. It can be reversed, to some extent.
✦ There are some specialist clinics where a woman can have surgery, called 'defibulation', to open her up and repair as much of the damage as possible.
✦ Gradually, and sometimes, the labia start to reform – but not the clitoris.

Do women who have had FGM/C ever enjoy sex?

✦ Yes. Depending on the type of FGM/C performed, some women enjoy an active sex life.
✦ However, many others, don't.

How can a man have sex with a woman who has had infibulation?

✦ He needs to be gentle and patient.
✦ It can take many months for a man to stretch the scar tissue enough to penetrate his wife if she has had infibulation, especially if there is thick scarring.
✦ Sometimes the husband uses a knife to cut her open enough to allow penetration to take place.
✦ Other times a local midwife is employed, in secret, to open the woman.
✦ Secrecy is important, to preserve the man's image of potency but there has to be a large enough opening for his penis to enter her vagina during intercourse.

How can women enjoy sex after FGM/C if their clitoris is so important for sexual enjoyment?

✦ Women who have not undergone the most severe forms of FGM/C can learn to enjoy sexual intercourse without a clitoris.
✦ This is because the clitoris is not the only sensitive area within the vulva.
✦ Both sides of the vulva contain deeper erectile tissue, which, along

with the labia majora *(large lips)* *(excised during Type 3 FGM/C)* contain erectile tissue, called vestibular or clitoral bulbs. These engorge *(fill)* with blood and swell during sexual arousal.
✦ This erectile tissue surfaces and joins at the top to form the 'super sensitive' clitoris but the severe forms of FGM/C destroy much or all of the vulval nerve endings, delaying arousal or impairing orgasm.
✦ Because erectile tissue remains following Types 1 & 2 FGM/C, a well motivated couple can develop techniques that allow her to relax and become sexually aroused enough to enjoy sex.
✦ However, large numbers of women who have undergone FGM/C merely tolerate sex, considering it to be a duty to please their husband.

Thinking about sex

✦ The brain is the biggest sexual organ and it controls how we feel and how we act.
✦ If a woman is unhappy, uncomfortable or not keen to have sex, she won't relax.
✦ If she's not relaxed, the glands in her vulva won't produce lubricating fluid.
✦ Without this fluid, dry sexual intercourse will be painful.
✦ Unsurprisingly, this leads to low libido and a lack of interest in sex.

What happens to the woman after she gives birth to a baby?

✦ When women are 'opened' during pregnancy to allow safe delivery of a baby, they sometimes want to be reinfibulated afterwards.
✦ Some young women only undergo FGM/C after having their first baby.
✦ Reinfibulation is illegal in the UK and many other countries.

Is reinfibulation requested at other times?

✦ Yes. Reinfibulation *(being sewn together again)* may be requested if a woman's husband is travelling away from home for a long time, to ensure she won't have sex with another man;
✦ if a couple divorces; or
✦ when an elderly woman is dying, to prepare her for death.
✦ As just mentioned, it is widely illegal to do so.

What happens with Type 4 FGM/C?

Type 4 FGM/C (unclassified) consists of all other operations on the female genitalia, including:

✦ pricking, piercing, stretching, or incision of the clitoris and/or labia;
✦ cauterization by burning the clitoris and surrounding tissues;
✦ incisions to the vaginal wall;
✦ scraping *(angurya cuts)* or cutting *(gishiri cuts)* of the vagina and tissue surrounding it; and
✦ introduction of corrosive substances or herbs into the vagina with the objective of tightening it.

World Health Organisation (WHO) examples of Type 4 FGM/C include:

✦ Stretching - e.g. in Tanzania and the Congo girls are told to stretch the clitoris and labia minora every day for 2–3 weeks - then an older woman uses sticks to hold the stretched parts in place before 'cutting' takes place.
✦ 'Gishiri' cutting involves cutting the vagina's anterior *(front)* wall to enlarge it.
✦ 'Angurya' cuts involve scraping tissue away from around the vagina.
✦ Another procedure is 'hymenotomy', the removal of a hymen regarded as too thick, which is practised by the Hausa people of West Africa.

Is cosmetic surgery to the vulva also classified as Type 4 FGM/C?

✦ No. The WHO does not include cosmetic procedures such as labiaplasty *(surgical alteration of the labia majora and/or minora)* or procedures used in sex reassignment surgery within its FGM/C categories.

How many young women and girls does FGM/C affect?

✦ UNICEF estimates that FGM/C affects over 130 million girls and women worldwide and over 8 million have had Type 3.
✦ They further estimate that although the practice is starting to decline in some areas, an additional 30 million more girls and young women will be affected within the next 10 years.
✦ In other words, this equates to
  — 57,000 per week
  — 8,250 per day
  — 344 per hour
  — 6 per minute
  — 1 girl mutilatedl every 10 seconds

Which methods of contraception can a woman use if she has had FGM/C and she can access modern methods?

✦ The contraceptive choice for a woman who has undergone FGM/C depends on the Type she has had, and whether she has received reversal surgery.
✦ Her choice of methods is, otherwise, the same as for a woman who hasn't undergone FGM/C.
✦ However "Fertility Awareness Methods" can be used by women who cannot easily access hormonal or intrauterine methods. *(See page 120)*

The Law & Sex - FGM/C

Where is FGM/C most commony practiced?

According to the World Health Organisation, FGM/C is known to be practiced in 39 countries *(listed here)*, but is most commonly practiced in the following 28 countries:
✦ Benin, Burkino Faso, Cameroon, Central African Republic, Chad, Côte d'Ivoire *(Ivory Coast)*, Djibouti, Egypt, Eritrea, Ethiopia, Gambia, Ghana, Guinea, Guinea-Gissau, Kenya, Liberia, Mali, Mauritania, Niger, Nigeria, Senegal, Sierra Leone, Somalia, Sudan *(northern)*, Togo, Uganda, United Republic of Tanzania, and Yemen.

It is also documented as occurring in:
✦ Australia, India, Indonesia, Iraq, Israel, Malaysia and the United Arab Emirates.

They have anecdotal reports from other countries, which include:
✦ Colombia, Democratic Republic of Congo, Oman, Peru and Sri Lanka.

✦ It has occurred, illegally, in the UK and other countries by immigrant populations. *(not listed here)*

Is the incidence of FGM/C declining?

✦ Yes. Thankfully the incidence of FGM is declining, but this is faster in some communities than others.
✦ UNICEF states that in 2013, the African countries where it is concentrated and the percentage of women affected are:
✦ Somalia (98%), Guinea (96%), Djibouti (93%), Egypt (91%), Eritrea (89%), Mali (89%), Sierra Leone (88%), Sudan (88%), Gambia (76%), Burkina Faso (76%), Ethiopia (74%), Mauritania (69%), Liberia (66%), Guinea-Bissau (50%), Chad (44%), Côte d'Ivoire (38%), Kenya (27%), Nigeria (27%), Senegal (26%), Central African Republic (24%), Yemen (23%), United Republic of Tanzania (15%), Benin (13%), Iraq (8%), Ghana (4%), Togo (4%), Niger (2%), Cameroon (1%), and Uganda (1%).
✦ Because FGM/C is practised by different ethnic groups within these countries, a country's overall rate can be affected by a high or low rate within any of these groups.

Do young women ever want to have this done to them?

✦ Yes. Some innocent young girls expect it as a social norm if they are brought up to expect it as a right of passage, and a thing that happens to girls.
✦ They have nothing to compare this practice with, and no exposure to girls and older women who don't undergo it.
✦ Because they have no access to alternative viewpoints, and people with whom they can talk and ask questions they don't realise that it is not common practice, for most girls around the world.
✦ They don't realise the excruciating pain involved or the physical and emotional implications.
✦ Their mothers, grandmothers and their aunts will have had it done to them and felt the same way, so they expect it and look forward to the time it will happen to them, too.

Is this attitude changing?

✦ Yes. With increased international travel, greater access to the media and associated campaigns publicising disapproval, improved access to education for girls, and the improving status of women, there is movement towards change.
✦ More mothers are speaking out against it, refusing to let it happen to their daughters and sometimes, this causes family conflict. So protecting their daughters can become problematic.

✦ Thankfully more young men are now speaking out against FGM/C.

✦ They don't want their sisters or other relatives to undergo the procedure and they are also more gentle and caring towards a partner who's had it.

Why is it important to have FGM/C on the school curriculum?

✦ It's important to have FGM/C on the school curriculum because nowadays, more children *(and parents)* from different cultures mix in school, and some will be vulnerable.

✦ We have a 'duty of care' towards each other, not just to our friends or family.

✦ Educating the next generation about FGM/C is the best way to influence change.

✦ Once FGM/C is better understood, children can help to protect each other; and increased disapproval of the practice can help to influence change.

✦ Greater understanding of what it involves can also help to support those who have been made to go through it.

What should I look out for if I think someone is at risk of having this done to them?

Signs to watch out for if you're worried that someone, from a community in which FGM/C is practiced, is at risk of being forced to have this done to them include, but are not limited to:

✦ talk of girls being taken abroad for a long holiday, especially during the school summer holidays — especially if this is with their grandmother or aunt(s);

✦ girls talking about a special ceremony that's going to happen when they go away;

✦ talk of a special family 'elder female' visiting from abroad;

✦ girls being in families in which the adult women have undergone FGM/C;

✦ overhearing children talking about it;

✦ a child talking about having a 'special procedure' to become a woman;

✦ the child appearing withdrawn and scared about something;

✦ the child opening up about what they fear will happen to them, asking for help.

What are the signs to watch for if someone has already undergone FGM/C?

Signs in a young person that it may have already taken place include, but are not limited to:

✦ a young girl or woman newly experiencing difficulty walking, sitting or standing;

✦ them taking longer in the toilet than usual, perhaps having recurrent urinary tract infections, or menstrual problems that they didn't have before their holiday;

✦ them being withdrawn, quiet and appearing to be depressed;

✦ prolonged or several absences from school and / or an unusual fear and / or reluctance to have medical examinations.

What can I do to help someone, if I'm worried that they might be at risk of FGM/C? Who do I tell?

✦ If you're worried, SPEAK OUT.

✦ Do all you can to keep them safe.

✦ Tell the police (UK = 999) or contact a trusted professional, such as their teacher, school nurse, social worker or GP, who will do it for you.

✦ Emergency care will be organised to protect them whilst investigations take place, so **DO NOT alert their family, friends or anyone from their community of your suspicion**.

✦ It doesn't matter if you are wrong.

✦ It's better to speak out than keep quiet and let someone be abused.

The Law & Sex - FGM/C

I've heard of a traditional practice called Girl-child Beading. What's that?

✦ 'Girl-child beading', which is a traditional practice amongst the Samburu people of Northern Kenya, started in 1780.

✦ Beads are worn and used by women the world over, for all sorts of reasons - from fashion to symbols of fertility or even as a form of birth control - and they can be used to convey coded messages that a community understands.

✦ But amongst the Samburu, a man enters his 'Moranhood' when he is circumcised between the age of 15-25, and he receives warrior status.

✦ He remains a Moran for the next 12-16 years, then becomes an 'elder' and can marry.

✦ In the meantime, he can choose a "temporary wife".

✦ He can have sex with her but he cannot marry or have children with her.

✦ The theory being, that this protects married women from the sexual advances of younger men.

✦ But this does not protect young women.

✦ The Moran chooses a young girl they fancy, who is a relative between 9 and 15 years of age, by placing beads over her shoulders to claims her as his 'temporary wife'.

✦ He later places more, red beads, over her shoulders when intimate relations commence.

✦ Her mother organises a 'singira' or hut, and he visits the child at night.

✦ He can then have unlimited sex with her but she is not allowed to get pregnant.

✦ If she gets pregnant the Moran leaves her immediately.

✦ Traditionally she is not allowed to keep the baby if she wishes to become a married woman in the future, so she is made to undergo a cruel abortion, performed by older women.

✦ The older women tell the 'elders' (older men) of the community that the girl is unwell.

✦ Her mother gets herbs called 'Sekotei' and treats her with these, and sheeps oil, to induce abortion.

✦ If this fails, the older women press the girl's abdomen with the palms of their hands, to induce abortion; followed, if that fails, by their heels, then their knee, supporting her back in the process and to prevent the foetus surviving, they also tie her abdomen.

✦ This is, of course, excruciatingly painful for the girl who could, effectively, die in the process.

✦ Only if she becomes critically unwell do the older women seek further advice on treatment from the elders - but they don't suggest that she is taken to hospital (abortion laws were relaxed in Kenya in 2010, but unsafe abortion continues).

✦ Amongst the Samburu people, FGM/C is performed on young women shortly before marriage, and only circumcised women are allowed to have babies.

✦ Uncircumcised children are not supposed to give birth, so if the girl has the baby instead of an abortion, the baby is considered an outcast, which brings bad omen to the family. So, again traditionally, it is taken from her at birth and thrown away, to die on its own.

✦ Now, there is an adoption / rescue centre which either gives the babies to disabled women or women who are unable to have their own baby; and the Samburu Girls Foundation helps rescued girls find safe haven.

✦ Sometimes, the girls are successfully supported back in to their family, with their baby. The rescuers also help the girls go to school and gain an education.

✦ Girl-child beading continues, despite it representing a form of child sex slavery and incest - both illegal in Kenya.

✦ Hopefully, like FGM/C, with greater awareness and understanding, this practice will eventually stop and there will be greater girl-child attendance at school .

✦ Sadly, that day is still too far away for many young girls and both FGM/C and being a 'temporary wife' bring risks of not only pregnancy but also HIV and other infections to the girls of the Samburu people, and their childhood remains stolen.

Ref: Samburu Women Trust
and Samburu Girl's Foundation

Population statistics

The UN states that:

◆ *the current global population is approximately 7.25 billion (or 7,250 thousand million). And, that this is will increase by 1 billion over the next 12 years and reach 9.6 billion by 2050;*

◆ *the population of developed regions will remain largely unchanged at around 1.3 billion from now until 2050.*

◆ *But, in contrast, the 49 least developed countries are projected to double in size from around 900 million people in 2013 to 1.8 billion in 2050.*

What is child marriage?

UNICEF states that:

◆ *child marriage, is a formal marriage or informal union* (sex) *before age 18;*

◆ *it is a reality for both boys and girls, although girls are, disproportionately, the most affected;*

◆ *about a third of women aged 20-24 years old in the developing world were married as children; and*

◆ *child marriage is most common in South Asia and Sub-Saharan Africa, but there are big differences in prevalence among countries of the same region.*

◆ They also state that *700 million women, who are alive today, were married before their 18th birthday.*

◆ *Of which, about 250 million entered in to this before they were 15 years of age.*

◆ Rates of child marriage vary, even within countries where it is common practice.

Why is it called child marriage when the young person is in their mid teens?

◆ In many countries, the legal system recognises that there is an age of majority, when childhood officially ends and adulthood legally starts.

◆ The term *'child marriage'* applies to anyone who is under the age of majority, so not yet considered to be an adult, in law.

◆ The age of majority ranges from 15 to 21, with 18 being the most common age.

Rural v city living; and education

◆ Rates of child marriage are twice as high amongst girls living in rural areas than urban *(city)* environments.

◆ Rates of child marriage *(or early union)* are higher in areas where girls have little or no formal education. *(e.g. see page 200)*

◆ Tradition and / or poverty may dictate that girls are married early, rather than an investment made in their educational.

◆ Increasing the availability of secondary education for girls decreases their risk of becoming a child bride. It improves their prospects and life chances, helping to reduce poverty and protect the lives of any future children.

Risks associated with becoming a child bride (early marriage/union)

Some of the increased risks for girls who marry as children *(under 15)* are listed here, but are not limited to:

◆ being socially isolated *(which can lead to: depression, self-harm, great unhappiness and related problems);*

◆ being financially and otherwise dependant on their husband;

◆ having low self-esteem;

◆ not having many opportunities in life, including employment and/or financial independence;

◆ not having their own friends or other sources of support;

◆ having lower levels of education, including literacy and numeracy;

◆ being unaware of the sexual health risks they may encounter;

◆ being less able to insist on, safer sex;

◆ being more vulnerable to sexual infections, including HIV and Hepatitis B;

◆ having early pregnancy;

◆ having multiple pregnancies, especially if they're compared with adult brides;

◆ not realising they're pregnant, or having baby safely, in a healthcare setting;

◆ not receiving adequate or any antenatal care during pregnancy;

◆ complications of pregnancy and / or childbirth, both for the girl and the baby as young girls are not physically mature enough to give birth;

◆ poverty - especially if the man leaves them, doesn't earn much or spends money unwisely / irresponsibly.

The Law & Sex — FGM / FGC
Child Marriage

Which girls are more at risk of becoming child brides?

✦ In general, poor, uneducated girls, often living in rural environments where child marriage is traditionally practiced are at greatest risk of being forced to become child brides.

✦ Others are at risk if their parents believe in child marriage; see their children as a currency *(a commodity to sell)* if someone offers them money for them, and / or if they are strongly influenced by other members of their community.

Are rates of child marriage declining?

✦ Thankfully, the rates of child marriage are going down in most countries where it is common practice. However, more still needs to be done to protect children in areas where this has not yet changed significantly.

Is it legal to force someone to marry?

✦ No. It is against the law to force anyone to marry; just as it is not legal to pay someone to marry another person.

✦ In the UK, the Home Office states that a forced marriage *"is one in which one or both spouses do not consent to the marriage but are coerced into it"* by means including *physical, psychological, financial, sexual and emotional pressure"*.

✦ It also says that *"in the cases of vulnerable adults who lack the capacity to consent to marriage, coercion is not required for a marriage to be forced"*.

✦ *For more on the law and forced marriage, see page 166.*

What does the future hold for present and future generations of girls?

UNICEF states that:
✦ *Of the world's 1.1 billion girls, 22 million are already married.*
✦ *Hundreds of millions more are at risk.*
✦ *The number will grow as populations increase.*

What's the difference between an arranged marriage and a forced marriage?

✦ Traditionally, an arranged marriage is when a child's parents choose a husband or wife for them and they ARE given a choice about whether they want to marry that person.

✦ A forced marriage, is just that. NO CHOICE is given to the person about whom they will marry, when or where and in the case of young brides, their future husband is often several years older.

✦ In both cases: in some societies he/his family may have paid an amount of money to her parents, to marry her *(bride price)*; and her father may have paid an amount of money to his parents *(a dowry)*.

At what age can young people marry in the UK?

✦ In the UK, young people can marry with parental consent at 16 or without their consent when they become adults at 18.

✦ There are young couples under the age of 18 who marry, voluntarily, for love, and it works well for them. There are others who marry young, then split up.

✦ Marriage that's entered in to freely is quite different from a forced marriage.

✦ All children deserve their childhood, wherever, and with whomsoever they live in the world. Marriage can, and should, wait!

✦ *For much more information on Child Marriage, see www.UNICEF.org and www.GirlsNotBrides.org*

Ending child marriage will help break the intergenerational cycle of poverty by allowing girls and women to participate more fully in society.

Empowered and educated girls are better able to nourish and care for their children, leading to healthier, smaller families.

When girls are allowed to be girls, everybody wins.

UNICEF 2013

What does the word fistula mean?

✦ Fistula *(fis-tu-la)* is the Latin word for tube or pipe.
✦ Medically, a fistula is an abnormal tube or passage between one organ, blood vessel, or two areas of the intestine, commonly caused by injury or surgery.
✦ Usually caused by injury or surgery, they may follow infection or inflammation.
✦ Single - fistula.
✦ Pleural - fistulas or fistulae *(fis-tu-lee)*.

What is an obstetric fistula?

✦ Obstetric fistulae are passages that either develop between the rectum and the vagina or the vagina and the bladder.
✦ It can affect any woman but it most commonly occurs amongst women who are: young; poor; illiterate, living in remote areas; unable to obtain good medical care during pregnancy; who have had Type 3 or 4 FGM; and / or forced abortion.

How do obstetric fistulae occur?

✦ Obstetric fistulae occur when there is obstructed or delayed labour and the baby presses hard against the vagina for a long time, cutting off blood supply to the vagina and rectum or to the vagina and bladder.
✦ Therefore oxygen is cut off to these areas, causing the tissues to die.
✦ This causes fistula formation.

What might the woman notice>?

The woman may notice one or more of the following after giving birth:
✦ flatulence *(excess 'wind')*;
✦ urinary incontinence *(being unable to hold her urine (wee))*;
✦ faecal incontinence *(being unable to hold her faeces (poo))*;
✦ a foul-smelling vaginal dicharge;
✦ recurrent vaginal infections;
✦ recurrent urinary tract infections;
✦ vulval pain or irritation - genital discomfort;
✦ pain during sex;

✦ vaginal ulceration;
✦ abscess formation;
✦ future infertility;
✦ 'foot drop' or paralysis of the lower limbs, making her unable to walk because of pressure on and damage to the pelvic nerves;
✦ although, if she is pregnant the baby may be stillborn *(die)*.
✦ Additionally, the woman may experience social isolation, psychological trauma, her health may deteriorate, she has an increased risk of poverty and of being socially stigmatised.

Can this be prevented?

✦ Yes. Good obstetric and antenatal care can prevent this happening.
✦ Improved education and empowerment of girls and women.
✦ Access to and use of contraception.
✦ Delayed sexual activity, marriage and childbirth.

Can obstetric fistulae be repaired?

✦ Yes. Surgery can be performed to repair obstetric fistulae and save the woman's life.
✦ She can also receive psychological and other support to rebuild life and self esteem.

Ref: UNFPA

References and further reading about FGM/C can be found at:
www.fco.gov.uk/fgm;
www.unicef.org;
www.path.org;
www.forwarduk.org.uk; and
www.who.int

Information about 'beading' can be found at:
http://www.wambuiwaithaka.com
http://www.iwgia.org

Information about obstetric fistula:
www.unfpa.org
www.endfistula.org

Safer Sex

Introduction

Information and advice provided here is universal and non-judgmental – i.e. it applies to anyone, regardless of sexual orientation.

It is offered on the basis that no-one can really tell, by looking at another person, whether they have a Sexually Acquired Infection (SAI).

Not all SAIs have instant signs or symptoms. Having one may adversely affect fertility and may be life-threatening.

Think about this!

Doctors, nurses, dentists and surgeons take universal precautions — i.e. they wear latex, polyurethane or nitrile gloves, masks etc. — to protect themselves from their patient during intimate examination.

They also wash their hands thoroughly before and after, touching someone.

In fact, in today's world, you would probably question somoene who didn't.

This protects the patient from them and them from their patient and they should treat all patients the same – i.e. as if there's a risk of infection.

Isn't it, therefore, sensible to assume that there is the same unknown risk when you have sex? Always protect yourself, since each of these scenarios involves contact with the blood or body fluids of another person.

Many people have infections without realising — therefore the aim of this section is to ensure you are protected from all sexually acquired infections, not just HIV*, which can lead to AIDS**.

✦   In the tiny amount of blood involved in a needle stick injury (stab or scratch with a syringe) the chance of getting HIV *(human immunodeficiency virus)*, if it's present, is less than 1 in 300 *(0.3%)*.
✦   BUT - if they're present, the chance of getting Hepatitis B is 1 in 3 *(30%)* and/or Hepatitis C is 1 in 10 *(10%)*.
✦   HIV dies quickly in the open air compared with Hepatitis B and Hepatitis C.

* HIV stands for Human Immunodeficiency Virus, is a virus that can be transmitted sexually, which attacks the immune system.
** AIDS stands for Acquired Immune Deficiency Syndrome, which is a series of conditions that the body can't fight without a healthy immune system.

Think about this!

✦   Certain sexual activities take place which aren't usually discussed openly by young people.
✦   The following is an assessment of the level of risk involved according to the sexual activity.

Safer Sex

Safer Sex

Safer Sex

The safest, if somewhat unromantic, steps to take before embarking on a sexual relationship would be to:

✦ confirm your partner's sexual health and wellbeing by each taking a test at a Sexual Health Clinic and re-test after three months, if necessary;
✦ use a condom properly and routinely, BUT remember that even the best of condoms can fail occasionally; and/or
✦ remain faithful.

When you are in a relationship, being unfaithful includes casual sex with male or female sex workers *(prostitutes)*, casual gay or bisexual sex, having several regular partners or being involved in group sex *(orgy / swinging)*, **without your partner's knowledge.**

Otherwise, you are at risk from the hundreds of millions of people with viral Hepatitis, HIV and others with major or minor SAIs throughout the world, who continue to have unprotected sex.

So, it's better to be safe than take unnecessary risks. You only have one life. Protect it. Practice safer sex !

Even if it's unrealistic, the safest kind of sex is 'no sex at all'!

Safer sex is the same for everyone, whether you're:

✦ **straight** – a man who is sexually attracted to women or a woman who is sexually attracted to men *(heterosexual)*;
✦ **a gay man** — a man who is sexually attracted to other men *(homosexual)*;
✦ **lesbian** — a woman who is sexually attracted to other women;
✦ **bisexual** – someone who is sexually attracted to both men and women;
✦ **transvestite** – someone who likes to wear clothing associated with the opposite sex;
✦ **transgender** – someone who believes that they belong to the opposite sex, and may undergo 'gender reassignment surgery' to make their external genitalia conform to their view of themselves.

For protection against all sexually acquired infections, it is recommended that you:
✦ employ precautions as a matter of routine – i.e. ensure condoms and/or dental dams are routinely used *(see page 210)*;
✦ consider the exchange or potential exchange of body fluid to be a risk — especially if it is blood-stained;
✦ cover any cuts or sores on the hand with waterproof plaster or wear latex gloves during foreplay / intimate contact.

Some sexual activities take place, which are seldom discussed openly by young people, or even by adults.

Safer Sex

Safer Sex

Sexplained Two — For Changing Times ® © 1999-2016

Safer Sex

This section assesses of the level of risk according to particular sexual activity; with an emphasis on the prevention of bacterial conditions, e.g. gonorrhoea, chlamydia and blood bourne conditions such as syphilis, Hepatitis B, and HIV.

Skin to skin viral conditions, such as genital warts or herpes cannot always be prevented.

High risk activities include — anything unprotected with someone whose infection status you do not know, e.g.:
✦ unprotected anal sex;
✦ unprotected vaginal sex;
✦ giving oral sex *(a blow job/fellatio)* to a man if his ejaculate enters your mouth;
✦ giving unprotected oral sex to *(going down on/cunnilingus)* a woman during menstruation / her period;
✦ unprotected finger insertion (anal or vaginal) if there are cuts, sores, bleeding piles *(haemorrhoids)* or a female partner has her period;
✦ withdrawal *(pulling out)* before ejaculation with a casual sexual partner, without wearing a condom;
✦ rimming – i.e. licking your partner's anus *(anilingus)* – without the protection of a barrier such as a dental dam;
✦ fisting — insertion of the hand or fist into the vagina or the rectum. With or without the protection of extra long latex or nitrile gloves, this activity carries serious health risks and should NEVER be attempted without fully understanding all of the risks that are involved.

For in depth information about genital conditions and sexually acquired infections, please see the author's other title:
Sexplained One — Sex & Your Health.
Available from
www.KnoxPublishing.com

Medium risk activities include:
✦ giving unprotected oral sex to a man without taking his ejaculate into your mouth;
✦ giving unprotected sex to a woman who is not on her period;
✦ protected vaginal or anal sex;
✦ rimming — i.e. licking your partner's anus – with the protection of a barrier such as a dental dam;
✦ finger insertion *(anal or vaginal)* but safer when broken skin, cuts, sores etc. are covered with waterproof plaster, condom over the finger or latex gloves are worn;
✦ wet kissing *(deep French kissing)*. Safety depends upon the health of your lips and mouth and those of your partner*(s)*.

Low risk activities for SAIs and alternatives to penetrative sex include:
✦ masturbating on your own;
✦ masturbating your partner (heavy petting) but, if any part of your hand enters their body you should make sure that cuts, rashes or sores are covered by waterproof plaster or latex gloves beforehand;
✦ dry kissing;
✦ hugging;
✦ love bites;
✦ sexual arousal; fully clothed and remaining so!
✦ And, anything else you can think of which doesn't involve the exchange of body fluids and gives mutual *(both of you)* pleasure by consent *(with permission)*.

IMPORTANT: If you use massage or body moisturising oils, they must be fully washed off the penis before using a latex/rubbr condom because the rubber may rot and the condom is likely to break. Non-latex condoms can be used with more lubricants.

Safer Sex — Oral Sex

Is oral sex when you 'talk dirty' to each other?

It may, but not in a sexual context. Oral sex also means mouth to genital contact to most people.

Performing oral sex on a man is called fellatio. It's commonly called a 'blow job' – but you don't blow – you lick – then suck his penis.

Oral sex performed on a woman is called cunnilingus or 'going down on' and, similarly, involves licking or sucking her clitoris, labia and vulva.

Oral sex can give your partner enough sexual pleasure to reach orgasm and some people prefer to have oral sex to penetrative sex

Other people don't enjoy oral sex and that's OK.

Is it really OK not to want oral sex?

Yes. It's quite OK not to want oral sex.

If you don't fancy it, simply tell your partner that you would rather not do it.

Tell them gently, so they don't feel you don't want them. It's simply that you don't want to do something that they want you to do.

Never allow anyone to pressure you in to oral sex. If you're going to do it, there are some things you may not realise.

(1) In the context of a long-term, loving, trusting relationship, where each of you has been fully tested for any SAIs before you have penetrative sex together, oral sex is a fairly safe, low risk type of sex.

(2) Sore throat germs can still pass either way, the risk of developing NGU, genital thrush or BV *(bacterial vaginosis)* is possible.

(3) The risk of infection increases considerably if you have casual unprotected oral sex with someone you later find out has gonorrhoea, herpes, warts, hepatitis, syphilis, or any other sexually transmittable infection – in their mouth.

(4) If you're unfaithful to your partner, you risk being found out if you transfer an infection to them after having unprotected oral sex with someone else.

(5) Since many SAI can be caught in, or transferred from, someone's mouth to your genitalia – or from their genitalia to your mouth – flavoured condoms are recommended when giving oral sex to a man.

Dental or oral dams are advised when giving oral sex to a woman – or, if you lick your partner's anus (anilingus / rimming).

(6) Alternatively, you can cut a flavoured condom along one side, open it out and place this over their genital area before oral sex, if you don't have a dental or oral dam.

(7) Hepatitis B and C viruses can be present in infected blood and blood-stained body fluids.

If you don't know whether your partner has hepatitis, you should ensure that cuts and sores on your fingers are covered with waterproof plaster or latex gloves before you start any genital foreplay. It's considered good sexual manners to wash your genital area before you receive oral sex.

Can a woman get pregnant if she only has oral sex?

✦ No, a woman cannot pregnant through oral sex, alone.

I've heard of the 69 position. What is that and how do you do it?

✦ The 69 position is one of the common positions used by a couple when having oral sex.
✦ You may face each other's feet and curl round to enable you to reach each other's genital area with your mouth.
✦ You then look like a 6 and 9 in position – hence the name, 69 position.
✦ It's also known as the Yin and Yang position.

Should condoms be used during oral sex?

✦ Yes. Just as you would use condoms routinely when having penetrative sex, it's sensible to protect your mouth when giving oral sex to your partner; or from being passed an infection they may have in their mouth.
✦ Flavoured condoms should be worn over a penis when giving oral sex to a man *(blow job/fellatio)*.

Safer Sex — Oral Sex

Safer Sex — Condoms

What are dental / oral dams? I've never heard of them before, and neither have my friends.

Dental dams are squares or oblongs of latex *(rubber)* or polyurethane, which are placed over the genital area before oral stimulation. Originally, these were simply sheets of latex *(rubber)* used by dentists, until someone decided to use them as barrier protection to keep their mouth safe during oral sex.

Just as you would use condoms routinely when having penetrative sex, it's sensible to protect your mouth when giving oral sex to your partner.

Condoms should be worn over a penis when giving oral sex to a man *(blow job / fellatio)*. There are flavoured condoms that are designed for this but any condom can be used.

Dental dams are expensive, should be used only once and don't have a 'this way up' sign on them so, you might want to mark them, yourself.

Otherwise, if the dam falls off and you replace it without checking, you could put it back the wrong way round, and defeat the purpose of using it, in the first place!

Alternatively, make your own by cutting a flavoured condom from base to tip, then open it out to make a barrier.

In an emergency, you could use some microwave cling film but this does not give as much protection as latex.

Also see the section on **Gel Charging**, on page 222.

Oral dams

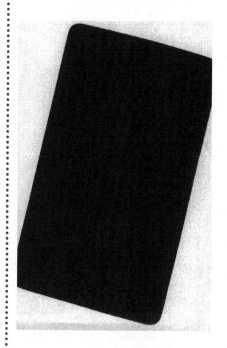

Safer Sex — Condoms

Can I use flavoured condoms during penetrative sex?

Yes. You can use flavoured condoms quite safely during penetrative sex.

BUT – if you WEAR LIPSTICK when performing oral sex, change the condom before having penetrative sex, since lipstick rots latex.

If you DON'T wear lipstick, you're safer to go from giving oral sex to having penetrative sex with the same condom, as long as it hasn't been otherwise damaged.

You may need to use extra lubricant to make penetrative sex more comfortable if the lubricant on the flavoured condom has come off.

A dry condom can cause stinging and general discomfort.

In this case, be careful to use water or silicone-based lubricant, NOT oil-based.

What if a partner tells me not to use condoms because they don't like them?

It's simple; don't have sex with them!

If they won't use condoms with you, it's more than likely they haven't used them with their previous partner(s).

Do you really want to receive all their germs?

Tell them: Sorry, no condoms, no sex. Try elsewhere. I value myself.

If someone carries condoms, does this mean she is promiscuous (easy / slack / sleep around)?

No. Carrying condoms does not mean a woman is promiscuous.

If she's sexually active, it means she's mature enough to take responsibility for her health and safety and that of her partner.

Her partner may not be sufficiently organised to protect them both.

If she's not sexually active at least she has the right idea about protecting herself when she does have sex.

Respecting herself and her partner's health is an important step to maturity.

Some adults dislike touching a condom. But being familiar with them is an important step in learning to look after yourself. It is good safer sexual practice and a good habit to develop.

But I can tell if she's a clean girl or a dirty girl

✦ No, you can't. It's impossible to tell, just by looking, or talking to someone if they have a transmittable infection.
✦ Your nose, eyes or brain aren't capable of detecting hidden bacteria or viruses lurking in someone's genitalia.

Should I practice using a condom on my own?

Yes. You should practice how to use a condom on your own. Large numbers of people are not skilled in their use. Everyone should know how to use a condom.

If not proficient at using them, men of all ages should practice using a condom until they can wear it quickly and correctly.

It is natural for men to wake up with an early morning erection so take advantage of this and practice, practice, practice!

If you're skilled at putting one on:
✦ you'll be less embarrassed with a new partner;
✦ you'll be less likely to make a mistake; or for the condom to fail.

Most men don't know how to use a condom properly. Many men weren't brought up to assume responsibility for pregnancy prevention or to think about sexual health protection.

You're a long way ahead of the competition if you know how to use a condom correctly. Who knows, by preventing infection / practicing safer sex, you could also be protecting your life.

Should I practice using a condom on my own if I am a woman?

Yes. Women of all ages should be condom proficient and should practice the skill of using condoms. Knowing how to use a condom correctly could protect you if your partner does not know how to use one or if you notice that he has done it incorrectly.

Obviously it won't be quite the same as practicing on an erect penis but since you can't practice on yourself, you can practice your condom application and removal skills using a vibrator, dildo or even a piece of fruit, such as a banana, instead.

When should male condoms be used?

Male condoms should be used to prevent infection and/or pregnancy.

It is vital that a condom is used BEFORE there is ANY genital contact whatsoever, with your partner.

There are approximately 3,000,000 sperm in the clear fluid that forms at the tip of an erect penis *(pre-ejaculate or pre-cum/come)*.

This is enough to cause pregnancy or pass infection in the right conditions, even without penetration occurring.

Important condom tips:

Check that you have more than one condom – in case one fails or you make a mistake.

Far Left:
BSI or British Standards kite mark
Left: CE mark

How are male condoms used?

Wash any massage oils, baby oil or creams off your hands and penis, using soap and water. Oils and latex/rubber do not mix and will split latex condoms. You will not be protected against pregnancy or infection if this happens.

Check the expiry date on the packet and make sure that the condom meets recognised standards – i.e. see if the box is marked with the British Standards kite mark, CE the European mark *(CE stands for Conformité Européenne / European Conformity)*, FDA (US Food and Drugs Administration) mark or the well recognised standard of the country of origin — and also of purchase.

Before taking a sealed condom from the packet, check that the wrapping hasn't been damaged and gently tear the wrapping to expose the condom and squeeze it out. Do NOT use your teeth!

Look at or feel the condom, to check which way round it is going to unroll. Check that the teat *(reservoir)* is easy to hold or if it doesn't have a teat, make your own by squeezing the top 2.5 cms (1 inch) of the condom, to empty the air.

Fig 1 - Take the condom from its wrapping and hold the teat.

Fig 2 - As you place it on top of your own or your partner's fully erect penis. Unroll it, outwards and down over your / his penis for at least 5 cm *(2 inches)* before letting go of the teat. This will ensure that no air slips back into the teat. *(If it does, the condom may burst in use.)*

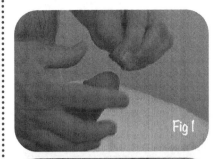

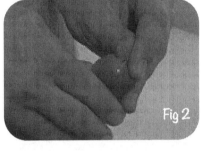

Fig 3 - Continue unrolling the condom

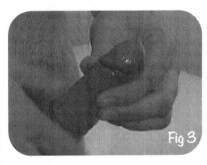

over the penis until - **Fig 4** - you reach the pubic hair line.

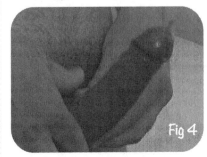

Correct Condom Application

Safer Sex — Condoms

During sex

It's sensible to check that the condom hasn't slipped slightly, as if coming off the penis. You may notice a slight change in sensation if it has.

If the condom has slipped, simply guide it back on to the shaft of the penis and continue.

Re-lubricate, as necessary, using only water-based or silicone lubricant.

If you have sex for a long time – say more than 10 minutes, or less if your partner isn't sufficiently moist/turned on – the condom may become too dry and will weaken. Also, your partner may become sore from dry friction and movement. To overcome this problem, you will need to use extra water based lubricant.

After Ejaculation

Ensure that the condom is held on the penis during withdrawal and that it is withdrawn before the penis starts to go soft/limp.

If you don't, there's a greater chance that the condom may slip off and sperm may spill inside your partner.

This would mean that using the condom was a waste of time and you risk pregnancy / infection.

Condoms should be used ONCE ONLY.

After use, the condom should be wrapped in a tissue and thrown in the bin.

Condoms float, so don't try to flush them down the toilet!

If anything goes wrong

If the condom splits or comes off before withdrawal, remember emergency contraception may be appropriate.

When it is taken within the first one to 24-72 hours *(three days)* after unprotected sex the most commonly used form of emergency contraception can prevent up to 95% of unplanned pregnancies. Containing a single progestogen, levonorgestrel, it is more reliable when taken within the first 24 hours.

Less widely available is another type of emergency hormonal pill, which is licensed for use up to 120 hours (five days) after unprotected sex, containing Ulipristal acetate.

Alternatively, an emergency IUD *(intrauterine contraceptive device)* can be inserted by a specially qualified practitioner, to prevent an unplanned pregnancy.

See Section 4, p75 about 'Emergency Contraception' for further information.

A Sexual Health Clinic can help if you are worried about infection. Many places are integrating contraception and sexual health services, so both concerns may be addressed with one visit. Other areas separate contraception and sexual health work, so you may have to visit two separate, but specialist facilities.

Emergency contraceptive pills can be obtained from family doctors, family planning / contraception clinics, Sexual Health Clinics, pharmacies — and it is commonly free of charge in the UK.

Safer Sex — Condoms

Don't take any extra risks. It is a very safe medication and, depending on circumstances, can be used more than once in a menstrual cycle.

Contact your local pharmacy, hospital, clinic or healthcare practitioner if you are concerned and do not know where to obtain this type of help locally.

What if the condom won't roll right down?

Check that the condom is round the right way – and not inside out. If it's inside out, throw it away and start again.

Longer condoms are available which may be more suitable.

Your local pharmacy may be able to obtain or help you source a range of different or longer condoms.

What if I make a mistake and put a condom on inside out?

If this happens, throw the condom away, immediately.

Do NOT turn it over and try again because any sperm or germs can be transferred directly inside your partner, risking pregnancy and/or infection.

It burst, it leaks, and it doesn't feel the same, why?

If your partner is not sufficiently moist or lubricated, the condom will dry out which will make it sore to use and, more likely to burst from increased tension and friction.

What if I don't get all the air out of the teat?

Air in the teat is said to be a contributing factor when condoms fail.

The pressure of ejaculation against the trapped air is thought to weaken the rubber and make the condom more likely to burst – usually along the shaft of the penis.

What if I have long nails, hang nails or rough nails?

Be careful. Your nails could puncture the rubber.

Condoms are too big for me, what should I do?

Condoms are available to accommodate all sizes of mature penis. Smaller and tighter condoms are available.

If you're young and they are too big for you, you could wait until you're fully grown before you have sex and are physically mature.

Your local clinic or pharmacist may be able to obtain or help you source a different range of condoms.

Some men suggest

Try thicker condoms, if you are concerned about ejaculating too quickly (premature ejaculation).

Try tighter/smaller condoms, or gel (jel) charging the condom carefully if you are concerned about a delay in ejaculation. This may help you ejaculate more easily but must be undertaken with care and is not suitable for all men.

Condoms are too small for me, so I can't wear them.

A few years ago you might have got away with the excuse, that condoms are too small. Today, however, there's a huge range from which to choose.

Try various brands, until you find one that suits you. Changing to a thinner condom on which the ring at the base is not so thick might make it more comfortable to wear, but better still find the correct size of condom for your requirements. A condom that is the right size for you doesn't have to stretch excessively to fit – in turn minimising any feelings of tightness or discomfort and meaning you'll feel more during use.

Condoms come with short teats, long teats or no teats; straight sides, flared sides; baggy tips or tight fit; with or without spermicide; with or without lubricant, various colours and flavours; various thickness; with or without ribbing; and different lengths.

There are hypo-allergenic (low allergy) condoms; polyurethane condoms; and condoms made from natural lamb membrane, so try each until you find one that suits you.

Since a British company (TheyFit.co.uk) entered the market in December 2011, the size range of condoms has changed for men around the world. They have introduced 'custom fit condoms' and with FDA* and EU** approval, **offer 95 sizes, ranging from a circumference of:**
—94-114mm (approx 3.5-4.5 ins) (USA);
—82-138mm (approx 4.5-5.5 ins) (EU).
And a length range of:
—80-240mm (approx 3.25-9.5 ins).

So, although it may be true of the average condom range available in most retail outlets, there is now no reason for a man to say that 'condoms are too big' or 'condoms are too small' for him! There is a condom to suit all men!

If I wear two condoms, I'll be double safe, won't I?

No. You won't be twice as safe if you wear two condoms. Although this is suggested in some parts of the world, condom manufacturers certainly don't recommend wearing two condoms at a time. Condoms are more likely to fail if they are used this way.

If you are concerned, you can use an extra or ultra strong variety of condom instead – with additional water or recommended silicone-based lubricant.

Can I use a flavoured condom for penetrative vaginal sex?

✦ Yes. Using a non-spermicidally lubricated or flavoured condom for vaginal penetrative sex correctly is thought to be equally effective.
✦ It's important to use extra lubricant with either type of condom when it becomes dry and uncomfortable. This reduces any discomfort.
✦ Some women develop thrush (candidiasis or yeast infection) or BV (bacterial vaginosis) afterwards but this is safer than having unprotected sex and an SAI!

* FDA - Food and Drug Administration (USA)
** EU - European Union

I'm allergic to condoms.

Nowadays, hypo-allergenic *(low allergy)* condoms are available.

It may not be the condom but the lubricant on it that's causing the discomfort and depending on where you are in the world, you may be using spermicidally lubricated condoms.

These are no longer recommended, especially for protected anal sex.

Spermicide is an irritant and an inflamed area of mucous membrane is vulnerable to infection.

Change from condoms with spermicide on them, *(nonoxynol 9 or 11)* to condoms that are lubricated, only.

Dryness can make sex very uncomfortable for both partners with or without condoms. To reduce this, use a lot of extra water-based or recommended silicone lubricant incase the allergy is friction based – i.e. from being too dry.

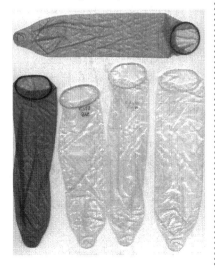

Are there any new male condoms?

Yes, there are polyurethane and also nitrile condoms available now.

The polyurethane ones are more expensive but the main differences and / or advantages are:
(a) any lubricant can be used with it – not just water-based ones;
(b) it doesn't stretch as much as a latex condom;
(c) it is much wider;.
(d) greater sensitivity can be expected;
(e) the polyurethane hardly smells;
(f) it's ideal for men or women who are allergic to all forms of latex, including the hypo-allergenic (low allergy) condoms.
✦ You must be careful to hold it on your penis after each ejaculation, when withdrawing after penetrative sex.

Other non-latex condoms

I've never heard of polyisoprene condoms. What are they like?

✦ Polyisoprene condoms are quite new, with only a few styles available.
✦ Polyisoprene is made by taking natural latex rubber and sending it through a process to removes any latex allergens.
✦ The result is a material that is very similar to latex but is better tolerated by a wide range of people.
✦ Also, the material is not expensive to produce.
✦ A drawback, for some people, is that it is possible to be allergic to it, and although this is rare, but not unheard of.

What is spermicide?

Spermicide is a chemical that kills sperm. It is powerful and can cause irritation and inflammation on areas of mucous membrane, making them vulnerable to infection.

Spermicide is no longer recommended with condoms. It is, however, still used by women who use a diaphragm of cervical cap for contraception.

NOTE: the chemicals in spermicides are strong enough to soften nail polish, so take extra care if your nails are manicured with varnish!

Should I use extra spermicide with my condoms?

No. You should not use extra spermicide with condoms. You should use extra water based lubricant instead.

Some studies show that by using extra spermicide you can reduce the chance of acquiring SAIs. However, with frequent use it may cause irritation and increase the risk of passing infection.

Although you'd have slightly more protection against unplanned pregnancy if the condom split or came off, the risk of irritation and infection advises against using it.

Should I use spermicidally or non-spermicidally lubricated condoms?

✦ Generally, it doesn't matter which type you use but spermicide can sometimes cause irritation and soreness, which can put people off using condoms.
✦ Some people think they're allergic to condoms when they are just reacting to the spermicide.
✦ Spermicidally lubricated condoms are no longer recommended in many countries because of this, which, in turn, stops many people who need it, from using protection.
✦ It was found that HIV *(human immunodeficiency virus)* may be transmitted more easily to women who used spermicides on a daily basis compared with those who use non-spermicidal products.
✦ Likewise, a dry condom can cause great discomfort and some people think they're allergic to condoms when they really need to use more lubricant with their chosen condom.

Should I use extra lubricant with any type of condom?

✦ Yes. Using extra lubricant is very wise, since a dry or poorly lubricated condom can cause discomfort.
✦ It's especially important if you are having sex for a long time and the condom begins to dry out.
✦ A dry condom can be uncomfortable for both partners.
✦ It is more likely to burst, can cause tiny friction burns and may cause thrush to develop.
✦ Use only water-based lubricants, spermicidal creams or gel *(jel)* from a reliable sales outlet or Sexual Health Clinic. NEVER use oil-based products with latex *(rubber)* condoms. They can ONLY be used with the non-latex products.

Safer Sex — Spermicide

Safer Sex — Lubricants

Which lubricants are safe to use with latex condoms or the female cap / diaphragm?

Anything that is oil-based is UNSAFE to use with latex condoms and / or with the female cap / diaphragm.

Unsafe Lubricants

Everyday products, which are considered UNSAFE to use with latex/rubber male condoms and the female cap/diaphragm include but are not limited to:

+ aromatherapy oils;
+ margarine;
+ butter;
+ low-fat spread;
+ ice cream;
+ suntan oil;
+ lipstick;
+ body oil;
+ cold cream;
+ baby oil;
+ cocoa butter;
+ massage oil;
+ skin softener;
+ hair conditioner;
+ Vaseline®;
+ Petroleum Jelly;
+ engine oil;
+ cream;
+ body paint;
+ chocolate spread/paint;
+ zinc and castor oil;
+ some vaginal medication, including Canesten® / clotrimazole cream;
+ some soaps *(oil based)*.

Plus, anything else that requires soap and water to wash them off your hands.

NOTE: If there is ANY risk of viral hepatitis infection, saliva must NOT be used as a lubricant.

Safe Lubricants

There are many vaginal and anal preparations that are considered to be SAFE to use with male latex/rubber condoms or the female cap / diaphragm and include, but are not limited to:

+ aqueous enemas;
+ silicone based lubricants;
+ spermicidal creams and gels;
+ water-based lubricant.

Check with the manufacturer or your local pharmacist about different products, especially if you are using vaginal or anal medication.

NOTE: if in doubt about a product, do not consider it to be safe until it is reliably confirmed to be so.

Ladies, please note!

+ If you wear nail polish when you put a spermicidally lubricated condom onto your partner, use spermicide with your cap, or diaphragm, the spermicide may soften your nail polish.

Safer Sex — Lubricants

To all men and women

NEVER use an oil-based lubricant with rubber/latex condoms. Oil based lubricants can damage the latex.

✦ Use water based lubricants ONLY or they will perish *(rot)* the latex in a very short time and make the condom more likely to burst.

✦ A damaged condom could put you at risk of pregnancy and/or infection.

✦ Water based lubricants are safe and can be washed off your hands with only water.

✦ Vaseline®, baby oil, massage oil, lipstick, petroleum jelly, hand cream, suntan oil, butter, margarine, or anything which needs soap and water to wash off your hands MUST NOT BE USED with latex condoms.

✦ If any oil gets onto your penis before sex *(massage oil etc.)*, it must be washed off with soap and water before the condom is put on. This is because there may be enough oil left on the penis to rot the condom!

✦ If you think you are at risk of sexually acquired infections you should visit a Sexual Health Clinic – and particularly if you if you notice any unusual lumps, bumps, discharges, smells or sores in your mouth or genital area after sex.

✦ Seek help if you're worried.

✦ Remember: Emergency Contraception is available should the condom fail.

✦ *For further information on Emergency Contraception, see page 75.*

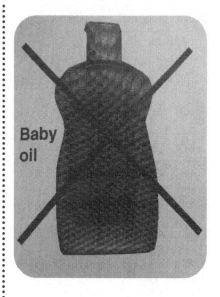

Baby oil

Is anal sex legal?

Yes. In the UK, anal sex became legal between consenting heterosexual *(opposite sex)* couples, over the age of 18, in April 1995.

Now, it is legal between consenting homosexual and heterosexual couples over the age of 16 in the UK and Northern Ireland.

Even today, anal sex between consenting homosexual *(same sex)* couples is illegal across one third of the world and it carries a wide range of penalties.

Different countries have different age limits and related laws.

Which condom can I use for anal sex?

There are no recognised anal sex quality 'standard' to which condoms can be tested. Therefore no condom is formally recommended for anal sex.

There are extra strong condoms available that some people prefer to use during anal sex but any non-spermicidally lubricated condom, used correctly, can provide protection during anal sex.

However, a dry or semi-dry condom is more likely to fail. Therefore, if indulging in anal sex, it is essential that plenty of additional water-based or recommended silicone-based lubricant is used to reduce stress on the condom and prevent failure.

Alternatively, a female condom, which is made of polyurethane or nitrile instead of latex, has been used successfully by men having anal sex with other men. They commonly adapt it by removing the inner positioning ring during use if using FC1 or FC2 *(see page 223)*.

Safer Sex — Anal Sex

Safer Sex — Gel Charging

Safer Sex — Gel Charging

What's Gel Charging?

Novice condom wearers should NOT try this.

Some men say that gel charging is 'wetter and better than sex without a condom'. But, before trying this, you must ensure you are proficient at the skills of condom application and gel charging BEFORE you decide to use a charged condom during sex.

Gel charging is when a small amount of water-based lubricant is placed inside the tip/teat of a condom before it's put on. The extra moistness of gel *(jel)* charging is said to increase the sensation and sensitivity, especially for circumcised men.

When using this, remember to expel the air carefully from the top 2.5 cms *(1 inch)* beyond the lubricant, before rolling the condom over the penis.

Be careful to only massage the lubricant over the glans *(helmet / hood)*. Do not get the lubricant down the shaft of the penis because it is likely to make the condom slip down or off.

Uncircumcised men may find that holding the foreskin right back before putting on a condom may help and additional lubricant may not be required.

Condom application and gel charging may seem a bit of a nuisance but, if when built in to foreplay, this can add enjoyment and increase the sensation — and a couple's communication together.

Gel charging is NOT suitable for all men.

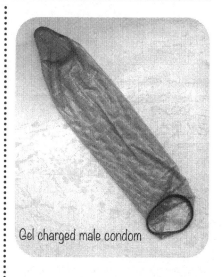

Gel charged male condom

Two types of female condom

Woman's / Female Condom

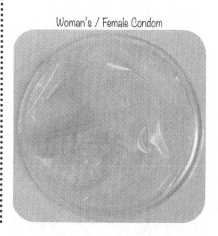

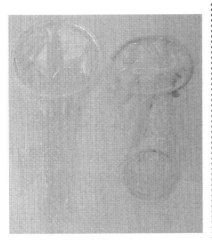

What are Female Condoms?

There are several different designs of female condom, made by a range of different manufacturers. They are designed to be used under the control of the woman rather than the man.

A woman inserts it into her vagina prior to sexual activity although it may be inserted by her partner during foreplay.

Alternatively, if the woman doesn't want to touch herself, her partner can wear it over his penis and penetrate her vagina to insert it.

It is designed to stay in place inside the vagina, as if lining it.

The Female Condom (FC1 and FC2), invented in the 1980s came to the market in the early 1990s, and is like a large, loose, lubricated condom with an outer ring to stop it from being pushed inside the vagina during sex and a loose inner ring that is used to help the woman insert it into her vagina. The inner ring holds the condom inside her vagina.

The Woman's Condom by PATH (Program for Appropriate Technology in Health), called here on it's packaging Female Condom, has a tampon shaped insertion device with four small dots of soft, absorbent foam instead of the inner ring. These hold the polyurethane condom securely in place during use and allow easy removal. It is not lubricated, so additional lubricant should be used with it, for comfort.

Although some people wash them and use them again, at present female condoms are licenced for single use.

The original (FC1) was made of polyurethane. Recently updated using nitrile (FC2), it is pre-lubricated and, because it is not made of latex (rubber), any lubricant can be used.

The man does not have to withdraw quickly after ejaculation. His penis can stay inside the vagina when it goes soft.

Female condoms are much more expensive than male condoms but offer an extremely viable alternative for a lot of women.

Designed for vaginal sex, they are sometimes used during anal sex. For comfort, the inner ring of FC1 or FC2 is generally removed prior to anal penetration and, whichever make, the condom is commonly worn by the man over his penis, as if it's an oversized condom.

Safer Sex — Gel Charging

How do I negotiate having safer sex when we have not been using condoms but have been together for a long time?

✦ This can be tricky!
✦ You could simply tell your partner that this is what you want to do, from now on. But how will they react?
✦ It's a question you will have to discuss together and examine your reasons for asking, very honestly.
✦ Introducing this question into your relationship for other reasons can be extremely difficult and is loaded with emotion.

You may have been advised, or wish:

(a) to change from other methods of contraception to condoms for medical reasons;
(b) to use protection in addition to hormonal methods at certain times;
(c) to take a rest from the responsibility of birth control and want to pass this to your partner;
(d) because it's now routine practise for sexual health staff to recommend a Double Dutch approach – ie. use condoms plus another method of birth control – plus the routine use of extra spermicide;
(e) your partner and furnishings stay drier after sex, as the ejaculate is contained within the condom!

What would this question imply if your partner asks to use a condom?

Would it mean:

– I don't trust you to be faithful;
– I want to be unfaithful and use condoms with you, too – just in case I catch an infection and bring it back home;
– it's a good idea, just in case either of us is unfaithful;
– I trust you and hope you really trust me. If we use condoms routinely, you'll have more peace of mind and feel safer *(just in case you don't really trust me but don't know how to tell me)*; or
– I'd like us to use them so I can relax and feel that you feel safer, with me?

✦ Should you make an absolute promise to remain faithful to each other and be honest, before either of you is unfaithful? This also gives you the chance to get your relationship back on course and avoid the so-called need to be unfaithful and the associated emotional hurt and pain.
✦ Should you go for a full sexual health check-up together, realise the implications of unfaithfulness and have an equal fear of the other's potential of being unfaithful. Then do you let that fear keep you faithful to your partner because of how you would feel if they were unfaithful to you and put your health at risk?
✦ Many people assume that it's OK to have unsafe sex with their regular partner but have safer sex with a casual partner.
✦ They think that using a condom is all the precaution necessary to keep their secret undiscovered.
✦ Not all sexually acquired infections have instant signs or symptoms, but can ruin the good thing you had, when your regular partner realises they've been cheated, deceived and their health put at risk!

Practise safer sex – ie:

(a) full STI check up before you have sex together. Re-testing after 3 months, if necessary.
(b) use a condom, routinely.
(c) be FAITHFUL or ABSTAIN *(NO SEX)!*

✦ Unfaithfulness is common, very unfair and brings nothing but misery when you're caught out.
✦ Being unfaithful includes casual sex with male or female sex workers (prostitutes), casual gay or bisexual sex, having several regular partners or being involved in group sex *(orgy / swinging)*.

REMEMBER

✦ Even the best condoms CAN fail.
✦ Condoms cannot protect against all, especially 'skin to skin' acquired infections.
✦ Not all sexually acquired infections show signs or give symptoms.
✦ Practising safer sex routinely, could literally save your life.

What if we always have safer sex but then want to have a baby?

✦ Each of you will want to know that you're safe from infection.
✦ The only sure way is for you and your partner to be fully tested at a Sexual Health Clinic before you have unprotected sex together.
✦ Again, you'll have to trust your partner isn't having sex outside your relationship – even if he/she uses a condom, you have no guarantee.
✦ After it's confirmed you can return to using condoms for protection throughout the pregnancy in case either of you has sex outside the relationship.
✦ Some men don't like to have sex with a pregnant woman. They find it impossible to remain faithful and stray towards someone else during this time – and make all kinds of excuses for their behaviour.
✦ If you're worried about having sex during pregnancy mention this to your midwife or doctor.
✦ It's usually safe for the woman *(and your baby)* to have sex well into pregnancy, so don't risk ruining a good relationship. Think very carefully before having sex elsewhere.
✦ Sex doesn't just mean penetration. There are many other ways to express close feelings and receive sexual pleasure and satisfaction.
✦ Potentially, it is serious for mother and baby to catch a sexually acquired infection – and, of course, you'd be caught out.
✦ If you can't control your penis during your partner's pregnancy, you will almost certainly regret it later. And for what? A few minutes fun which you could still enjoy without penetration.
✦ Remember: respect your lady and you will enjoy the closeness of your family and new baby.

Negotiating Safer Sex

What about artificial insemination?

✦ Artificial insemination is where a female receives the sperm of a man without having sexual intercourse.

✦ Sperm donated to clinics specialising in this type of assisted conception has, for many years, been tested for HIV and some other infections.

✦ Sperm donated by a male friend for this purpose may put you at risk unless he has been fully tested for infection and counselled about the legal and emotional implications of donating sperm.

✦ Becoming pregnant through a one-night stand or other form of casual sex as a single parent *(or part of a lesbian couple bringing up a child together)* involves high-risk sex and you are strongly advised against it.

A sobering thought

✦ A woman is many times more likely to catch HIV from a man than a man is from a woman.

✦ Most men get HIV from one-night stands.

✦ Most women get HIV in long-term relationships.

✦ Many of these women find out that their partner has been unfaithful with another woman – although many find out it was with another man.

✦ A large number of men are closet *(secret)* bisexuals. They have sex with other men but are in denial. They don't consider themselves to be unfaithful to their female partner. They don't identify themselves as being gay or bisexual.

✦ Since many missed out on the information passed on throughout the gay community when HIV was first identified as an extremely serious infection, they don't employ safer sex correctly or sufficiently.

✦ Large numbers of people *(whatever their sexuality)* fail to enquire about the sexual history or infection status of a new partner before having sex.

✦ Having any SAI increases your risk of contracting Hepatitis or HIV – and vice-versa.

✦ Hepatitis B virus can live for two weeks and Hepatitis C virus can live for three weeks in dried blood.

✦ 80% of the intravenous / injecting drug users *(junkies)* in the UK are said to be Hepatitis C positive.

✦ There is a vaccine against Hepatitis A and B – but NOT against Hepatitis C.

✦ Hepatitis B and C cause 82% of the world's liver cancer.

✦ By denying that you're at risk or failing to practise safer sex, you put your regular partner and, even perhaps your family, at risk – as well as yourself.

✦ You can only know your own sexual history, not that of your partner*(s)*.

Safer Sex

Safer Sex

Some general points to remember

✦ You should: cover any broken or scabbed areas of skin or bleeding hang nails with waterproof plasters; or wear latex gloves for best protection from infection during foreplay.

✦ There's a risk of getting infection from unprotected oral sex. Germs can travel easily this way.

✦ If you get a sore throat after oral sex, don't be shy to tell the doctor you see, so they can treat you properly.

✦ Unprotected anal sex is the highest risk form of sex.

✦ Having vaginal sex immediately after anal sex without changing to a new condom, is particularly dangerous. Germs from the bowel can pass easily into the vagina, womb and tubes unless you are meticulous about changing condoms.

✦ Vaginal sex before anal sex is safer if the condom cannot be changed.

✦ All sexually active people go to a Sexual Health Clinic for a check up periodically.

✦ SAIs are the most common infection caught after the common cold, so let's reduce the misery they cause and become more responsible.

Please note

✦ You may be at risk from Hepatitis B or C if you share cigarettes, spliffs, water pipes, crack pipes, hubble-bubble; or notes used to snort cocaine, with an infectious person.

✦ When kissing someone the risk of cross infection depends upon the state of both mouths – and whether there's blood in either person's saliva. In particular, a tiny amount of infected blood is sufficient to pass on the Hepatitis or Herpes Simplex Virus (HSV).

Think Twice

✦ If you're a virgin, and your partner's also a virgin, you're having sex and contact with the germs of just one person.

✦ If you're a virgin and your first partner has had sex with, for example, 5 people, you're having sex and contact with the germs of a minimum of 6 people – the other 5 plus your partner.

✦ If you change partner (now with your second partner) and use the same theory, you have sex and contact with the germs of a minimum of 30 people (their 5 partners and the 5 each of those have had).

✦ Change to your 3rd partner = a minimum of 155 people.

✦ Change again. Your 4th partner = a minimum of 780 people.

✦ 5th partner change = 3,905

✦ 6th partner change = 19,530

✦ 7th partner change = 97,655

✦ 8th partner change = 488,280

✦ 9th partner change = 2,441,405

✦ 10th partner change = 12,207,030

✦ Plus, of course, all the people – all those other people – with whom they have had sex, too!

Safer Sex

A WISE PENIS SHOULD

1. Behave with dignity and allow his owner to have a wee in the morning, since his bladder is probably quite full after a night's sleep – despite his morning's glorious erection.

2. On a daily basis, change the underpants he lives within.

3. Be considerate of showing off his size and strength whilst in auto-erect mode within his owner's clothing and remain hidden from the view of others – except when invited out to play in private.

4. Ask his owner to treat him with respect during masturbation.

5. Have a wash at least once a day and clean away the smegma from around his glans (hood/helmet).

6. Be completely familiar with the look, feel and smell of condoms so he doesn't let himself or his owner down when he encounters another's genitalia, . He'll be competent at the skill of applying, using and, after ejaculation, removing them before he has his first sexual encounter.

7. Communicate with his owner and his testicular relatives on a regular basis. They must ensure they have no abnormal lumps, bumps, discharge or sores.

8. Be aware that condoms float, so used ones must be wrapped in a tissue and placed in a bin or other utensil for disposal, NOT flushed down the loo.

9. Treat himself to regular check ups at a Sexual Health Clinic when he is sexually active.

10. Be aware of emergency contraception should his condom slip off during a sexual encounter with a female partner.

11. Behave with care and dignity when he finds a partner wanting him to visit, in order to encourage a return visit.

12. Ask permission to enter and clarify the situation before entry, rather than just assume it's alright to have sex with someone; otherwise he may get a knock back, be rather embarrassed and risk serious legal problems.

13. Stop, if his partner tells him to stop, or face the possibility of being charged with rape or sexual assault and going to prison for quite some time. And, no sensible penis wants to do that!!

Image © Sylvia Rawsthorn

A WISE PENIS SHOULD NOT

1. Embarrass his owner by becoming erect every time he senses an attractive person nearby. He'll learn to control these urges as he gets older or risk embarrassment by his continual desire to stand to attention.

2. Force himself or his presence onto or into anyone. He must only enter and exercise himself with the full and express consent (permission) of his partner.

3. Get trapped in trouser zips (ouch)!

4. Complain if he overdoes foreplay. His testicular accomplices may complain of an ache (blue ball) the next day. They won't be harmed, but this can be relieved by masturbation.

5. Worry about getting trapped inside his partner during sex, for he needs to be erect and strong to gain entry. He can pull out at any time. He'll return to his pre-erect size and softness after ejaculating, so he can slip out unharmed – but must not forget to hold his condom in place as he withdraws.

6. Even attempt to have sex with anyone who is under the legal age of consent for the country in which he is erect at the time.

7. Assume it's a green light to proceed to sex just because someone allows a certain amount of intimate foreplay. No means No.

8. Even think of having sex without wearing a condom to protect himself from invisible invading bugs or lurgy.

9. When wearing a condom, he'll withdraw before he goes limp after ejaculation; otherwise it's likely to remain inside his partner, rendering its use ineffective. In other words, he must withdraw whilst still hard, holding the condom in place as he does so, to ensure that it doesn't get left inside his partner.

10. Have sex if he fears he might have an infection. He should get thoroughly checked by the Sexual Health Clinic, before he resumes sexual activity.

11. Rub himself up, down or around his partner's genitalia without wearing a condom.

12. Assume that a female partner is using birth control, but wear a condom at all times when encountering female genitalia. The only exception is if his owner is fully prepared for the consequences of unplanned pregnancy and he has a healthy bank balance to support his partner and any future offspring.

13. Continue if he senses that his condom has slipped down or off. He must stop and reconsider the situation. It may be wise for his female partner to seek Emergency Contraception in order to prevent an unplanned pregnancy and/or if he's been put risk of HIV, he considers PEP (post exposure prophylaxis).

Penis Manners Sexplained®

The Pyramid Risk of Infection

Regular sexual health screening helps to shorten the potential pyramid of infection risk

Me   You

The Ex   The Ex

THEIR POTENTIAL PAST

Their Regular Ex   Casual Ex   Casual Ex   Casual Ex
Casual Ex   Their Regular Ex   Their Regular Ex   Casual Ex
         Their Regular Ex   Their Regular Ex
Casual Ex   Their Regular Ex Casual Ex   Their Regular Ex   Casual Ex
Their Regular Ex Their Regular Ex Casual Ex   Casual Ex   Their Regular Ex
Casual Ex   Their Regular Ex   Casual Ex   Their Regular Ex
Casual Ex   Their Regular Ex   Casual Ex Their Regular Ex
    Their Regular Ex Casual Ex   Casual Ex   Casual Ex
       Their Regular Ex Casual Ex   Casual Ex   Casual Ex
       Their Regular Ex   Their Regular Ex
     Their Regular Ex Casual Ex   Casual Ex   Their Regular Ex
        Casual Ex   Casual Ex   Casual Ex   Their Regular Ex Casual Ex
Their Regular Ex   Casual Ex   Casual Ex   Their Regular Ex
     Casual Ex   Casual Ex   Casual Ex   Casual Ex
  Their Regular Ex   Casual Ex   Their Regular Ex
  Their Regular Ex Their Regular Ex   Casual Ex Their Regular Ex
Their Regular Ex Casual Ex   Casual Ex   Casual Ex
      Casual Ex   Casual Ex   Casual Ex
  Casual Ex   Casual Ex   Their Regular Ex Casual Ex
  Casual Ex   Casual Ex   Their Regular Ex Their Regular Ex
Casual Ex   Casual Ex   Casual Ex   Casual Ex   Casual Ex
   Casual Ex Their Regular Ex Casual Ex   Their Regular Ex
Casual Ex Their Regular Ex Their Regular Ex Casual Ex   Casual Ex
Casual Ex   Their Regular Ex   Their Regular Ex   Their Regular Ex
    Casual Ex   Casual Ex   Their Regular Ex Their Regular Ex
Casual Ex   Casual Ex   Their Regular Ex
     Casual Ex Their Regular Ex Their Regular Ex   Casual Ex
Their Regular Ex Their Regular Ex   Their Regular Ex Their Regular Ex
    Casual Ex   Their Regular Ex
Casual Ex   Casual Ex Their Regular Ex   Their Regular Ex
    Their Regular Ex Casual Ex   Casual Ex   Their Regular Ex
     Their Regular Ex   Their Regular Ex Their Regular Ex
Their Regular Ex Their Regular Ex   Casual Ex
  Their Regular Ex Casual Ex   Casual Ex   Their Regular Ex Casual Ex
Casual Ex Their Regular Ex Their Regular Ex   Their Regular Ex
Their Regular Ex Casual Ex   Casual Ex   Their Regular Ex Their Regular Ex
  Their Regular Ex Their Regular Ex Their Regular Ex Their Regular Ex
Casual Ex Their Regular Ex   Their Regular Ex Their Regular Ex   Casual Ex

Safer Sex

Social Media

Social Media

Introduction : The Internet is a fabulous resource and one that is taken for granted nowadays.

✦ It's here to stay and the way we communicate with each other has changed dramatically over the last few years.

✦ In real life, when we see and speak to people, we pick up on the many 'non-verbal clues' they give off (body language) - for example, their facial expression, tone of voice, appearance, etc.

✦ When it comes to meeting new people, we make up our mind about them within seconds of first meeting them.

✦ Online, unless we are using a webcam, we can't do this or pick up on other small clues, which this puts us at a disadvantage.

✦ Language can be misunderstood.

✦ We may read things in to comments that the writer has not intended, which may cause arguments and / or upset.

✦ Depending on our mood and emotional vulnerability, we may assume someone cares about us, is genuine, telling us the truth in reply to our comments and is someone we can trust - when they may not be.

✦ The term 'stranger danger' is, sadly, something to take seriously when it comes to life online.

What is Social Media?

Social media is any electronic platform that allows a user over 13 to interact with others.

✦ The Internet *(Web 1.0)* used to be a pretty static environment, in which websites provided information, allowed people to download content, and search a site before moving on to visit another site.

✦ Newsgroups and interactive forums were the start of user interaction.

✦ Now, the Internet *(Web 2.0 and 3.0)* allows people to have all of that, plus almost endless forms of interaction and connectivity with others; to upload their own information, photographs, videos, music etc.; play interactive games in real time with other players across the world - and even see and speak to each other across time zones.

✦ This is all amazing and fantastic but it also allows virtual strangers to enter someone's home, where and when they should always be able to feel safe.

✦ Many young people have a computer in their bedroom. They lock themselves away in a virtual world for hours on end, and this takes over their day-to-day life.

✦ Many are safe, but some are not, and it is important to learn how to stay safe online.

Language and Respect

✦ Our spoken language can let us down or help us.

✦ People make as many instant judgements about us by the language we use and the accent with which we speak as they do by our appearance and our body language.

✦ In the same way, the language that is used electronically should be the same as that used towards people in real life.

✦ We only get one chance to make a first impression and however much you may think it's funny to swear, or you've formed a habit of scattering offensive language in to your conversations, whatever they say, it may not always appreciated by recipients.

✦ You may not think that using bad language matters, but it can come back to haunt you.

✦ Think twice before you respond to an email that upsets you, and read it again, a different way. It may 'sound' quite different.

✦ Respect others, and treat them as you would like to be treated online, as well as off.

✦ Most people don't set out to offend.

Manners

✦ The saying *'manners maketh man'* holds true online as well as off; and it also holds true for women.

✦ Think how you feel when you're ignored. If someone writes a personal email or message to you, it is polite to reply promptly, even if this is just to acknowledge receipt of their communication, explaining that you will respond fully at another time.

✦ You can set up an 'auto-respond' reply in your e-mail system, so that the person knows their communication has been received and will be dealt with as soon as possible.

✦ Ignoring someone conveys the message that they are just not important or that they just don't matter to you!

✦ You may be surprised by how a simple things like this can earn you a better reputation.

Sexplained ᵀʷᵒ — For Changing Times ® © 1999-2016

Geo-tagging

✦ Geo-tagging stands for geographical tagging or marking.

✦ In the UK, the *Service Provider's Code of Practice 2004* states that geo-tagging should not be allowed without parental consent under the age of 16.

✦ In other words, the device embeds information about where you are posting your information, or photographs, from and the time you do so beside your post.

✦ This may show that you are not at home; and depending on what else you post *(e.g. that you're having a lovely time on an overseas holiday with your family for the next two weeks)*, you may be telling strangers that your home is empty, which allows someone to work out how long it is likely to remain so and available for break-in, either for burglary, squatting, using as a party venue etc. All from simply posting your present location online!

✦ Later on, your geo-tagged information can help someone form a picture of your whereabouts and your movements. This may be from innocent curiosity but it may not.

✦ It is simply safer not to allow electonic devices to geo-tag such information.

Stranger Danger

✦ Don't be too open, familiar or friendly with people you have only met online.

✦ They may not be who or what they say they are. It is very easy to get 'sucked in' and believe what a new 'virtual friend' says.

✦ If you have known the person in real life before linking to them online, you can generally speak to them and share things safely — but even then, be careful.

✦ Sometimes 'hackers' break in to someone's profile / account and take over, locking the genuine person out.

✦ If a post from a friend appears different from how they usually correspond, don't reply online.

✦ Contact them offline (e.g. by text, not email) and check that they did, in fact, contact you online at the time in question.

✦ A genuine friend won't mind.

Password Protection

✦ Your password is like the key to your front door — so protect it.

✦ It is sensible to change your passwords every month and not to use the same one across several websites.

✦ This helps to reduce your vulnerability to hacking and identity theft.

✦ Make your password a mixture of upper and lower case, include at least one number and an additional, non-alphabetic character.

Who Gets Hired – Who Gets Fired?

✦ What happens when the pictures and comments that you post online for 'friends' to see are also seen by potential employers?

✦ If it was your business, and you were looking to hire someone, what would you be looking for in an individual? After all, they will effectively represent your company during working hours — but increasingly, their non-working hours behaviour can reflect on their employer, too.

✦ Be brutally honest with yourself. If you had worked hard to grow a business that has to compete against others for work *(sales/contracts/income, etc.)*, which, in turn supports x-many people to pay their mortgage etc., would you really want someone to present themselves to you in one way, but present themselves to friends and family in a completely different way when you were hiring somoene?

✦ Or would you want to know that the person you are interviewing, is an open, honest, trustworthy individual, who can deliver consistently good quality work; and not risk bringing your company's name in to disrepute?

✦ Increasingly, employers are doing online background checks on job applicants, which take in to account what is posted by or about them on social networking sites.

✦ As professional as you may appear on paper, they don't always have to be your 'friend' to access enough information to make a 'behind the scenes decision' that may result in you not getting an invitation to interview.

✦ You may not hear anything further about that application which may not be fair, but life's not always fair.

persoSocial Media

Good Times Come Back To Haunt

✦ You may not feel that posting sexy, provocative pictures of yourself — or someone else 'tagging' you in some they have taken of you - is much of a problem.

✦ Likewise, that comments or photographs in which you often appear to be at wild parties, drinking lots of alcohol, taking or smoking drugs should be a problem offline.

✦ Complaining about your colleagues or your job online is not very wise, especially if you are in a probationary period, working to contract, seeking promotion or a pay rise!

✦ It's not always what you post about yourself that can cause a problem. Posting comments about someone else can have a detrimental (bad) effect on them, as well as you.

✦ Before you push 'send', remember that you are actually publishing something when you post a comment or an article online, not just having a chat with a group of 'friends' and can be considered a legal document (likewise texts!).

✦ Discretion should be used when communicating electronically, because you don't know really who it may effect, when or, even, if it may be used as evidence in the future!

Privacy Settings

✦ Each social media site has to provide privacy controls for its users to control who can see the information or pictures they post.

✦ Some sites have more detailed controls than others, so it is sensible to understand the limitations of the sites you intend to use before you post personal information, pictures or comments.

✦ The minimum age for use of most social media sites is 13 without parental consent.

✦ This is the age at which the US distinguishes children from teenagers for the purpose of privacy / data protection.

✦ Double check your settings regularly and the rules of the sites you use.

Profile Pictures

✦ Be careful when you accept a 'friend' you don't already know as an offline friend.

✦ Their profile picture may not be of them but of someone else.

✦ And, if someone hides behind a logo or an 'avatar' (symbol) instead of a photograph of themselves, it may be wise to delay or decline accepting their 'friend' request.

✦ If you accept someone and they seem over friendly or sexually suggestive, ignore them. And if, after ignoring them, they become offensive, delete and if possible, block them.

✦ Do not engage with someone you don't feel completely comfortable talking to and if you don't know them in person, don't allow them access to all your posts or pictures.

✦ Keep your real life and online friendships separate.

Posting Pictures Online

✦ Each social media website will have a description of what they will or won't allow people to post on their site in the way of language, pictures / video and audio material, so check their 'terms and conditions' carefully before posting items.

✦ Although people can take pictures of others in a public place without their permission, posting them online without their consent is not always so simple or wise.

✦ If you post a picture of someone on, for example, Facebook, and tag them, they can remove the tag. Removing the picture, if someone asks you to, is a wise thing to do.

✦ Think how you would feel about someone if they posted a picture online you that you didn't want them to show and they removed it when you asked, and also if they refuse.

✦ Which is the nicer way to behave?

✦ Finally, beware: whatever your age, in the UK it is illegal to take or post pictures online of a sexual nature of anyone under the age of 18 and other countries will have similar rules.

✦ Check before posting anything that could lead to legal problems!

✦ *See p160 for information on Indecent Images.*

Social Media

Online Bullying

✦ Bullying others is one of the nastiest online and offline crimes.

✦ *See p184 in Section 6, "The Law and Sex", for more information about Cyber Bullying.*

Lock Your Device(s)

✦ Most, if not all devices have a locking facility — use it — and don't let other people know the access code to your device(s).

✦ If you think someone knows it or has worked out your passcode, change it — and change it regularly, for added security.

False Accounts

✦ It is easy for someone to create a false account and then invite someone to be their 'friend' online.

✦ If you don't know the person in real life, don't accept them online.

✦ You don't know who they are and they could be an 'undesirable' adult pretending to be a young person.

F-raping (Facebook® raping)

✦ Don't leave your device unlocked when you leave it in the company of other people.

✦ Although most people don't, some people may think that it's funny to post comments on your profile page, making it look as if it's from you.

✦ Likewise, if you see posts from friends that don't look like their usual style, contact them another way - by text or phone - and ask them if you posted it.

✦ If you are wrong, it's OK.

✦ If you are right, they will be grateful.

Spam

✦ Everybody get 'spam' or annoying e-mails from strangers trying to sell all sorts of things that most people don't want.

✦ Delete them — don't click on them.

✦ Some have tracker code embedded that tells the sender if they have sent an e-mail to a 'live' address, in which case, they send even more!

✦ Do not write back to them, or the same annoyance continues.

✦ If you don't already have one, install a 'spam filter' which catches most of these and keeps them separate from your wanted e-mail.

✦ But always check through the 'spam' folder before you 'delete forever' incase a wanted e-mail has fallen there by mistake.

Friends Of Friends

✦ Because someone is a 'friend' of a 'friend' online, it doesn't mean you should accept them as your 'friend'.

✦ Only accept people YOU know in person.

Screen Prints From Video

✦ Even if it's your boyfriend / girlfriend asking you, don't risk stripping on camera or webcam.

✦ *Definitely* don't strip for strangers.

✦ Screenshots (pictures of what's seen on screen) can be taken easily and, depending on someone's motives, may end up posted to various websites without your permission.

✦ Once uploaded, the image remains in cyber space.

✦ If they are taken with a digital device rather than a formal camera, the geo-tagging information may be embedded in to the image's background information.

✦ That, in turn, could end up in the hands of someone you wouldn't want knocking on your front door one day!

✦ *Be very, very careful and don't be too trusting online.*

Do Things Ever Really Disappear

✦ Once text or images are published online, they remain in cyber space, even if the website agrees to take them off general view for you.

✦ Each website is 'cached' *(saved)* by search engines on a regular basis, and what's there is archived.

✦ It's easy to view copies of old webites!

DOs and DON'Ts of Using Social Media Safely

The Internet is a fabulous resource but there are some important things to be aware of whilst using it. Sadly, people are not always honest, nor who or what they present themselves to be. This is especially true online.

Do NOT:

+ talk to strangers in chat programs;
+ trust other people too quickly;
+ share your passwords;
+ believe everything someone tells you;
+ publicise your home, school, or college address;
+ give out your email address;
+ give out your mobile or landline phone number;
+ share your bank account information;
+ accept 'friend' invitations from strangers;
+ take your clothes off on webcam if you're asked to;
+ let anyone take a screen shot of you in skimpy or no clothing;
+ do sexy poses on webcam;
+ take your clothes off on webcam;
+ arrange to meet up with someone you've only met online;
+ open e-mails from strangers;
+ click on e-mail hyperlinks;
+ open e-mail attachments from strangers;
+ reply to emails from strangers;
+ visit 'adult' websites if you're under age;
+ explore sexually explicit websites;
+ visit websites that contain prohibited images;
+ leave your device(s) lying around unlocked;
+ post language that you wouldn't want your grandmother to read;
+ post offensive language or images online;
+ post information about parties where strangers can see;
+ try to frighten or stalk someone online;
+ think you can't be traced if you stalk, bully or frighten someone online;
+ forget that your every move online can be recorded.

Do:

+ enjoy using the Internet safely;
+ keep your personal information personal!;
+ change your password regularly;
+ tell others about what you're doing;
+ update your virus checker every week;
+ remove 'cookies' from your browser;
+ tell someone who you're speaking to;
+ keep your address secret;
+ keep your location secret;
+ if you do meet, do so in a public place;
+ take a friend with you if you meet;
+ choose the websites you visit carefully;
+ tell a trusted adult if anything you see or read online worries you;
+ minimise you public profile;
+ check your privacy settings regularly;
+ put 'friends' into lists so different people access different things;
+ be careful with you language and what you say online;
+ remember that employers increasingly check social media sites before offering interviews;
+ speak to the police if someone frightens or bullies you online;
+ report offensive behaviour, language or images to the website and/or the police;
+ go to a website directly by name, rather than following the hyperlink to one;
+ hover your mouse over an e-mail hyperlink so you can check if the underlying information is from the site is says it's is;
+ reclaim your life - stop using social media if anyone frightens or bullies you;
+ 'block' people who upset you;
+ remember to live your life offline as well as online.

Social Media

Safer Dating
&
Clubbing

Identification
Clothing
Theft and pickpockets
Mobile phones and handbags
Men hunt in packs
Lone danger
Casual sex
Look after each other better
Accepting a lift
Mini cabs (taxis)
Advice when entering someone's home for the first time
Being alone with strangers
Date rape
Rape
Sexual Assault
What to do
Are there any organisations around that help men with a history of violence?
Swapping addresses and phone numbers
Don't accept things from strangers or acquaintances
Drink, drugs and fights

When to contact the police
Will I have to make a formal complaint?
If I'm being harassed, why is it so important to contact the police?
PEP / PEPSE — What is it?
PrEP — What is it?
Safer dating for people with physical or mental disability
LAST BUT NOT LEAST
Conditional Consent

Identification

It's wise to carry photographic ID *(identification)* as proof of your age and to prevent any embarrassing moments when trying to gain entry to clubs – especially if you look younger than your age.

Clothing

✦ No-one has the right to touch you without permission. However much you may dislike it, you'll be judged by the clothes you wear.

✦ It can be dangerous to try to be more grown up than your years, to tease or act provocatively, just to experience adult life!

✦ Your self-confidence will grow with age and experience but it's wise to wear clothes in which you feel comfortable, especially in relation to the comments or actions you'll provoke.

✦ You may want to dress provocatively – eg. in skintight clothes – to attract others, but beware of the non-verbal signals you give to others.

✦ Do wear underwear, even if you do want to conceal your panty lines, otherwise you will invite trouble.

✦ Don't make the mistake of thinking an attack couldn't happen to me, it could and it can.

✦ Be perfectly clear about the behaviour you will or won't allow.

✦ Carry an attack alarm in your handbag and don't be afraid to use it, if you feel frightened or need help.

Theft and pickpockets

✦ Don't flash your cash!

✦ Pickpockets abound. Nightclubs are no safer than crowded tube trains when it comes to theft.

✦ Be particularly careful when carrying cash and credit cards. You may be watched when, after use, you return them to your bag or pocket.

✦ Don't carry more money or credit cards than you need to use at any one time.

✦ Don't carry a chequebook. Just carry one or two cheques. Keep them away from your cheque-card.

✦ Always try to keep enough money for a cab fare home and if necessary keep this in a separate place. Even if you go out with friends, you may find you want to leave before or after them and to have the cab fare handy may save your life.

✦ It's always much safer to go to and leave a club or party in a group.

✦ It's safer to take a licensed cab than risk walking alone at night. NEVER accept a lift from a stranger.

✦ Only use a recognised mini-cab company.

✦ If you can't afford to get home, you can't afford to go out!

Mobile phones and handbags

✦ Beware of someone who gives you a mobile phone number – but no land line number. Maybe they live with someone or it may simply be a precaution since they don't know you. If in doubt, wonder why, then ask!

✦ Take care of your mobile phone. Don't leave it lying around while you go to dance. Don't leave it in your coat pocket in a cloakroom.

✦ Avoid handbags if possible. Use a bum bag/belt bag or something else you can wear while dancing.

✦ For security reasons, remove combs, nail files, sprays etc. from your handbag before entering a club – or leave them at home – since they are considered potential weapons. If you don't, the door supervisor may confiscate them until you leave the club.

✦ Don't put your handbag on the floor or by your feet when standing in a crowd having a drink; or while dancing.

✦ Don't put your handbag by your side when seated unless it's zipped up or closed properly.

✦ Keep the closed end of the zip or flap nearest your front and keep the bag closely attached to you in some way, at all times.

✦ Even when it's over your shoulder, in your hand or on the floor by your feet, a clever pickpocket can take contents from it without you even feeling their presence! Be very careful.

Men hunt in packs

✦ Go to a club or a party in a crowd and leave with that crowd. NEVER go off alone with a stranger – or someone you've been chatting to all evening. He/she is still a stranger.

✦ If you notice a group of young men watching you with your friends before you go to dance, be particularly careful not to leave your drink where it could be 'spiked' *(have a drug slipped into it without you knowing)*.

✦ When you flirt or tease, make sure you don't lead a man on – unless you're prepared for the consequences.

✦ Avoid being over friendly, since you may give off the wrong signals. It could lead to trouble you may not be able to handle.

Lone danger

✦ Beware of the attention of lone men and don't become isolated from your friends.

✦ Bring anyone or anything you feel uncomfortable about to the attention of the club's security staff. They should be able to help you.

Casual sex

✦ Today, casual sex is more dangerous. Medical advances and expensive treatments don't necessarily provide a cure for all infections passed on through casual sex.

✦ If you buy condoms from a vending machine in a club, make sure they're still in date and that they're not gimmick condoms.

✦ Check for the British Standard kitemark, the CE or EN600 mark on the packet or understand the standard to which they are made.

✦ It's impossible to know someone's sexual history or whether they have a sexually acquired infection in just one evening.

✦ Think of tomorrow, not just the moment! Look after yourself and if they care about you at all, they'll wait – if they won't wait, then you've lost nothing!

✦ Don't put yourself at risk for the sake of a thrill or someone else's ego.

✦ If you decide to have casual sex make sure you use a condom and other protection correctly, especially if you're just giving or receiving oral sex *(blow job)*.

Safer Dating & Clubbing

Safer Dating & Clubbing

Look after each other better

✦ If you see your female friends OR your male friends drunk or otherwise under the weather whilst out clubbing, look out for their safety – not just your own. In this state they are vulnerable and a potential victim of crime.

✦ By keeping a watchful eye on them, you could prevent them from harm.

Accepting a lift

✦ Don't accept a lift if you feel uncomfortable, particularly if the driver has been drinking alcohol, or taking drugs.

✦ When you get into someone's car, you're entering their territory. You can't get out when you want – the driver will be in control.

✦ You won't know how well they can drive but your life may well depend on it.

Mini cabs (taxis)

✦ If you're uncomfortable about someone who's offering you a lift home, get a cab home.

✦ Phone for a licensed, on duty and properly insured, identifiable cabdriver, from a legitimate company. Always ask for – and write down – the name of the driver and their cab driver's ID number.

✦ Ask for a pre-arranged code word to identify them further, when they arrive.

✦ Wait in a well lit place with someone else – if possible.

✦ Don't approach him/her first. When the driver approaches, ask him/her to give his/her name.

✦ Don't simply ask: are you eg. John Smith. A genuine cabbie won't mind at all.

✦ Ask to see their photographic ID.

✦ Touts often offer to get young women cabs. These are often unlicensed and sometimes operated by criminal gangs for the purpose of gaining money, sex – or both – from female groups or single passengers.

✦ Many criminals evade police checks and work as pirate cabbies – often without insurance.

✦ Even if it's late and you have to wait for a cab, NEVER take a pirate cab. Don't accept identification in the form of a business card. Anyone can have business cards. They don't prove a thing!

✦ Some pirate cabbies clock off from a shift with a legitimate firm and work for themselves for a few hours, to avoid paying commission to their employer.

✦ A pirate cabbie won't be in regular radio contact with his base, even if they've got a radio in their car, with an extra arial. This is to trick you into thinking they're genuine.

✦ Don't assume that because a door supervisor *(bouncer)* hails you a cab, you'll be safe – and don't take his/her word for it that you'll be OK. He doesn't know that for sure.

Advice when entering someone's home for the first time

✦ Being alone with someone for the first time may be exciting but it can also make you feel a little nervous. It is sensible, therefore, to be cautious. Ensure that you tell someone where you're going and with whom. Arrange to call this friend to check in when you arrive and as you leave – or by an agreed time. If your friend doesn't hear from you by the agreed time, they can then decide whether or not to contact the Police and ask them to check up on your safety.

✦ A genuine friend won't mind how many precautions you take.

When you arrive:
(a) check whether anyone else is there – especially if you expect to be alone with your host;
(b) make a mental note of the layout when you arrive;
(c) check your exit routes in case of fire or fear;
(d) let your host know that someone is waiting to hear from you, knows where you are and who you're with, by name. Your host now knows that someone else is looking out for your safety;
(e) observe your surroundings to ensure it's their home or whether it's a place used for seduction/sex!
(f) if you feel uncomfortable, make an excuse and leave quickly;
(g) call to check in – as pre-arranged.

Being alone with strangers

✦ Be especially careful if you invite a stranger into your home. NEVER give your address to someone you've just met – however charming s/he may seem. Get to know and trust them.

✦ Love yourself enough to take time to get to know a person on neutral territory *(out in public)* – eg. a cafe, with friends etc.

✦ It's safer, but not foolproof, if they're already known to someone you know well, who can vouch for their good character.

✦ NEVER invite a stranger into your home, even for coffee, until you feel safe and secure with them.

Safer Dating & Clubbing

Rape

There are three types of rapist:
(a) stranger rapist.
(b) acquaintance rapist.
(c) date rapist.

✦ It's an alarming fact that more rapes are carried out by men known to their victims than by strangers.

✦ Usually, rapists are unpredictable bullies of any shape, size, colour or creed.

✦ Many are good looking, likeable and often, charming men. Indeed they may be the last person you'd think would ever need to rape a woman.

✦ But rape has little to do with sex. It has far more to do with exerting power and control over another person.

✦ They get off on terrorising their victim.

✦ Some don't accept they've done anything wrong – and spend years in denial. Many are very devious conmen.

✦ Many excuse their behaviour by saying that their victim was 'up for it' (wanting sex) – ie. by their suggestive clothing or actions – and cried rape after the event.

✦ Some men are not confident about their sexuality. They may even believe it's their right to have sex with someone who flirts innocently with them, goes out for a meal or spends time alone with them.

✦ They don't stop to think how they would feel if their mother, sister or even their son or daughter was the victim.

✦ Every victim has a mother – as does every attacker.

✦ Few men are rapists. But any man could rape and any woman could be raped.

✦ Male rape happens too. Men need to be equally aware. No matter how big and strong you are, you'd be weak against a gang intent on rape.

✦ Female or male – no one has the right to force another person to do ANYTHING against their will.

WARNING:

✦ Sadly, in some inner city areas, gang rape – rape by more than one man – appears to be increasing, so be vigilent.

✦ Rather than risk being caught carrying a gun or a knife, gang rape of rival gang members' girlfriends or sisters, is being used as a 'weapon' against members of opposing gangs.

✦ They anticipate that their victim is unlikely to report the incident to the police because of the fear or reprisals if they do.

Date rape

✦ Be aware of date rape drugs.

✦ A certain type of man may plan to rape (force someone to have sex without consent) before they leave home, and take date rape drugs with them.

✦ Stranger rape, when the attacker is unknown to the victim, is what most people associate with rape.

✦ Date rape is when someone you know and feel you can trust, rapes you.

✦ Date rape and acquaintance rape (not a stranger but not someone you know well) is far more common than stranger rape.

✦ Men (gay or straight) are also at risk of rape and sexual assault.

✦ Drugs such as roofies, (Rohypnol®) or another type of mind-altering drug, are slipped into your drink.

✦ In the dark, you'll be unaware of any change in the colour or taste of your drink. The change of colour – which shows blue in a light coloured drink – takes 20 minutes. By which time, you'll probably have consumed it, anyway.

✦ Their method of operation is to lead you away to a lonely corner – eg. toilet or car park – or even perhaps go home with you or invite you to their place.

✦ The drugs make you fall asleep. You could be raped and, because you'd be so sleepy, you wouldn't

Safer Dating & Clubbing

remember much about the incident (or them). The drugs have an amnesic (loss of memory) effect. You'd wake up to realise something's not right and may feel that you've been raped.

✦ Some rapists even wear a condom, in an attempt to conceal (hide) evidence.

✦ If you see anyone slip something into a drink, you MUST first report it to the nightclub security AND the Police. If they suspect rape, they will arrange for a medical examination, emergency contraception and SAI advice and check up as soon as possible.

✦ Even if you don't want an examination or aren't sure what happened but feel you may have been raped, it's important to get to the Police within 24 hours (or as soon as possible) after feeling odd (or as if you've been raped) to have a special blood or urine test. This will be used as evidence and will help the Police find your attacker.

Sexual Assault

If you are sexually assaulted, whether you are a man or a woman, PEP and/or Emergency Contraception may be advised.

It is important that advise is sought as soon as possible, even though it may be the last thing you want to think about at the time. The local police will know where your nearest SARC or 'sexual assault referral centre' is located and they will see you as soon as possible. You do not have to go ahead with a prosecution for assualt or rape, but you do need to seek approriate help as soon as possible.

Rape Crisis centres exist in many countries. If you need their help, or just someone to talk to, they can help in many ways.

What to do

✦ If you're ever sexually assaulted or raped, DO tell the Police.

✦ Remember, however terrified you may be, your attacker WILL strike again. He could kill his next victim. An attacker must be caught and stopped. Give the Police all they need – eg. clothing, bedding, towels etc. used during or straight after the incident – as soon as possible. This will help secure a conviction and other people will be safe from your attacker.

✦ **Note:** It is a serious offence to accuse someone of rape without justification.

Are there any organisations around that help men with a history of violence?

✦ There are a few excellent organisations. They specialise in helping men who have a history of violence either towards their partner or who hate women, despite an outward display of adulation.

✦ Whatever excuse you use for losing your temper, which leads to violence – eg. alcohol, drugs, history of abuse or simply something someone does to upset you, you should NEVER take your anger out on others.

✦ You may think you've got to appear big and tough but remember, it takes a big man to admit he has problems and a bigger man to seek help in dealing with them.

✦ Be brave, pick up the phone and get help before it's too late.

Useful websites:
http://rapecrisis.org.uk
https://rainn.org

Safer Dating & Clubbing

Swapping addresses and phone numbers

✦ Don't give your address or phone number to someone you don't know without thinking of the consequences.
✦ Make sure you're not overheard when giving out details in public – eg. shop, club, etc.
✦ In the wrong hands, your address and telephone number could be used to commit crime – either in your name (!) or with you as a victim of crime.

Don't accept things from strangers or acquaintances

✦ **A drink**. It may be laced (mixed) with a date rape drug or other drug.
✦ **Chewing gum.** It may be laced with LSD/speed.
✦ **Ecstacy.** It may be laced with heroin.
✦ **Cigarettes** (or spliffs or joints). They may be laced with cocaine and/or heroin.
✦ **Viagra**®. Unless you're being treated for impotence, it may seriously affect your erectile function. It MUST only be used under medical supervision since it interacts badly with some other drugs and could be fatal.

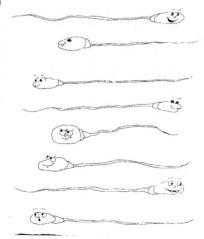

Drink, drugs and fights

✦ Unprotected sex is often a consequence of too much alcohol – so don't have too much – or mix types of alcohol. Getting drunk means you're likely to take more risks and go home with someone to whom you'd not normally be attracted.
✦ When a person is under the influence of drink, drugs or both, they lose their inhibitions, and common sense. They often get carried away sexually – taking more risks. They then worry about pregnancy and/or infection the next day!
✦ Don't leave your drink at a table or at the bar when you go to dance.
✦ It's safer to drink from a can or bottle.
✦ Keep your drink with you at ALL times so it can't be 'spiked' (a drug slipped into it without you realising). Someone may do this for 'fun' but it is a criminal offence. Also, they are unlikely to know your medical history or whether you are taking any medication. They could find themselves facing serious criminal charges – for example, murder, attempted murder or manslaughter if you react seriously to the combination and collapse.
✦ In addition – alcohol mixed with some drugs can cause serious complications – and could be fatal.
✦ So, if you put your drink down or leave it – even with a friend – don't touch it again. Buy a new drink from the bar.
✦ If you're involved in a fight and blood is drawn, assume you're at risk of catching hepatitis and seek medical advice within 24 hours.

When to contact the police

Contact the police when:

✦ If you're particularly frightened or uncomfortable about a situation – or by a particular person. They may already know the person in connection with similar or worse things. Even if they don't, they should be aware of people who make others frightened.

✦ Remember: the Police can't do anything to help the public, without information.

Will I have to make a formal complaint?

✦ No, you won't have to make a formal complaint. You can tell them what's happened and let them guide you from there.

✦ Even if you make an allegation against someone – but don't want to proceed with a charge against them – if you have clear reasons for not wanting to proceed, the Police won't think you're wasting their time.

✦ It's not being silly or making a fuss about nothing. You should always trust your instincts.

If I'm being harassed, why is it so important to contact the police?

It's important to contact the police for several reasons:

✦ harassment is a crime and is against the Law. The Law is there to protect you – stand firm and use it to protect yourself;

✦ most bullies are basically cowards and if they are not stopped they will continue to frighten more victims;

✦ sometimes, just realising that a victim refuses to be bullied any more – even if it means they have asked the Police to help them – the bully stops his disgraceful behaviour; and

✦ you may also need support from friends or family but don't let a bully – of any description – get away with intimidating you.

I'm not being harassed but I want the police to know about something. I don't want to give them my name, so what can I do?

✦ Many countries now operate an anonymous crime reporting phone call system.

✦ In the UK, you can ring Crimestoppers on their freephone number – 0800 555 111.

✦ You don't need to give your name.

✦ Your call could help to protect others.

✦ Your call could prevent a crime.

✦ You could receive a cash reward.

Safer Dating & Clubbing

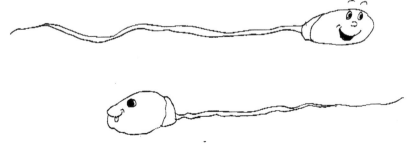

PEP / PEPSE — What is it?

PEP stands for **Post Exposure Prophylaxis** / PEPSE stands for **Post Exposure Prophylaxis for Sexual Exposure** and is available for people who have a high risk of exposure to HIV within the previous 24-72 hours.

PEP involves taking highly active anti-retroviral treatments for 28 days. This is the same as given to people with HIV disease, with the aim of stopping the virus replicating shortly after infection.

Apart from risky sexual exposure, PEP is given to healthcare workers, who have or may have been exposed to HIV through 'needlestick injury' – accidentally pricking themselves with a used syringe.

Generally dictated by what has happened, with whom, from where and exactly which risk activities occurred, PEP is offered on a case-by-case basis and to strict criteria at the discretion of the doctor prescribing it.

For treatment to be given, the benefits should outweigh the risks. These include the risk of someone not fully completing the treatment course.

It is only available from specific centres; not yet widely available from pharmacies, general practitioners, etc. So, if you feel you have been put in a position that worries you, call your local hospital's A&E *(ER / Casualty)* Department or your local Sexual Health Clinic for advice about how to obtain it.

Side effects used to be problematic but with modern treatment, they are minimised.

You may be advised to have an HIV test before treatment, as a base guide and another for comparison a few weeks after treatment.

PrEP — What is it?

PrEP stands for **Pre-Exposure Prophylaxis** and is not yet widely available. It is an approach to HIV prevention that uses antiretroviral medications *(ARVs)* to reduce the risk of HIV infection in HIV-negative people. ARV treatment is increasingly given to pregnant women with HIV infection to protect their unborn babies, with good effect.

Outside this use, daily basis for the wider public is under discussion.

Trials of PrEP are ongoing in various countries.

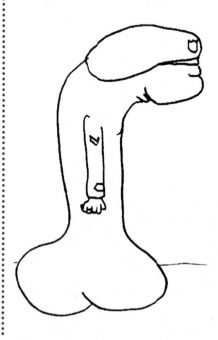

Safer dating for people with physical or mental disability

✦ Don't walk on the other side because any one of us could become disabled.

✦ The information provided in this book is as much for able bodied as it is for people with a physical or mental disability.

✦ Just because someone is disabled or has learning difficulties it doesn't preclude them from wanting to be loved emotionally and physically.

✦ Those of us who are fortunate enough to be able bodied should stop to think for a minute. How would I feel if I was less able bodied or if I had learning difficulties?

✦ If you know someone in this situation, do what you can to help him/her to have an enjoyable social life.

✦ It's harder to find nightclubs, restaurants etc. with suitable provision for wheelchairs but they do exist and there's an increasing amount of information and support available from disability related organisations.

✦ Girls with certain learning difficulties – eg. Down's syndrome – often start their periods slightly earlier than other girls and may appear to be less inhibited sexually.

✦ They are equally at risk of unplanned pregnancy, or sexually acquired infections.

✦ BUT they are often less able to give their informed consent to have sex.

✦ Sometimes, people who've suffered a severe head injury – eg. from a car crash or boxing accident – behave in a way which is sexually inappropriate. This needs to be understood by friends and family. They may need gentle help to understand and re-learn how to behave with other people.

✦ Young men with spinal injuries who are unable to get an erection need to discuss their difficulties with their doctor.

✦ Various products are available to help all forms of impotence.

LAST BUT NOT LEAST

Conditional Consent

✦ A person may agree to give consent under certain conditions.

✦ If those conditions are not met, there is no consent.

✦ An example of this would be if a man tells another person that they will use a condom in order for them to agree to have penetrative sex – but having started with a condom, they remove it without the other person's permission (consent).

✦ They have changed the conditions under which consent was given, and this becomes an offence and could, in theory, put the other person's life at risk.

✦ Sex without consent is RAPE.

✦ Sex when consent is removed when a conditon changes is either rape / sexual assault / assault and could result in a criminal conviction and being placed on the Violent and Sex Offender Register (ViSOR).

✦ Simple! So take it seriously.

✦ For more information on consent, see the section called The Law & Sex - page 149.

Safer Dating & Clubbing

Language & Respect

Language and Respect

Discussion Points

Language and Respect

✦ People are judged by their appearance but also by the words their language; the words they use.

✦ You'll want to be respected by others but to get respect you have to give respect and it's not always what you say, but how you say it that matters.

✦ Some people choose to show off and use bad language – but most people don't like loud mouths!

✦ Just like your 'body language', with which your facial and other expressions portray silent messages that are recognised by other people, the words you use tell your listener things about you.

✦ Using disrespectful terms can have the opposite effect from what you want, which is one sure way to lose other people's respect!

✦ How would you feel about someone if you heard them describe your mother, sister, partner or friend in disrespectful terms?

✦ Most probably, not much, so think about your language before you speak.

Discussion Points

Think of some respectful words to describe the following and how you feel when you hear people using slang, disrespectful terms for the same topics:

✦ sexual intercourse;
✦ vagina and penis;
✦ external genitalia;
✦ breasts;
✦ oral sex;
✦ masturbation;
✦ erection;
✦ bisexual;
✦ homosexual man;
✦ lesbian;
✦ trans-sexual;
✦ transvestite;
✦ sexually experienced male;
✦ sexually experienced female.

✦ How do you think your best friend, brother or sister would feel about you if they heard you talking offensively, if they were hoping to confide in you that they are homosexual or bisexual?

✦ If they heard you use discriminatory terms you'd probably lose their close friendship and not know why.

✦ The damage from that could prove to be too much to allow your broken friendship to ever repair.

✦ You will also realise that virtually all the words for sexually experienced men portray the opposite image to the words used for sexually experienced women. That is neither right, not fair – why?

✦ Apart from portraying considerable disrespect, many sexually explicit slang terms suggest violence against women and girls.

✦ Before you use words, which may discriminate towards or offend other people, think for a moment about how you would feel if you were called un-kind names – even in fun.

✦ And, if you wouldn't like to hear someone talk about your mother, father, brother or sister with these unkind words, should you use them about other people?

✦ Using them actually says more about you, than it does about them!. Simple!

Language & Respect

The Sexplained® Column

Addicted to Porn

I've just realised that my boyfriend is addicted to watching porn online. This worries me because he's also been making different sexual demands of me recently. He's changed and I don't feel comfortable any more. It's as if I'm some sort of sex object rather than his girlfriend these days and I don't want to do some of the things he's pestering me for. I feel bullied. I don't like rough sex or bad language and he wants sex that includes both of these. Looking back over the last few months, it's now obvious that his attitude towards other women also seems to have changed, and not for the better! He describes women disrespectfully when he's speaking to his friends and I'm not comfortable inviting my girlfriends round any more. It's turning me off him and I'm not sure what to do. It's as if he's a stranger at times and I don't like it, even though I love him. What should I do?

— AJ

Dear AJ

I'm sorry that your relationship has changed and it's understandable that you don't feel the the same as you did about him. Don't let him make you do anything you don't want to do. No relationship that's worth being in should make you feel uncomfortable. Have you tried to talk to him about this yet? If not, that's a good place to start and it will give you some insight as to whether he is aware that he's changed, and if he isn't, at least you can point this out to him. Whether he takes that on board, and modifies his behaviour is another thing but at least you will know that he knows how you feel. Only you can decide whether you can put up with it if he continues, or not. But, since the Internet has brought porn to the home of everyone at the click of a mouse, it may be difficult for him to leave it behind without accepting that it's an addiction that's harming other areas of his life. The obvious and evident danger from what he's doing is that he's becoming desensitised to the mutually respectful behaviour that you fell in love with him for. Porn is here to stay and most men (and many women) look at it from time to time. It's when it becomes a problem that affects other areas of life that something needs to be done about it. He has to want to change and you have to decide if you want to stay if he continues. If he feels he needs help, his doctor or sexual health clinic can refer him to a sex therapist who can help him unravel why he's become so hooked on porn and help him reduce his dependence on it. Good luck, AJ.

I hope things work out well after you open up to each other.

— Helen

The Sexplained® Column

In a Quandry

After speaking to my friends about their relationships, I don't think things are quite right with mine. One of them said mine is not healthy but how can I tell the difference between a healthy and an unhealthy relationship?

— Alison

Dear Alison

I'm sorry the conversation with your friends has caused you to doubt your relationship and that you are now questioning your feelings — but, the mere fact that you are doing so suggests that this may have been a useful chat to have had, after all. If things were great in your relationship, you would be unlikely to be wondering about it.

There are many different types of relationship, ranging from healthy to unhealthy and also abusive. Obviously, 'healthy' is the type that's most desirable. Sadly, unhealthy and abusive relationships are what many people endure, often for too long, and for a wide variety of reasons.

Usually, new friendships and relationships start off as healthy, with people feeling happy, good about things, about themselves and about each other; and they share interests. They like and respect each other; make decisions together, communicate well and share the same level of power, control and values. They have occasional disagreements but these settle quickly and without any fear or nastiness between them. Both partners maintain contact with their friends and family, and their relationship is just one part of their life.

In unhealthy relationships, with time and depending on the personalities involved, things change and it becomes time to get out of the relationship — but it can sometimes be incredibly difficult to do this. They don't want to accept that change has taken place. They may have just drifted apart but stay together out of habit, or from fear of what other people might say. They stay in the relationship but are unhappy. One may have hurt the other by breaking their trust or hurt them physically. Arguments don't settle easily, or in the way they used to. One may be overdependent on the other, leaving that person feeling smothered and unhappy. Sometimes, it's easier to stay than face the fear of starting over again — or of failing.

Sometimes things become happy and healthy again. Other times, they don't. After holding on, or feeling that they are in too deep to feel safe getting out, things may go from bad to worse. Abusive relationships are not about love, care and respect for each other but about one person having power over the other, dominating and controlling them. The dominant partner gradually erases the other's self-esteem, stops them doing things they enjoy or seeing people they care about. They isolate them, bit by bit. They pretend they are the centre of their world and they can't bear to be without them. They may use threats, insults, or frighten them to get their own way. They wear the other person down. They make them feel worthless and helpless. They may take control of their finances, leaving their partner in a postition where they have to ask for their own money; or they may expect the partner to pay for their living costs and their entertainment, while they use their own money for fun, leaving the partner at home. They have no respect for their partner. Indeed, they become strangers, with one feeling that they are 'walking on eggshells', too terrified to leave, especially if threats and violence have become the 'norm' between them. Sometimes, the fear of what will happen if they leave is worse than putting up with the physical and emotional abuse. Dominators often pull their victim back in by saying things like 'I'm sorry. Don't leave me. It won't happen again.' — but of course it does and it escalates. The first violent act is a sign that it's time to 'get out'.

You are not responsible for someone else's behaviour, only your own. Healthy relationships are based on good friendships, with open communication, genuine care and the desire to give and receive the best of each other. Just having sex together does not mean that it is a good relationship. Having good sex but a bad friendship means that it's time to think about what you're doing, and why you're doing it.

It takes a lot of courage to leave an abusive relationship and you will probably need a lot of ongoing support, from friends, family and perhaps even the police — but being able to smile again and feel good about yourself once more will make it all worthwhile. You only have one life, so enjoy it as much as possible.

Of course, there is much more to a healthy relationship than this. However, for now I hope this helps you consider your relationship carefully, so you are sure you want to continue spending your precious life with this partner.

— Helen

Ballooning Belly

I'm 27 and have always suffered with bloating around the time of my period but I have recently realised that it happens throughout the month now, too. Is this a normal 'bowel thing' for my belly to be ballooning like this?

— Sherie

Dear Sherie

If you cannot equate the bloating with your period or what you have been eating recently, it may be a 'bowel thing' or, even though you are only 27, it may suggest a more sinister problem related to your ovaries. More commonly a problem of older women, younger women can be affected by ovarian cancer, too. It's a tricky disease but symptoms such as persistent bloating, pelvic and abdominal pain, loss of appetite or feeling full quite quickly, extreme fatigue or even urinary problems could point to something other than a 'bowel thing'. I'm not saying that everyone who is bloated has ovarian cancer! ... but I am saying that a change in bowel habits should be investigated further. So if you haven't changed your diet or been eating lots of 'baked beans' recently, do yourself a favour and let your doctor guide you. I hope this helps, that it has a simple explanation - and that it's nothing serious.

— Helen

Fun Sex

All my friends have arguments with their partner but we're really happy. My partner and I have been together for five years now and we laugh together all the time, talk about everything, have a fun sex life and enjoy seeing our own friends as well as spending time together. Is this normal?

— Peter

Dear Peter

This is lovely to hear. What you have together describes a very normal, happy and healthy relationship which many others would envy having. You obviously love and respect each other and are good friends as well as lovers. I hope you have many more years of such happiness together.

— Helen

Scared About Being Examined

When I go to a clinic to get The Pill, will I have to have an internal examination by a doctor or nurse before I can get it?

— D

Dear D

No, you won't have to be examined beyond having your blood pressure taken, your height and your weight checked before getting hormonal contraception. If, however, you have pelvic pain, abnormal vaginal discharge or other worries 'down there' that may indicate that you have a problem, it would be wise to be examined. But just to be given hormonal contraception, such an examination is not necessary.

— Helen

Tantric Tootsies

This is embarrassing, but I must confess that I get extremely aroused when my boyfriend sucks my toes and nibbles my ear. When having sex, things move from good to great the second he starts to play with my toes and ears, and I consistently orgasm as a result. Is this weird?

— K

Dear K

No, this is not 'weird'. It's quite common. Toes and ears are two of the top ten female erogenous zones (areas of the body that respond to gentle touching, massaging, licking, sucking or kissing in a pleasurable way). Likewise soles, toes and ankles can respond in the same way for many people, even if they're ticklish, as long as it's done in a gentle way. Some guys like the smell and taste of sweaty feet but others prefer feet and toes to be washed before orally stimulating (sucking) them — each to his or her own, there! This form of foreplay is harmless and fun; and as you have already found out, very stimulating when the recipient is relaxed enough to get lost in the sensations. It is a form of 'tantric sex', with which penetration is not involved. Continue enjoying this form of pleasurable and very safe sex. And, remember: the most responsive sexual organ is your brain. Enjoy.

— Helen

Seeing Spots

I'm 24 and I've been on a very common COC Pill for 18 months, but for the last couple of days I've bled. I'm in the middle of my packet and this has never happened before. I'm worried. What could it be?

I read the manufacturer's leaflet and have not vomited, missed or taken any pills late. I have not been taking St Johns Wort. I have been with my partner for two years and we always use condoms as well - and we were both virgins before hand. He has not slept with anyone else and neither have I.

The only thing I can think of is that in the last cycle a condom split while we were having sex, but he hadn't 'come' and we didn't continue. However, I got my bleed when I should have but I'm still worried. Could I be pregnant from this condom mishap? I started taking multivitamins and iron tablets a week before the bleeding started. Could there be a link?

— Jess

Dear Jess,

From your description, no you won't be pregnant from that 'mishap' as you put it. You haven't done or taken anything to interact with the absorption of your COC Pill.

By using routine dual protection, you are superbly protected from pregnancy and since you were both virgins and are faithful, that rules out the risk of Chlamydia and / or gonorrhoea; a classic sign of which is abnormal bleeding.

The COC Pill is extremely reliable when taken correctly. It's quite likely to be a what's called a second generation Pill, not one of the latest, so very well tried, tested, and safe if you're medically fit to use it.

I can't tell what has caused this 'blip' Jess. If it is a 'one off' don't panic. Please keep a diary of what's happening, when, and discuss it when you go for your next check-up. But, you don't have to wait for months for a check-up if there's something you're worried about.

Sudden weight loss can have odd effects on us at the best of times but keep an eye on the spotting and see how it goes. Also, be careful taking the iron and multivitamins. The COC Pill helps to prevent anaemia, raising iron levels in the blood, so check with your doctor whether you really need to be taking these if they were not prescribed for you. If you are eating a healthy, balanced diet, you shouldn't really need to take supplements at your age.

Do you smoke? If you do, that can cause an interaction. Apart from all the other nasties it does to the body it sometimes causes women using combined hormonal methods of contraception to spot *or* bleed when not expected - e.g. COC Pill, Vaginal Hormonal Ring or Contraceptive Patch.

If it continues your doctor MAY change the dose of COC Pill you are taking and they may suggest taking a cervical smear test, if you haven't had one recently. They may also screen you for Chlamydia and gonorrohoea, even though you, and they, will fully expect that to be negative. It's sometimes a process of elimination, whilst hoping not to find anything untoward to worry about.

— Helen

A Pinching Problem

There has been a lot of talk in the news recently about older men touching younger women, and sometimes boys, in a sexual way. If someone pinches another person's bottom, is that a sexual offence? Or is it only if they touch someone's genitals or breasts that there's a problem?

— TJ

Dear TJ

Yes, it's an offence to pinch someone's bottom. It's very simple really. Any touching of a sexual nature, which takes place without someone's consent, is illegal. Touching or feeling someone's breasts or genital area without their consent, is also a sexual offence. For more on sexual assault, see the section called "The Law and Sex".

— Helen

Sugary Daddy

I overheard one of my friends say that a mutual friend of ours had a 'sugar daddy'. I don't understand what this is but I didn't want to look stupid by asking what they meant. What is a 'sugar daddy'?

— MA

Dear MA

A 'sugar daddy' is usually an older man (often married) who offers to support a young woman (or young man) financially after establishing a relationship with them; which is usually sexual. This may be seen in the same way as a man having an affair, with a 'mistress', who generally doesn't have sex with other people, in return.

— Helen

Conception Without Intercourse

Can a woman get pregnant without having intercourse?

— JJ

Dear JJ

Yes, it is possible to get pregnant without having sex. Expensive fertility treatment is only one way to get pregnant without having sex. In fact, a virgin can get pregnant and remain, technically, a virgin because the ejaculation of sperm is not always necessary to create a pregnancy. Many people get this fact wrong!

How come? Well, when a young man gets an erection, there are about 3 million sperm in the drop of clear fluid that appears at the tip of his penis. That's enough sperm to populate the whole of the Central American country of Honduras!

If her partner just rubs his erection around the entrance to her vagina (without inserting it inside her), sperm could get into the fertile mucus she makes before ovulation (egg release) and travel up to her fallopian tubes. If they meet an egg there, then an unplanned pregnancy may occur. This may not result in pregnancy very often but don't take the risk and don't forget, where sperm can go, so can germs! Use a condom and remember: if ever in doubt or worried, emergency contraception is available!!

— Helen

Expanding Vaginas

I've read that the average vagina is only 3 to 4 inches deep, but this seems way too small because the average penis is longer than that. Does the vagina elongate during intercourse to accommodate the entire length of the average penis?

— Ryan

Dear Ryan

Yes. The vagina expands during sex, when respected. Your information is correct - but it doesn't explain that the vagina is a passage that can expand considerably. It's lined with folds or 'rugae', which stretch and expand enough to allow a baby to pass through the vagina (birth canal) during delivery. Nature is very clever and an expandable vagina ensures survival of the human race. It also allows any size of penis to fit inside a well lubricated and willing vagina during sexual intercourse. But for this to happen, the woman needs to be relaxed, feel safe and be happy to have sex with the penis owner who is wanting to have sex with her.

She also has to give her consent to have sex. Without this, the man should stop and not try to force the issue or he could find himself in trouble with the law!

I hope this helps to clarify things for you.

— Helen

Too Drunk To Consent

Is it true that if a man has sex with a woman who is drunk it's considered to be rape?

— DJ

Dear DJ

Yes, it's considered rape if a man has sex with a woman, or another man, who is under the influence of alcohol or another a mind altering chemical (drug). This is because, in this state, they cannot give consent - and sex without consent is rape. For more on this, see the section called "The Law & Sex".

— Helen

The Sexplained® Column

Forever Bladdered

Whenever my boyfriend and I have unprotected sex, I develop a bladder infection and need to take antibiotics. My doctor has suggested that this is because my boyfriend is not circumcised. So, now he is considering getting circumcised! I find it hard to believe that if he keeps his penis clean, that an infection could be passed on to me this regularly. What do you think?

— Sick and Tired

Dear Sick and Tired

I take it that there's no problem with protected sex so having a circumcision is a bit drastic! I think the best thing your boyfriend can do is to help you break the cycle of expectation and use a condom, routinely. Whether you develop a laboratory diagnosed bladder infection after sex or feel that you may have one, being circumcised or not has little to do with this other than that his general hygiene may need a bit of improvement. Millions of men with a foreskin have sex and their partner(s) don't develop a bladder infection. Washing himself (with warm water, not soap) before and after sex and both of you passing urine before and after sex are likely to help. Whether he likes condoms or not, maybe he needs to learn to like them! There are loads of different styles, makes and types on the market, so why not try to reduce the risk of bladder discomfort with some 'condom experimentation'.

If size is the problem and nothing helps, locally, get him to log in to www.TheyFit.com where he can input his measurements and receive a custom fit condom by post. The company is based in London and offers 95 custom sized condoms in their range so no man can get away with saying 'the condom is too small / large / tight / loose' any more. Instructions are online and all he has to do is follow them.

I hope this helps.

— Helen

PS If he adds the code 'KP', the company will know he's heard of them through me and I will get to know that I've helped someone (but not who or any details).

Friend said ... Cancer Comes From Sex!

Is it true that having sex at a young age, especially for girls, increases the chance of developing certain types of cancer? I am 17 years old and my closest girlfriends are worried since they have been sexually active for at least two years and we just found this out.

— Melanie

Dear Melanie

Sex, by itself, does not lead to cancer but certain sexual conditions are associated with it. Namely, HPV or human papilloma virus, of which there are over 100 types. Luckily, only a few types are associated with cervical and other genital cancers. Unfortunately, the more sexual partners someone has, the more opportunity there is for HPV to be passed from a lover who probably doesn't even realise they carry the virus. The cervix (neck of the womb) does not mature until you are about 23 years of age and is vulnerable to various problems that take time to show. Having a healthy cervix is a great reason why using a condom routinely, consistently and correctly, is so important. Condoms protect people from a lot more than just HIV and/or pregnancy and sexual infections!

In view of the fact that there is now a vaccine available to protect young people against the four most problematic strains of HPV (two that are linked to genital cancers and two that are linked to some of the most annoying and common genital warts) I would urge you to speak to your doctor about having the vaccination. Also, even though your friends have been sexually active, and it's most helpful before sexual activity starts, it should still be possible for them to have it, too. Depending where you are in the world, you may have to pay for it, but it's definitely something to take advantage of, rather than hope you won't encounter this problematic little virus. Statistically, you are very likely to!

I hope this helps.

— Helen

Oops! Something's Wrong!

I've heard about emergency contraception but when might I need to use it?
— JA

Dear JA

Emergency contraception (EC) is contraception used after unprotected sexual intercourse or contraceptive failure e.g. a broken condom) to prevent pregnancy.

Common times that emergency contraception is used include:
- after a broken or slipped condom;
- when contraceptive pills have been restarted late, after the 7 day break between packets and condom use was forgotten or went wrong;
- getting carried away and not thinking about protection at the time;
- having too much to drink and then sex, without thinking about contraception;
- being persuaded that it will be OK not to use protection (for example, when the boy or man says 'it's OK, I'll be careful' or 'it's OK, I'll pull out' ... this is very risky and not reliable!); and/or
- being forced to have sex (rape).

EC is not as reliable as contraception used ahead of, or during sex, but is increasingly, significantly helpful at preventing an unwanted pregnancy if obtained within five days (120 hours) of unprotected sex (not just the next morning).

Nowadays, there are three types of emergency contraception - 1) Levonorgestrel based, commonly called Levonelle, Plan B or Postinor (although it has different names in different countries)(72hrs for Type 1) ; 2) Ulipristol acetate based, such as el-laOne® / ella®, and 3) the non-hormonal and well known IUD (copper coil or intra uterine device) (120 hours Types 2 and 3).

The medication is widely available but in some countries it can only be obtained via prescription. This means that it can't be bought or handed to you over the counter without prescription from a doctor, nurse prescriber or some pharmacists.

The first method can be used more than once in a menstrual cycle, while the second can only be used once in a cycle. An emergency IUD can be inserted up to day 19 of a regular 28 day cycle, and if desired, it can remain in-situ as an ongoing method of contraception for up to 10 years.

The IUD, however, requires specialist insertion so might be a little more difficult to obtain in time. The up side is, though, that both Ulipristol acetate and an emergency IUD have a lower failure rate than the first method, which if you have an accident, is still more reliable than keeping your fingers crossed. The best method for a particular situation will be worked out when you are asked questions about your menstrual cycle, when your last period started and when, exactly, you first had unprotected sex during that menstrual cycle.

Obviously, when any form of emergency contraception is used, there has been unprotected sex. The risk of pregnancy is one thing, but there will also be the risk of sexual infections to consider.

A full sexual health screen may be advised at the time as background information and again, perhaps three weeks later to rule out Chlamydia and gonorrhoea, followed three months later by blood tests to rule out syphilis and HIV.

It may seem a lot of fuss but preventing unplanned and perhaps unwanted pregnancy is important and if an infection has been passed, treating that or knowing about its existence is important for long term health, too.

After using EC, it is wise to take a pregnancy test three weeks later. The next period should have occurred within that time but if it is lighter or different from usual, it is important to see your doctor or pop along to a Sexual Health Clinic in case you are pregnant.

I hope that helps to answer your questions JA.

— Helen

A Tangled Web

I used a spray on my penis to enhance my erection and keep me from climaxing too quickly. It worked well. However, about two days afterwards I got a burning feeling in my penis after I passed water. I also noticed bumps around my foreskin. Do you think it is the spray that affected me or could it be due to something else, as I did not use a condom with the woman? But I'm sure she is clean as her husband and I are friends.

— EH

Dear EH,

The fact that you and your lover's husband are friends means zilch. How do you – or he – know that she hasn't had sex elsewhere? How do you know for sure that your friend hasn't had sex elsewhere, then had sex with her? After all, does he, your friend, know you are having sex with his wife? I suspect not... at least not yet!

If he's been playing away and if he's brought home an infection to his wife that she's given to you, and if you've had sex with your wife or regular partner (if you have one) . . . The spider's tangled web of deception broadens out.

Your penile bumps could be anything. You could have herpes, you could have warts, you could have an allergic reaction. The pain when passing urine may have been due to local irritation at the tip of your glans (the meatus or opening) but this came on two days after you used the spray, not shortly after, and you didn't use a condom. You may merely have NSU (non-specific urethritis) to have stinging or burning when passing urine you have urethritis, inflammation of the urethra – but you may have gonorrhoea or Chlamydia, which can present similarly.

You don't say your age but don't rule out infection if you are in your later years (which you may be by feeling the need to use artificial erection aids). You have no choice at all here. You must go and get checked. You do not know her sexual history and you should NEVER assume anyone is free of infection, so, make condoms part of your sexual routine and protect yourself, routinely.

— Helen

What's Wrong With Vaseline®?

I always use condoms but I've read on several websites that using Vaseline as a sexual lubricant is discouraged, but no one states the reason. Why can't I use Vaseline? And can you give me some alternative suggestions?
— Stefan

Dear Stefan

The reason you must NOT use Vaseline® *(or any oil-based product)* with a latex condom is that they interact badly and the oil rots the latex, making the condom burst during use. Any water-based lubricant can be used as an alternative, especially if it is found on sale next to condoms in a pharmacy. There are loads of different brands on the market so I won't name anything, here, but I do know they are widely available. I hope this helps.
— Helen

To Masturbate or Not to Masturbate... That is the Question!

Is it OK to masturbate?

Masturbation is viewed as a form of safer sex. With masturbation there is no risk of pregnancy and there is no risk of catching a sexual infection from yourself. It's natural and done in private, it's harmless. However, in most countries, if it's done in public, it's frowned upon and you could risk being arrested for exposing yourself.

Some people believe it will badly affect future sexual relationships but in moderation, it is much safer to masturbate than have casual sex with other people just for the sake of it.

But if you become obsessed with masturbating to the extent that it virtually takes over your life, then perhaps should you seek help to calm your addiction down!

— Helen

The Bottom Line

My new boyfriend loves having oral sex but one night he put his finger into my bottom. Although it was uncomfortable at first, it felt okay afterwards. He is now asking me to have anal intercourse. I have refused, but don't want to lose him. He told me I'll enjoy it, but I'm not so sure. Should I let him? Won't it be painful?

— Help

Dear Help,

Interest in anal sex is increasingly being shown as porn is more easily accessedonline, but it's important to tell your boyfriend how you feel. Widely practised heterosexually in some communities as a form of contraception, it is still possible for a woman to get pregnant folowing anal sex (if this occurs at the fertile time of the month and if sperm gets into her fertile mucus). Once sperm get into that, they are on their way! And unprotected anal sex carries an 18 times higher risk for transmission of HIV than vaginal sex, if it's present.

Surely there's no point in exchanging body fluids with someone, whilst being too shy to talk to them or share your worries. You should not do anything to please him and not yourself. Spell out your fears, and if he cannot accept your decision not to do it, then you know what sort of person he really is.

The bottom line: If he doesn't respect your wishes, tries to coerce or force you into doing it, or threatens to leave you if you don't do it, let him go; he's a bully and it's not YOU he wants. He only wants to use YOUR body! And, if you don't give your consent, freely, and he goes ahead, he will be committing a crime!

Gentle anal foreplay can be made safer by him putting a well-lubricated condom or latex glove over his finger before insertion. The more the anus is stretched, the more chance there is of the skin tearing and causing discomfort. If you decide to consent to anal sex it is important to take it very slowly and use a LOT of water-based or silicone (condom friendly) lubricant to assist entry, and at all times ensure he correctly wears a condom.

Unless you are able to relax your anal sphincter sufficiently to allow gentle entry, it may be painful. And, to prevent bowel germs entering your vagina, it is extremely important NOT to go from having anal sex to vaginal sex with the same condom. Either change condoms, or go from vaginal penetration to anal with the same condom if you decide to consent to anal sex.

— Helen

NOTE: anal sex is NOT recommended as a form or contraception (birth control).

Two Women

I have two women: my wife and my girlfriend. I do not use a condom with either and, knock on wood, neither of them have come down with any infections yet. But I know I should be taking precautions just in case. My outside girl does not like condoms as they make her itch badly. Is there some cream or ointment I can use after she and I have sex to kill anything I may have picked up from her before I go home and have sex with my wife?

— Help

Dear Help,

I'm glad you know you should be using precautions! And 'NO', there is no reliable cream or lotion you can rub on yourself to stop from catching an infection. Only a condom can do that to keep this genital triangle as safe as you can. Your outside girl's itch may be related to the lubricant on the condom, to thrush (yeast infection), or she may be sensitive to latex — with the first being the most likely.

Try using a variety of different lubricants with your condom — you'll be amazed at the results and at least you will keep the three of you safer! Think, though, how you would feel if your wife was the one having an affair... would you really like it. If you wouldn't, doesn't she deserves a bit more respect?

— Helen

NOTE: Don't mix latex condoms and any oil-based product. Oil rots latex and renders the condom useless. Use only water-based or silicone condom-friendly lubricants designed for the job.

Tell Me Yours

Can you tell me if it's true that a doctor can tell that a woman had abortion just by examining her although it may be as long as 12 years ago? I'm asking because when I was 17, in a moment of stupidity encouraged by too much alcohol, I had sex for the first time and got pregnant. I didn't want it and my mother helped me to obtain a termination. I took the proper time to heal – in fact, I didn't have sex again for five years and no one knows what I went through except her and the doctor. I've never told anyone because it's something I am ashamed of – my only mistake in an otherwise perfect life. The problem is that I'm going with someone who has medical training and I'm scared he could be fooling around and realise I had this done. I would not want him to know this as it may make him change his mind about me.

— Urgent

Dear Urgent,

First, please relax. Unless your partner inserted a speculum into your vagina to visualise your cervix he wouldn't be able to tell anything by looking at you.

However traumatic, you were also very lucky to have such a supportive relationship with your Mother. Others turn to a friend for support but many women go through this experience totally alone and it can have a devastating effect on them. At least you were able to share your feelings, fears and the experience with her, and however much she may have worried, she would have been far more upset if she found out about it by chance one day and realised you hadn't felt able to turn to her.

What you don't say is how far pregnant you were when the abortion was carried out or how it was done, as there are both medical and surgical options available. But in general an early abortion leaves no obvious signs; especially up to nine weeks, when it can be medically induced.

During a surgical abortion, the cervix or neck of the womb is gently stretched by insertion of a series of dilators (metal instruments) to allow the suction equipment entry to the womb without damaging the cervix. The muscle of the cervix then tightens and everything appears as it did before. Later terminations involve the use of different instruments but the cervix is only opened as much as is required to remove contents safely. If a pregnancy is so advanced that delivery has to be induced, the cervix, in this situation, does stretch differently to allow passage of larger contents which alters the shape of the cervical os (opening of the cervix). How long and to what extent will depend on the gestation and the procedure. Why don't you – to be comfortable and sure – go and have a chat with a doctor and ask them to have a look. Or, ask when you next have a cervical smear test (which all women should do regularly).

But, if this man is as important to you as you imply, why are you in such great fear of the truth? You never know, he may have had the same experience, but the other way around, and be scared of telling you. There is a saying: "the truth can set you free", and in most cases this is true. It's not just the woman's experience, either, which we commonly forget to consider. Your past is in the past and you were young. Everyone's allowed a mistake or two in their life, otherwise how do we learn from them?

Good luck, Urgent, and try not to worry so much. . . if your past scares him away now, isn't that better than scaring him away later, when you have shared much more together? He won't be the nicest of characters if he leaves you for something that happened 12 years ago. You were certainly a very different person then and unless he's a saint, I am sure there will be something in his past that he's not too proud of, so start sharing – 'you tell me yours and I'll tell you mine' (secrets)' – and let the pain of the past leave you both. You don't have to take this risk, of course, but one day, if he's as nice as he appears, you may feel safe enough to do so.

He is medically trained, so he most certainly shouldn't be interested in judging anyone, only caring for and about them – and that includes you.

I can just hear the anti-abortion shouts from some readers for this but unless and until you walk in another person's shoes, don't judge them. No woman wants to have a termination (abortion) but for many, it is the best decision at a particular time and it is rarely a decision taken lightly.

Some regret it later, others don't, but it has to be the woman's decision. So, good luck with whatever you decide to do next, Urgent.

— Helen

Shocking Syndrome

I have heard that it's dangerous to use tampons during a period. I'd like to use them some of the time but now, I'm too scared to try. Are they really problematic?

— Lizzie

Dear Lizzie

No, tampons are not dangeous to use, most of the time. It's advisable to wash your hands before and after inserting or removing a tampon. The instructions should be followed and the tampon should be changed regularly. If this doesn't happen, then sometimes rare problems, such as toxic shock syndrome (TSS) can occur.

This is an infection caused by the bacteria called 'staphylococcus aureus' which is just one of the many bacteria that usually live harmlessly in the vagina. But, if tampons are left inside the vagina for a long time (or forgotten), in the presence of this bacteria, the normal vaginal conditions are altered, causing problems. Using sanitary towels instead of tampons on light flow days may be helpful and does not carry the same risk.

Symptoms of TSS can include one or more of the following: headachess, sore throat, aching muscles and joints, high temperature (fever), a rash, dizziness, diarrhoea and even coma from septicaemia (blood poisoning), which is a life threatening condition. This has to be treated quickly with antibiotics, and probably in hospital.

It's surprising how common it is for women to forget to remove their last tampon and then worry about an unpleasant smell coming from their genital area a few days later. Some develop an unpleasant vaginal discharge which prompts them to seek medical advice and examination - only to feel mortified when a rather smelly tampon is removed from their vagina.

Age is irrelevant and there are other conditions that cause a discharge that smells 'down there' but this seems to happen to women of any age. If you notice an abnormal odour 'down below', to avoid embarrassment, just check that you haven't left a tampon inside before seeking help.

— Helen

Loverboys Galore

What are loverboys? I heard this term used recently but it didn't really make sense. Are they boys, who are lovers, or are they something else?
— Confused

Dear Confused

Although the term 'loverboys' could mean boys, who are lovers, sadly, this term has a much darker meaning today. 'Loverboy' is the slang term for young men who lure, usually innocent and vulnerable young women, who are under the age of consent, in to the dangerous world of child prostitution. Internationally, child sexual exploitation is an increasingly organised criminal activity.

They start grooming their victim using their various looks, charm, power, status, smoothe talk and 'bad boy' image to attract and impress. They isolate them from their peers, their family or carers. They promise the world, make them feel special and as if they are the only person who really matters to them; and that they are the only person who really cares what happens to them. They make them play truant from school, buy them gifts and hook them in quite quickly. Initially, their victim may look up to them and although under age, agree to have sex with them, believing this to be the grown up thing to do, and that it's expected.

However, they are not what they seem. They operate using coercion, intimidation, threats of or actual violence, alcohol and drugs. They have no conscience and don't care. They merely see an opportunity to make money for themselves by forcing their victim in to a dark and dangerous world of child sexual exploitation. They terrorise their victim using gang rape and /or kidnap if they're not 'willingly' obeyed. They arrange for other men to have sex with them and terrorise their victim so much that they feel this is 'normal'. They are usually a few years older than their victim and of an age difference that some young people, and even some parents may not agree with, but tolerate.

If you are ever worried that a friend is in this position, speak out. Tell the police. Tell your parents. Tell your teachers. Tell a trusted adult. Ask them to tell the police if you haven't or can't. You may just save their life. And, even if you are wrong, it is better to be wrong than keep quiet and let someone suffer. Eventually, they will thank you.

— Helen

LGBTQI - What's That?

I've have heard the term LGBT for many years but I recently heard it extended to LGBTQI. What do the new letters stand for?

— DC

Dear DC

The letters in the phrase 'LGBTQI' stand for lesbian, gay, bisexual, transgender, questioning (sexuality) and intersex.

Many people question their sexuality and are curious to explore different activities. This is a normal part of human development. Some people act on this, others don't. Some people explore and experiment with people of the same and/or opposite sex during adolescence whilst others wait until later. Others merely fantasise, but don't question their sexuality.

Intersex is more complicated and intersexed people (also called hermaphrodite), are born with reproductive organs and genitals that are less easily identifiable as belonging to someone of a particular sex. Intersex is NOT the same as homosexual. Estimates suggest that instead of being born appearing to be a boy or a girl, approximately 1 in 1,500 people are born with some degree of intermediate sex – or intersex. For example, someone may have a penis and vaginal opening, but ovaries instead or testicles – although other combinations also occur. This is a huge and complicated subject, so for more information, support and links to a wealth of national and international information about intersex check the website: www.oiiinternational.com – the online home of Organisation Intersex International.

They state that "Intersex is always congenital and can originate from genetic, chromosomal or hormonal variations. Environmental influences such as endocrine disruptors can also play a role in some intersex differences. The term is not applicable to situations where individuals deliberately alter their own anatomical characteristics."

I hope this helps.

— Helen

```
C O M B I N E D O R A L S F V P A D G
O C Z P G A S E A E O U Y A Z L P I P
N B L A F T R V I C Q B S M T A H B M
T D R P L U T I N J E C T I O N E J K
R V T A M F S C O C A T E L T N O N E
A L F V M A L E A A T E M Y H I V I R
C O I L U L G C X R O M A N C N B U T
E M E R G E N C Y G E J C E H G F M A
P O P S T E R I L I S A T I O N B D F
T H E C A P A C O N D O M C R U M B A
I N T R A U T E R I N E S Y S T E M S
V C E L I B A C Y U M T Y N R E T R O
E F E M A L E Y O D I A P H R A G M G
P R O G E S T O G E N O N L Y P I L L
I M P L A N T P A T C H T I C R U E S
L T I T C H P S F R A B R L O M S T A
L O V E R S Y S E X P L A I N E D H K
```

No Shame

Is it true that men can be victims of domestic violence (DV) and/or domestic abuse, as well as women?

— AZ

Dear AZ

Yes. It's true that men can be victims of domestic violence/abuse, as well as women. Age, ethnicity, race, gender identity, sexuality, profession, religion, class, health, wealth, ability, disability and/or background are no barriers, or protection, against it happening.

DV/abuse can happen to anyone. Indeed, the UK's House of Commons published information stating that in '2012/13, there were 1.2 million female and 700,000 male victims of domestic abuse in England and Wales', alone. Only the person involved will know when they are ready to seek help but they deserve to feel, and be, safe. There is NO SHAME in being a survivor of domestic abuse. Survivors are people who cope well with difficulties in their life. Men in this situation can check out www.MensAdviceLine.org.uk and www.Mankind.org.uk for what to do to keep safe and speaking to the police.

It is hard for a anyone to take this first step but it's usually well worth while.

— Helen

Overview

of

Sexually Acquired Infections

(SAIs)

Bacterial Causes

Names:
BV / Chancroid / Chlamydia / Donovanosis / Gonorrhoea / Lymphogranuloma Venereum/ Mycoplasma Genitalium / NGU / Syphilis / Ureaplasma Urealyticum

Cause and mode of transmission:
The bacteria can live inside cells of the cervix, urethra, rectum and sometimes in the throat and eyes. It may be passed from a mother to her baby during pregnancy or birth. Each of the above can be passed from one person to another during unprotected anal, oral or vaginal sex, or by sharing unwashed sex toys.

Male symptoms:
Often nothing, but there may be: unusual discharge from the tip of the penis, which may be white, yellow or green, inflammation of the foreskin, pain passing urine, painful or tender testicles, rash or open sores.

Female symptoms:
Often nothing, but there may be: unusual vaginal discharge, which may be thin, watery, white, yellow, green or grey, pain passing urine, lower abdominal pain or tenderness, bleeding between periods or after sex and, sometimes, a rash and/or open sores.

Treatment:
Depending on the infection, antibiotic tablets or injections may be advised.

Abstain from sex:
Sex should be avoided during treatment or for seven days after it ends. Also, until seven days after the sexual partner has also been treated.

Partner notification / treatment required:
Sexual partner(s) should be informed, tested and treated appropriately. This may also include previous partner(s), depending on the situation.

Test of cure required: A test of cure may or may not be advised, depending on the infection involved.

Viral Causes

Names:
Genital Warts and HPV / Hepatitis / Herpes / HIV / Molluscum

Cause and mode of transmission:
The virus enters the body through small cracks in the skin or through the moist soft lining (mucous membranes) of the mouth, vagina, rectum, or urethra. It may cause symptoms or become dormant (inactive) and hide in the body.

Symptoms are the same for both men and women:
There may be no symptoms to indicate infection or, there may be a feeling of being generally unwell, with flu-like symptoms. For example, fever, tiredness, headache, swollen glands, aches and pains in the lower back, legs or groin.

There may be stinging, tingling or itching in the genital or anal area and/or small, fluid-filled blisters or small hard raised bumps or lumps, which appear on the skin or on shiny wet areas of mucous membrane. There may be pain when passing urine or opening bowels.

Treatment:
Depending on the infection, anti-viral tablets or creams may be given or other treatment may be applied to the area(s) of concern.

Abstain from sex:
Sex should be avoided during treatment and / or for seven days after it ends.

Partner notification / treatment required:
Yes. This may also include previous partner(s), depending on the situation.

Test of cure required:
No.

Non-Bacterial — Non-Viral Causes

Names:
Candidiasis (Thrush) / Lice / Scabies / Trichomonas Vaginalis (Trichomoniasis or TV)

Cause:
Thrush is usually caused by the fungus, Candida albicans. It lives harmlessly in warm, moist areas of the body unless conditions change and is not sexually transmitted. Lice and scabies are tiny creatures, which attach to hair or burrow into folds in the skin. They are not necessarily transmitted sexually. Trichomonas vaginalis is a tiny protozoan parasite, which is commonly transmitted sexually.

Symptoms:
Thrush is famous for causing an uncomfortable itch and thick white vaginal discharge in women or inflammation and discomfort of the glans penis, in uncircumcised men. Lice and scabies cause itching, irritation and inflamed skin in the areas they are found. TV causes an unusual vaginal discharge in women or discharge from the penis and discomfort passing urine, although many people are unaware of its presence.

Treatment:
Thrush is treated with an antifungal cream, vaginal pessary or oral medication. Lice and scabies are treated with different lotions.
TV is treated with antibiotics.

Abstain from sex:
For each of these conditions, sex should be avoided during treatment and for seven days afterwards while healing continues. To avoid reinfection, because TV is considered to be sexually transmitted, partners must also be screened and treated before sex can be resumed seven days after their treatment ends.

Partner notification / treatment required:
Partners do not need to be treated for thrush, but they should be examined, screened and treated for lice, scabies and/or TV.

Test of cure required:
A test of cure may be advised for TV if symptoms remain.

Index

I hope you have found this book interesting.

Also, that it helps to keep you and those around you safe.

HJK

www.Sexplained.com
www.KnoxPublishing.com
www.WillyWorries.com